BILL MADDEN

My 25 Years Covering Baseball's Heroes, Scoundrels, Triumphs and Tragedies

BILL MADDEN

WWW.SPORTSPUBLISHINGLLC.COM

Managing editors: Susan M. Moyer and Joseph J. Bannon Jr.
Project manager: Greg Hickman
Developmental editor: Erin Linden-Levy
Dust jacket design: Joseph Brumleve
Copy editors: Holly Birch and Cynthia L. McNew
Imaging: Kerri Baker

Front cover photo by Neil L. Waingrow

ISBN: 1-58261-529-2

Printed in the United States.

This book is dedicated to Lillian Madden, my life partner and an admittedly biased critic on whom baseball is no longer lost.

It is also dedicated to Steven and Thomas Madden, who both lived through most of these columns and are in every way a father's pride.

CONTENTS

Acknowledgments vi

Introduction vii

Chapter 1
Scoops and Exclusives 1

Chapter 2
Heroes and Legends 37

Chapter 3
Villains and Scoundrels 103

Chapter 4
Colorful Characters 131

Chapter 5
Remembered Friends 181

Chapter 6
Labor Pains 197

Chapter 7
Events 217

Chapter 8
Tragedies and Travesties 237

Chapter 9

The Rivalry 269

Chapter 10

General 281

ACKNOWLEDGMENTS

The author gratefully acknowledges the following people for making both my career and this book possible: Les Goodstein, who makes it all happen at the *Daily News*, especially this book; Martin Dunn, who made sure I stayed at the *Daily News*; Leon Carter, a sports editor who has trusted my judgment and given me the freedom to "do my thing;" Buddy Martin, who had the foresight to hire me; Dick Young, a mentor who taught me just about everything I know about reporting; Milton Richman, a mentor who introduced me to everyone who was important in baseball; Fred Down, a mentor who taught me how to do it "under the gun;" Phil Pepe, who taught me the ropes on the Yankee beat; Bob Raissman and Mark Kriegel, colleagues who always supported me; Delores Thompson, who has always looked out for me; Scotty Browne, Jimmy Converso, Alan Delaqueriere, Pete Edelman, Dawn Jackson, Ellen Locker, Shirley Wong and Faigi Rosenthal from the *Daily News* library, who faithfully and tirelessly assisted me through the years in researching material for my baseball writings; Eric Meskauskas and the *Daily News* photography department, especially Angela Troisi, who helped research, gather and scan the photos in this book; Elaine Kauffman, my toughest critic; Joe Bannon Jr., who hatched this idea for Sports Publishing L.L.C.; and Erin Linden-Levy and the rest of the SP staff who implemented it.

INTRODUCTION

To paraphrase Tommy Lasorda, who always liked to say he bled Dodger blue, I feel like I bleed *Daily News* black. Twenty-five years at one New York newspaper, covering baseball, has been a dream job for me. Anyone who's been around the New York newspaper scene knows this is a transient business. I've been at *The News* through three ownerships and 10 sports editors. George Steinbrenner once said to me: "How the hell can you criticize me for changing managers all the time? You've had more sports editors than I've had managers!"

I couldn't argue with him on that one, but there were plenty of other issues on which we butted heads during our mutual quarter-century of coexistence on the New York baseball scene. I have to believe there's no tougher beat anywhere than New York baseball, especially the Yankees. I was Yankees beat writer for *The News* from 1980-88, but I always tell people you have to multiply that by seven (as in dog years) to take into account the Steinbrenner/Billy Martin/Reggie Jackson factor. It's been both a grind and a joy—as any great job is.

My greatest satisfaction is running into a player years after I covered him and being greeted warmly. The writer-athlete relationship is a strained one—there's no getting around this—and the key is to gain the player's trust. You do that, and as my old sports editor and mentor, Milton Richman at United Press International, always told me, "They'll all want to tell you things." That's kind of the way it's been, from Joe DiMaggio to Mickey Mantle, Reggie Jackson, Lou Piniella, Tom Seaver, Goose Gossage, Don Mattingly and Mike Piazza.

I hope the *Daily News* readers have enjoyed it all as much as I have.

CHAPTER 1

Scoops and Exclusives

The Mets leaving Tom Seaver unprotected in the free agent compensation draft was unthinkable, and the source in the commissioner's office at the time who tipped me off to this is still working in baseball. He knows who he is. ...Bill White turned out to be an inspired choice as National League president, and it didn't matter what color he was. I only wish he hadn't left the game as bitterly as he did. ...I was one of the few reporters Joe DiMaggio ever let into his private circle, and when, at the end, he came under the influence of Morris Engelberg, I was both saddened and outraged—and determined to get the real story out. ...The Steve Phillips column generated the most hate mail I ever got (all from enraged Mets fans).

TOM-FOOLERY LETS CHISOX NAB SEAVER

JANUARY 21, 1984

The incredible, unthinkable, impossible notion that Tom Seaver would again have to leave New York became a shocking reality yesterday when the Chicago White Sox stunned the Mets by selecting their 1984 Opening Day pitcher and most popular player ever from the free agent compensation pool.

And shocked was the only way to describe the reaction of both Seaver and the Mets' braintrust at a hastily called news conference, which could have easily been mistaken for a wake. The 39-year-old Seaver, who was in Chicago Thursday night meeting with White Sox co-owners Jerry Reinsdorf and Eddie Einhorn, said he was still not certain he would report to his new team. At the same time, he expressed his hurt and anger at the Mets' braintrust for subjecting him to this predicament. (The White Sox got to take a player from the compensation pool for having lost "Type A" free agent Dennis Lamp to the Toronto Blue Jays.)

"It's an unfortunate situation that has sprung up," Seaver said. "I've gotten a little more upset as things have gone along. I'm not here to blast anybody, though. They [the Mets] had their meetings and they have to do what they think is best. I don't agree with what they did. They made a mistake, that's for sure. I just don't understand their thinking behind it."

Seaver, whose reluctance to leave New York again is based on wanting to be near his wife and two young daughters, admitted his only alternative appears to be retirement. The White Sox owners spent an hour Thursday night selling him on the advantages of pitching for a pennant contender (he needs just 27 wins for 300). In addition, it has been learned they will show Seaver further good faith by re-negotiating his contract with a no-trade provision and a raise from his present $750,000 salary.

Mets general manager Frank Cashen, on whom the burden of this worst blunder in the Amazins' 23-year history must fall, could not disagree with Seaver that a terrible mistake had been made. Looking somber and stunned by the disastrous turn of events, Cashen admitted that "black ties and black armbands" should have been the proper attire on such a dark day.

Cashen again took pains to explain that his prime reason for leaving Seaver unprotected to the White Sox was because of Chicago's obvious strength in starting pitching.

"If we felt there was even a slight chance he [Seaver] would have been taken, I would have never brought this embar-rassment to the owners of this ballclub," Cashen said. "We made a mistake and we are not here to

Tom Seaver is stunned by the news of his selection by the White Sox. (Dennis Caruso/Daily News)

tell you we didn't. We looked at their [Chicago's] club and the fact that they won their division by 20 games and we figured they might be more apt to go for a prospect—which is why we protected as many of ours as we could."

But to hear White Sox general manager Roland Hemond explain it, the Mets really shouldn't have been surprised to lose Seaver.

"When I saw Tom Seaver's name on that list, I jumped right out of my chair," Hemond told the *Daily News* by phone. "In our opinion he was clearly the best player available. We took him, not only because our scouts assured us he is still a first-rate pitcher, but because he is the sort of class person we want on our ballclub."

And according to Hemond, where the Mets miscalculated was not so much with the White Sox, but rather with the Oakland A's, who will also get a compensation pick from the pool once their Type A free agent pitcher Tom Underwood signs with another team.

"I can understand how people in New York might think we wronged the Mets," Hemond said, "But this was a business decision. It was our thinking that if we didn't take Seaver, the A's certainly would, and they're in our division."

Of course, Seaver feels the Mets have wronged him…again. As he said, when the baseball strike of 1981 was finally settled with the creation of free agent compensation, it was inevitable that someone would get hurt by it. "I felt at the time it was a farce and a joke and that people were gonna get hurt," Seaver said. "I just never thought it would be me."

Then again, the Mets were hurt even more. They lose their greatest and most popular player ever—and get nothing in return.

NL TARGETS WHITE FOR JOB AS PREXY

JANUARY 31, 1989

National League owners have zeroed in on longtime Yankee broadcaster Bill White as their new president, the *Daily News* has learned. He likely will be offered the job this week to succeed Bart Giamatti.

The league owners have been seeking a black to be their new leader ever since Giamatti was elected September 8 to a five-year term to replace Peter Ueberroth as commissioner.

Reached at his home last night, White said, "I have no comment. I really can't say anything. I don't know anything."

But, as one high-level National League executive told *The News*: "From what I've been told, it'll be his if he wants it."

Wilpon: No decision.

Dodger president Peter O'Malley, head of the NL search committee, could not be reached for comment. However, Mets president Fred Wilpon, a member of the committee, insisted that no decision has been reached as yet.

"There are quite a few candidates that we've talked to, all of them very impressive," said Wilpon.

It also was learned that O'Malley is due in New York this week for a meeting with the committee, at which time it is expected that a choice will be made.

If White, 55, is that choice, he would be the first black man ever to head a professional sports league.

The NL owners had talked to Simon Gourdine, the former deputy commissioner of the National Basketball Association, and Gil Griffin, the vice president of labor relations for Bristol Myers.

Longtime Yankee broadcaster Bill White (right) may be leaving Phil Rizzuto to run the National League. (Daily News)

Although both of those black men were considered highly qualified, it was apparently felt by the owners that neither had a close enough association with baseball.

As a result, the search in recent weeks was shifted to former black players and narrowed to White, a slugging first baseman with the Giants, Cardinals and Phillies in the '50s and '60s, and Joe Morgan, the former two-time Most Valuable Player second baseman with the Reds.

But according to one source, Morgan asked that his name be removed from consideration because the salary, believed to be in the $200,000 range, could not match what he is making both as a broadcaster and in his numerous private business endeavors.

Morgan also turned down the opportunity to become manager or general manager of the Astros in recent years.

That left the field open to White, who also would have to give up his lucrative broadcasting deal with WPIX-TV as well as undergo a major change in lifestyle.

A spokesman for WPIX said the station had no comment on the White situation, but it has been learned that contingency plans are being made to find a replacement for him as Phil Rizzuto's partner in the TV booth.

As a broadcaster of the Yankee games for the last 18 seasons, White has commuted to Yankee Stadium from his home in the Philadelphia area. In addition to adopting nine-to-five hours as league president, he presumably would have to move to the New York area.

"He was a late starter in the field," said one National League executive, "but he's become a very firm candidate. Something is very close to being completed."

As one of the first black announcers in sport, White has long been held in high esteem by the baseball hierarchy. A few years back, George Steinbrenner approached him about managing the Yankees, and White showed his good sense then by saying he had no interest in the job.

Yankee Officials Cut Fay Down to Size

August 5, 1992

It turns out that was quite a saucy exchange that took place between Fay Vincent and the three Yankee officials he called on the carpet on July 1. As a result, it appears the imperial commissioner of baseball has created a heap of trouble for himself with the Players Association, the National Labor Relations Board and, most significantly, baseball arbitrator George Nicolau.

In public documents obtained by the *Daily News* from the NLRB's New York office, Yankee manager Buck Showalter, GM Gene Michael and vice president Jack Lawn all testified that Vincent threatened them with disciplinary action for appearing as character witnesses on behalf of Steve Howe at the pitcher's drug hearing. In other words, the imperial commissioner stands charged with tampering with witnesses in a formal grievance proceeding.

Although Showalter and Michael were clearly rattled by Vincent's intimidating tactics, Lawn, the former head of the Drug Enforcement Agency, went toe-to-toe with the imperial commissioner and his deputy, Steve Greenberg.

After being told by Vincent that he, Lawn, had "effectively resigned when you agreed to appear at that hearing" and "you should not have testified for the other team," Lawn shot back: "You don't understand—if you're called to testify, you testify, and you tell the truth."

To that, Vincent is quoted as saying: "You should not have testified on behalf of the Players Association."

Responded Lawn: "It was not for the Players Association. I testified for Steve Howe."

Vincent: "I could not believe that you would all testify because of your interest in seeing Steve Howe in a Yankee uniform."

Lawn: "That's not why we testified. We testified to tell the truth."

Vincent: "But then why would you want to testify?"

Lawn: "If a month from now, I pick up the paper and see that Steve Howe killed himself, at least I would have known I tried to help."

Later, Greenberg asked Lawn again: "Why did you do this for Steve Howe?"

Lawn replied: "Well, as I learned in the Marine Corps, you don't abandon the wounded."

Lawn confirmed the dialogue in the NLRB document, including the quote attributed to Vincent after Lawn explained that he was sworn to tell the truth and he only testified in accordance with his conscience and his principles. Replied Vincent: "You should have left your conscience and your principles outside the room."

That quote is now destined to go down in Yankee lore right alongside Billy Martin's infamous sum-up of Reggie Jackson and George Steinbrenner—"One's a born liar and the other's convicted."

"I wrote it down on an index card," Lawn told *The News*, "because I couldn't believe it. To be honest, I was confounded that he called us in. I think the reason was that Greenberg pumped him up by telling him, 'They trashed your drug policy.'

"At one point in the hearing, Greenberg started to say something about how he interpreted what I said, and I told him: 'I don't care how you interpreted it.' The fact is I supported the drug policy and said so. I also acknowledged the commissioner's power to suspend."

Vincent's interrogation and treatment of Michael as some sort of enemy to baseball makes chilling reading, and ought to set off alarms among club owners, who could just as easily find themselves on the commissioner's carpet some day. Repeatedly the imperial commissioner tells Michael, "You have effectively resigned from baseball," and "You have quit your baseball job," as if to drive home his intention to suspend the Yankee GM.

Again, it should be made clear that Lawn, Michael and Showalter did not volunteer to testify on Howe's behalf. They were requested to testify—and could have been subpoenaed had they refused. But Vincent still threatened them with suspensions.

A week prior to this hearing, Vincent had called Michael in for testimony on George Steinbrenner and informed him he could not bring his attorney with him. The commissioner made reference to that at the conclusion of the July 1 meeting with another veiled threat of suspension, saying: "This is where you need an attorney, not last week. The Yankees didn't brief you well. Yankee lawyers have not served you well."

Those were the almost identical words Vincent used reflecting on Steinbrenner's decision to take a lifetime ban rather than a two-year suspension back in August 1990. "George's lawyers didn't serve him well," he told the media.

Maybe one reason they didn't serve him well was because when Steinbrenner arrived at his meeting with Vincent, the imperial commissioner informed The Boss's co-counsel, U.S. attorney Paul Curran: "You are not welcome at this proceeding" and told him to leave.

That seems to be the pattern of Fay Vincent's imperial commissionership, especially in regard to the Yankees. He calls them in, denies them legal counsel, suspends them, then tells them their lawyers didn't serve them well.

FAY DECIDES NOT TO STAY

SEPTEMBER 8, 1992

Fay Vincent has taken himself out of the ballgame "in the best interests of baseball."

Recognizing the difficulty of trying to remain in office without the support of a majority of owners, Vincent yesterday resigned as commissioner. Vincent's resignation comes just four days after owners called for it by an 18-9 vote, with one abstention.

Informed of that no-confidence vote Thursday, Vincent had vowed to fight any effort to remove him from office through a court suit. But he reconsidered over the holiday weekend.

"I've concluded that resignation—not litigation—should be my final act as commissioner in the best interests of baseball," Vincent wrote in a letter to owners yesterday. "It would be an even greater disservice to baseball if it were to precipitate a protracted fight over the office of the commissioner."

Vincent was forced out by owners angry at his refusal to relinquish the commissioner's "best interests" power on collective bargaining, his unilateral order to realign the National League and his stance against superstations.

The group was led by Jerry Reinsdorf of the Chicago White Sox, Bud Selig of Milwaukee, Stanton Cook of the Chicago Cubs and Peter O'Malley of the Los Angeles Dodgers.

The threat of litigation was Vincent's only weapon for remaining in office. However, even though he had retained the services of high-powered Washington, D.C., attorney Brendan Sullivan, legal sources had concluded that it would have been unlikely Vincent could have prevailed since owners have offered to pay him for the remaining 14 months of contract.

"To obtain a temporary restraining order to remain in office, he would have had to have damages," said Robert Costello, an attorney who represented Gene Michael and Leonard Kleinman of the Yankees against Vincent. "And he had none."

Had Vincent not resigned, owners were prepared to take a vote to fire him at a meeting the next day in St. Louis. A leader of the movement to oust Vincent said plans had been discussed to "if necessary" to bar Vincent from their joint meeting Thursday and even change the locks at the commissioner's office at 350 Park Avenue if he tried to remain in office.

"After the vote at the meeting last week, I can no longer justify imposing on baseball, nor should baseball be required to endure, a bitter legal battle—even though I am confident that in the end I would win," Vincent's letter said. "But what would that accomplish? What will the right have been worth if, 14 months from now, prior to electing a new commissioner, the owners change the Major League Agreement to create a 'figurehead' commissioner. This is certainly the goal of some."

In adopting their resolution calling for Vincent's resignation, owners announced they would form a committee to study restructuring the commissioner's job, according to a press release from owners. It is the aim of the majority of them that future commissioners would serve as chief executive officers, answerable to owners, and that the all-encompassing "best interests of baseball" powers (which most felt Vincent abused) be eliminated.

In the interim, the office will remain vacant, and under the baseball agreement, the 10-member Executive Council (composed of four owners from each league and the league presidents) will govern baseball. It is believed the council will appoint a "caretaker" to handle the day-to-day duties of the commissioner. There was no immediate indication of whom owners will select to fill that role. In all likelihood, it will be a retired baseball executive, such as former American League president Lee MacPhail or former Expos boss John McHale. However, Blue Jays president Paul Beeston, selected to chair last week's emergency meeting on Vincent, is looked upon now as a strong candidate for the permanent job after the job is redefined.

For the most part, the owners were just grateful Vincent decided to resign and not take them to court. For although they were confident they would prevail against him if he did, there was some concern one of the teams supporting him would file suit against the majority that opposed him, charging they had violated the major league agreement by firing him.

"I was not surprised he resigned," said Phillies owner Bill Giles, one of Vincent's most outspoken opponents. "I couldn't believe any human being in his situation could think he could operate any kind of organization when so many people had no confidence in him. I believed in my heart he would do the smart thing and he did."

Vincent apparently agreed, concluding his letter: "I cannot govern as commissioner without the consent of the owners to be governed. I do not believe that consent is now available to me."

FATHERS AND SONS

JUNE 19, 1994

It was a few minutes before 11 a.m. and Mickey Mantle was sitting at the bar in his restaurant just as he had with Billy Martin on so many other "mornings after" in what was the boozy haze of his baseball after-life.

On this day, though, Mantle's "breakfast of champions" was a diet root beer, and the haze that he was seeing through the window of the restaurant was the real thing, the product of the oppressive heat outside.

"People don't believe this," Mantle said, wiping his brow, "but I haven't had the urge to have a drink since I got out of the Betty Ford clinic. I thought I would. The day before they let me go home I was walking around the track they have there, thinking that as soon as I get on the plane I'll order a glass of wine. But I never did, which makes me

believe that they do a lot more with you there than you realize."

He is trim, 20 pounds lighter than when he entered the clinic last January for treatment for a lifetime of alcohol abuse. The eyes are clear now, and most importantly, so is the mind.

A smile came over his face as he looked across the room at his two sons, Danny and David, who were having makeup applied in preparation for a Father's Day TV special they were all doing together. And then, just as quickly, it vanished at the mention of his own late father, to whom he was required to write a letter as part of the program at Betty Ford.

"That was the hardest thing I ever had to do," Mantle said. "Part of the program is grief. I told my dad in the letter how badly I felt for having let him down, for not being the ballplayer I should have been. If he had lived

I don't think I would have drank. I wouldn't have wanted him to see me with a beer. I sure as hell wouldn't have drank in front of him the way I did in front of my sons."

But now, at 62 and in what he regards as his second chance in life, he is finally bonding with his sons, all of them except Billy, the unlucky one who contracted the Hodgkin's disease that killed Mickey's father, grandfather and uncle.

After a long bout with painkiller addiction, Billy Mantle died at 36 of a heart attack last March, just two weeks after Mickey left the clinic. "I told my wife I picked a helluva time to quit drinking," Mantle said, "but in truth if I hadn't quit that might have been the thing that put me over."

His regret at not having been the father to his sons that his father had been to him is understandable. Mutt Mantle would trudge home from the Oklahoma lead mines every day and throw baseballs to young Mickey until twilight, teaching him how to switch hit. When Mickey's kids were growing up, he was seldom there.

But when he says he let the old man down too, maybe he's being too hard on himself. After

Mantle's three sons (l. to r.) Mickey Jr., Daniel and David throw out the first balls before a NY Yankees vs. Seattle Mariners game (John Roca/Daily News)

all, as his millions of fans have told him, nobody felt short-changed by 536 home runs or the record 18 more he hit in the World Series. Or his three Most Valuable Player awards and his leading role on 12 Yankee pennant winners. Surely Mutt Mantle would have been proud of all that, too.

"You have to understand," Mantle said, "I didn't have a good year after I was 33 years old. When I was playing, they always used to compare me, Willie Mays and Duke Snider. But just look at the final stats. Willie played 20 years, injury-free. If I had taken better care of myself I might have been the player he was."

For however many years he has left, Mantle has vowed to take care of himself. If, in his mind, he wasn't the role model he should have been as a ballplayer, he hopes to be looked upon as one now.

"I would like to tell kids, 'Don't fall off the mountain before you get to the top,'" he said. "I want them to know how bad it was for me. I always did what I wanted to do. I'd drink to enjoy it and then I'd wake up and not remember anything. I'd be told how I embarrassed people and I couldn't believe that was me."

Regrets? Yes, he's had more than a few, and there are times, even now when he can see clearly, that he finds himself having to come to grips with them all over again. He cannot bring back those years he feels he wasted as a player any more than he can bring back Billy Martin, the best friend who didn't make it to Betty Ford.

"The last time I saw Billy, right before he died, we were sitting right here in this bar, drinking," Mantle said. "He was crying. He wasn't happy with anything in his life, and I said to myself: 'Man, this would be a good time for both of us to stop drinking, right now.'

"Lou Gehrig said he considered himself the luckiest man on the earth. That's the way I feel now, except when I think about Billy. Both of them."

FEDS TO TAG STRAW WITH TAX CHARGES

DECEMBER 8, 1994

Former Mets slugger Darryl Strawberry will be indicted today on federal tax charges, his attorney has confirmed to the *Daily News*.

Strawberry, 32, who finished last season with the San Francisco Giants, could face more than 18 months in prison if found guilty of not paying taxes on under-the-table money from signing autographs at card and memorabilia shows.

The indictment is the culmination of a three-year investigation by the U.S. attorney's office in White Plains. *The News* on June 20, 1993, exclusively reported that Strawberry was the target of a federal probe of unreported cash payments to professional athletes.

According to Marty Gelfand, Strawberry's Los Angeles-based attorney, arraignment is set for December 14 in White Plains.

"It [the arraignment] will be very brief because he's not guilty," Gelfand told *The News* yesterday.

"Darryl is innocent, and he will plead not guilty. This is the end of a long investigation, but in our opinion it is a case that has no merit."

However, a tax attorney familiar with the investigation contends that the government's case against Strawberry is strong. "They've got all the receipts," the attorney said.

Federal tax officials determined through grand jury testimony and interviews with card show promoters that Strawberry had failed to disclose "in excess of $300,000" of income derived from signing autographs at card and memorabilia shows over a five-year period, sources said.

If convicted, Strawberry could face from 18 to 24 months in prison. Strawberry's agent, Eric Goldschmidt, also will be indicted, according to sources familiar with the investigation. The only professional baseball player to be indicted and convicted of tax evasion for card shows is Pete Rose, who was sentenced to five months in prison and fined $50,000 in January 1990 for failing to report $345,967 in income.

The indictment of Strawberry and Goldschmidt is only the first shot fired by the feds in a wide-scale investigation of tax evasion by pro athlete superstars, sources said. The L.A.-based Goldschmidt also is the agent and financial adviser for a half-dozen other prominent major league baseball players including Cincinnati Reds stars Barry Larkin and Reggie Sanders.

Last month, Goldschmidt successfully convinced the Giants to offer Strawberry salary arbitration—which in effect makes him a signed player for 1995. "We've been apprised of the forthcoming indictments," San Francisco general manager Bob Quinn said yesterday. "We've known this was a pending situation, but we remain committed to Darryl."

Several sources told *The News* that negotiations by Strawberry's attorneys for a plea bargain finally broke down a few months ago, prompting the feds to seek the indictment. And despite the indictment, the investigation is still ongoing.

As recently as nine days ago, Joe Esposito, a memorabilia dealer from Westchester, testified to the feds that he paid Strawberry $2,800 in cash for signing autographs at a September 1986 card show. It also has been learned that a number of prominent dealers including Alan (Mr. Mint) Rosen of Montvale, N.J., and Wanda Marcus, who hosted two national card collectors conventions in Dallas, have been told by the feds to be prepared to testify at Strawberry's trial. Rosen previously testified that he paid Strawberry $7,000 in cash to sign autographs at a 1988 card show in Madison Square Garden.

Besides the dealers, the feds have called dozens of prominent players to testify in the probe, including Dwight Gooden, Lenny Dykstra, Gary Carter, Ron Darling and Kevin McReynolds. However, it was not clear if they were called as potential targets in the investigation or as corroborating witnesses against Strawberry.

It is believed that the probe's initial focus was on members of the Mets' 86 world championship team but that it later expanded to include other baseball teams and other sports.

Since *The News'* revelations of the tax probe, Strawberry has had more than his share of career setbacks. Once one of the most productive sluggers in baseball— he remains the Mets' all-time leading home run hitter with

Darryl Strawberry signs autographs at no charge before a game in 1995. (Keith Torrie/Daily News)

252—he was struck down by a herniated disc in his back that required surgery and sidelined him for most of the 1993 season. During the off season last winter, he touched off a public furor in Los Angeles with his off-the-cuff "let it burn" comment about the brush fires that had ravaged Southern California.

Then last April, after going AWOL for a day in spring training, Strawberry admitted to a substance abuse problem and checked into the Betty Ford Clinic. When he was released from the clinic four weeks later, the Dodgers bought out the remaining year and a half of his five-year, $20.4 million contract that he signed after leaving the Mets as a free agent in November 1990.

The Giants, in desperate need of a left-handed power hitter to replace Will Clark, signed Strawberry on June 19 last season. In 29 games for them leading up to the players' strike, he hit .239 with four homers and 17 RBI.

As part of what he termed his "new life" with the Giants, Strawberry was accompanied everywhere by his older brother, a former L.A. policeman who was paid by the club to serve as his chaperone. But while Strawberry was able to convince the Giants that his drug and back problems were behind him, he was unable to resolve his tax situation.

FROM DAY 1, BOSS SECOND-GUESSING

APRIL 27, 1995

TAMPA—He was with you all the way, Buck.

Well, most of the way. There was a little problem early on. Like from the moment the game came on the big screen and the lineup card was flashed, showing Mattingly hitting in the five hole and O'Neill hitting third.

"I don't like that," George Steinbrenner mumbled. "Nothing against O'Neill. He's been a great hitter for me, but why isn't Donnie batting third?"

I was sitting at a booth in Damon's Ribs, the sports bar/restaurant in Steinbrenner's hotel that is equipped with three giant TV screens and accompanying satellite dishes. It was here we found The Boss in his "doctor's orders exile"—prohibited from flying to New York for Opening Day at Yankee Stadium because of recent surgery for a detached retina.

I thought he might like some company, even if I wasn't The Donald, Fugie, Elaine or any of his customary Opening Day companions. While they were feasting on champagne and smoke salmon in the owner's box at the Stadium, The Boss and I shared a bowl of popcorn and drank iced tea.

"In 20 years I think I've missed only four or five Opening Days," Steinbrenner said. "Of course, most of them were from my two suspensions, which I don't count. All I know is I really wanted to be at this opener, but at least here I don't have to worry about taking care of everyone, making sure they've got their seats and enough to eat. And I can really watch the game."

Actually, *two* of them. Because he owns the hotel and controls the satellite dishes, Steinbrenner was able to get the MSG and ESPN feeds—and critique two sets of announcers as well as his manager and his ballclub.

If you're Steinbrenner, the supreme critic and grandstand manager, it doesn't get any better than this.

"The Yankees are the team to beat," said Al Trautwig in his opening MSG monologue.

"Damn it, Al," Steinbrenner screamed at the screen, "don't say that! I hate everybody picking us to win!"

But before he got a chance to grouse any further over his team's preseason accolades or Buck Showalter's lineup, we were joined by his four secretaries, all of whom had been given the day off in honor of the Yanks' opener.

"Some gift, Boss," huffed Joanne Nastal, who is somewhat of a miracle woman in that she has worked for Steinbrenner for 23 years and never has missed a paycheck for ordering the wrong sandwich. "We thought when you told us you were taking us to Opening Day, it was in *New York* with all the theatres and restaurants."

"Whaddaya mean?" Steinbrenner laughed. "Look what I've got for you. Front-row seats!"

"Yeah," retorted Joanne, "well, next time I'll be sure to ask for the details."

As they introduced Yankee players on both networks, Steinbrenner provided me with inside scouting dope on his players, the stuff you don't get from Jim Kaat.

"Bernie Williams has bulked up. I think we're going to see a lot more power from him this year. And Tartabull...he's got to hang right in there and not stay off the plate so much. There's no way he should be buried by Canseco. He should hit as many homers as anyone in the league."

Having filed those bits of insight, I dug into the popcorn and settled in for Jimmy Key's first pitch—which was promptly lined into right field by Otis Nixon for a single.

"That's a hell of a way to start," Steinbrenner fumed.

Fortunately for all of us, Key quickly settled into his 1994 form, and when Tartabull homered to left center to put the Yankees up 1-0 in the second, Steinbrenner let out a yelp and hugged his six-year-old grandson, Steven, who had saddled up next to him.

"Atta boy, Danny! That's the way to hang in there! Did you see that? He didn't bail out!"

We all nodded, even Steven. Hey, when you're right...

In the third, Texas used a squeeze play to tie the score, but

Steinbrenner, perhaps buoyed by his call on Tartabull, seemed unperturbed.

"Give me the power," he grumped. "I'm an Earl Weaver guy. We'll get that run back and more."

Sure enough, the Yankees proved him right again, and as they were scoring three runs in the fourth, ESPN showed a highlight of the Brewers going ahead of the White Sox, 6-2.

"Look at those Brewers beating up on the White Sox," said Steinbrenner. "And they talk like they're small-market."

He was laughing and everyone was laughing along with him, and it was shaping up as a joyous and festive Opening Day in Tampa until Key suddenly lost it in the sixth inning in New York. It was here, Buck, that you lost him again.

"Too long," Steinbrenner agonized. "He stayed with him too long! You can't stretch those guys out so long this early with so little spring training."

Even after Bob Wickman came in to preserve a one-run lead by getting Mickey Tettleton to ground into a double play, I sensed an uneasiness with everyone in the restaurant except maybe Steven, whose attention was divided between a ginger ale and a bowl of ice cream. We definitely needed someone to restore the happy mood, and when Bernie Williams homered, you could hear our collective sigh above all the crowd noise from the two screens.

"You see?" Steinbrenner exclaimed, nudging me. "Bernie's not a kid anymore. Look at that strength now that he's bulked up! Didn't I tell you?"

Yeah, I thought, Bernie may not be a kid any more, but in many ways The Boss is.

There were, to be sure, a few more hairy moments before the Yankees tucked this one away. From where we were watching, Buck, you made all the right moves after the sixth—especially bringing in Wetteland to close it out. The Boss really liked that.

"You know," Steinbrenner said, "as much as I missed seeing everyone, I really enjoyed this because I got to see the whole game."

Got to *manage* the whole game, too.

JOE D & MORRIS: THE FINAL DAYS

Yogi Berra, Whitey Ford and Phil Rizzuto were among those at the Stadium on April 25, 1999 at 1:15 p.m. as a monument to Joe DiMaggio was unveiled. It is only the fifth such memorial in the Yankees' 97-year history—the others are to Babe Ruth, Lou Gehrig, Mickey Mantle and Miller Huggins.

As Joe DiMaggio lay dying, hooked up to tubes in intensive care and slowly succumbing to lung cancer, an old friend, Angelo Sapio, tried to cheer up the ailing legend.

Sapio was DiMaggio's barber, and he told Joe how he'd recently spoken with a man who claimed to have seen the Yankee Clipper's fabled 58-game hitting streak halted in Cleveland in the summer of 1941.

Barely able to speak, "Joe grabbed me by the sleeve, pulled me down and whispered, 'It's 56,'" Sapio recalled. "Even sick as he was, he kept track of the details."

But while the stricken DiMaggio could correct a flawed recollection of his most famous record, he was able to control little else during his final months.

His will, his legacy, his carefully crafted image, and even his friendships now belonged to someone else: a litigious Florida tax lawyer, Morris Engelberg, who is now the sole trustee for DiMaggio's multimillion-dollar estate.

For years, Engelberg had been known as DiMaggio's "longtime friend and attorney," and anyone who wanted to strike a business deal with "baseball's greatest living player" had to go through him.

In DiMaggio's final months, from the time he began a 99-day hospital stay Oct. 12 until he died peacefully March 8 at his Hollywood, Florida, home,

Engelberg was DiMaggio's link to the rest of the world.

It was not always a dependable link. Initially, Engelberg refused to divulge the truth of DiMaggio's cancer, then later told stories of DiMaggio's "miracle recovery."

Said Engelberg on November 24, "I said, 'Joe, the Dow is up,' and he made a fist and smiled. Tell the world Joe is not going to die."

The truth was grimmer. Throughout his ordeal, DiMaggio was a terminal cancer patient.

As early as September, Engelberg said DiMaggio was spitting up blood, but still trying to keep to his schedule of public appearances. "He didn't want anyone to know," he said. "He told me not to tell anyone."

Engelberg enforced DiMaggio's privacy orders ruthlessly, not even disclosing the Yankee Clipper's condition to Dominic DiMaggio, his only surviving brother.

That led to a confrontation with Dominic outside DiMaggio's room at Memorial Regional Hospital in Hollywood. "We had our scuffle in the hallway," Engelberg said. "Dom wanted to know what was wrong. But I couldn't tell him. Joe made it totally 100 percent clear."

But Engelberg's isolation of DiMaggio was self-serving, say those who were ostracized from the inner circle of the man they adored. For them, DiMaggio's last days left a trail of get-well wishes never received, questions never answered, goodbyes never said.

"I tried. I really tried. Fifteen times I called Morris. I wrote letters to Morris," said Bert Padell, who managed DiMaggio's business affairs in the 1970s through the mid-'80s. "When Joe was really sick, I called Morris at least twice a week, and he never got back to me. I knew him since 1948. Since 1948!"

Now, in the weeks since his death, there are whispers among DiMaggio's friends that Engelberg's actions were more to help the lawyer than the client.

Engelberg rejects such suggestions. "A lot of people don't like me," he said. "Know why? I protected Joe for 15 years."

But there were signs in the final year of his life that DiMaggio was losing patience with his representative.

Around Old Timers' Day at Yankee Stadium last year, sources say DiMaggio became aware that Engelberg, through his brother, Lester Engel, had approached at least one entertainment company thought to be the Walt Disney Co. about a deal involving the use of Joe's likeness and name.

Engelberg had "no comment" about any entertainment deal.

Engelberg flatly denies knowing of any approach to Disney. He acknowledges exploring with other producers the possibility of an animated cartoon series using DiMaggio's name, but said the idea was DiMaggio's. "I never started a deal without him," Engelberg said.

But other DiMaggio friends insist that Joltin' Joe complained of an overture to Disney made without his knowledge and erupted when he found out.

"Joe was furious," said one longtime DiMaggio friend. "How furious? On a scale of one to 10, how about a 10 and a half?"

Friends also say DiMaggio recently sought the advice of longtime William Morris CEO Norman Brokaw. "In the last couple of years we had a series of dinners together, and he asked me for advice on certain business matters," Brokaw said. "The Disney thing was one of them." DiMaggio also tried to set up a meeting with former baseball commissioner Fay Vincent. "He said he wanted to discuss business," Vincent said. "But I don't know what it was. He got sick, and we never did meet."

Another DiMaggio associate was convinced Joe considered

Engelberg attends a memorial for DiMaggio. (Howard Simmons/Daily News)

cutting ties to Engelberg last summer. If Joe were alive today, the associate believes, "Morris would not be handling his affairs."

Engelberg maintains DiMaggio and he were closer than ever toward the end. He told a story Friday in which DiMaggio introduced Engelberg to Joe Pepitone, saying, "Pepi, this is Morris, my main man."

Legend's Protector

In any case, after he entered the hospital in October, DiMaggio, famous for cutting off anyone he suspected of trying to make money off him, was in no shape for a battle with Engelberg, or anyone else. "You gotta understand something," said a longtime DiMaggio confidant. "Joe was 83 years old. He was frail and sick and wasn't anywhere near the tiger he used to be."

The notion of a rift between DiMaggio and Engelberg will come as a shock to anyone who observed Engelberg after DiMaggio was admitted to Memorial Regional. Engelberg repeatedly identified himself as DiMaggio's "friend and attorney," personal representative of his estate, accountant, spokesman and protector of the Yankee legend's good name.

In a letter to the mayor of Hollywood, Florida, Engelberg explained why he wanted to stop an attempt by city leaders to name a landmark after DiMaggio. "There will be absolutely no approval to naming the Presidential Circle [in Hollywood]," the letter says. "I control the license and use of Mr. DiMaggio's name in perpetuity as long as I am alive."

A similar suggestion from San Francisco officials to name a park for him in the city DiMaggio grew up in was met by Engelberg with unreturned phone calls.

"San Francisco wasn't right for Joe DiMaggio," he said last week.

In a letter to Mayor Giuliani, Engelberg criticized Gov. Pataki for his proposal to rename the Major Deegan Expressway for DiMaggio. While Engelberg approved of Giuliani's idea to rename the West Side Highway for Joe D, he slammed Pataki's initiative.

"Gov. Pataki should be made aware that there cannot be anything named after Joe DiMaggio anywhere, without my approval," Engelberg wrote.

While Engelberg controls licensing rights to the DiMaggio name, it is doubtful he has power to stop all uses.

Friends Kept Out

"The public is not likely to be confused into believing that Mr. DiMaggio sponsored or endorsed the highway, park or memorial service," said Barbara Friedman, a New York intellectual property attorney. "Rather, they will likely perceive it as it is an honorary memorial. It does not appear to be a commercial use under the right of publicity laws."

As acrimonious as attempts to honor the great ballplayer have become, DiMaggio's friends were more hurt that Engelberg shut them out during Joe's last months.

In the final days of DiMaggio's life first on the heavily guarded second floor of Memorial Regional and later in the large, airy "Florida room" at DiMaggio's Hollywood home, Engelberg took it upon himself to determine whom Joe could see and blockaded those he didn't want to let in.

He says it was logistical, not personal. "I'm not returning 100 calls a day," he said. "I work 100 hours a week. I'm an attorney. Joe got thousands of letters and cards. All I really cared about was Joe getting better."

With DiMaggio on a respirator, only Engelberg could comment on DiMaggio's condition during his long hospital stay.

When Barry Halper, a memorabilia collector, Yankee limited partner and 25-year DiMaggio friend, wrote a guest column about their friendship in this newspaper after DiMaggio's death, Engelberg wrote a cease-and-desist letter that said, "He was never your friend, he only tolerated you."

Such actions were intended to protect Joe's name from profiteers, Engelberg said.

But Engelberg has his own financial interests as the lone trustee for each of the seven trusts created in DiMaggio's will for DiMaggio's two granddaughters, four great-grandchildren and son, Joe Jr. According to Florida law, trustees are paid under a "reasonable compensation" standard, which means that Engelberg has wide latitude in setting his own fees for administering the trusts.

The will also makes it clear that Engelberg represents the estate, currently estimated to be worth $30 million, in all matters connected with the licensing and use of DiMaggio's name, likeness, image, signature or memorabilia items.

That all could be worth millions more. Dead celebrities are a hot commodity. The estate of Babe Ruth earns more than $1 million a year for using his image to sell things such as Lipton iced tea, and it is widely believed the DiMaggio estate will be worth at least as much as Ruth's.

Sullied Image

Few celebrities enjoyed as crystalline a public image as Joe DiMaggio. But Engelberg, the legal custodian of that image and gatekeeper of that good name, has been muddied more than once in court documents obtained by the *Daily News.*

One document, buried in a sexual-harassment suit filed by Robin Wolfer, a former employee at Engelberg's law firm, is full of assertions of wrongdoing by Engelberg.

Drafted by attorneys for Les Kushner, a former law partner of Engelberg's who was himself drawn into litigation with Engelberg, it alleges that: Engelberg bragged of refusing to do deals while DiMaggio was alive in order to beef up the value of the estate, thus driving up the fees he could collect from the estate.

Engelberg had DiMaggio sign hundreds of items of memorabilia, which the attorney accepted in lieu of payment for services and was stashing away until after DiMaggio's death. "Purportedly," the document says, "none of the items received were reported on his individual tax returns even though he has received these items in lieu of fees."

Engelberg regularly divulged attorney-client confidences, allegedly referring to one well-heeled client as "a nymphomaniac," and revealing secrets about Joe Jr., Joe's only son. The document also says Engelberg "discussed with numerous people that Joe D is extremely cheap, will never go into his pocket to pay for a meal and didn't even bring a gift to [Engelberg's] daughter Laurie's wedding."

In the Kushner suit, which initially was unrelated to DiMaggio, Engelberg nonetheless brought DiMaggio into it. The court file shows that after Engelberg wrote a threatening letter to Kushner and copied it to DiMaggio, the Clipper was subpoenaed. The case was settled out of court before DiMaggio was compelled to testify.

Neither Wolfer nor Kushner would comment, citing

confidentiality agreements made as part of their settlements.

But Engelberg, who denied the allegations in court documents and accused Wolfer and Kushner of trying to defame him in the lawsuits, did comment Friday.

The Kushner case, he said, "was about a stockholder suit where we threw a partner out of the office. He tried to subpoena Joe, but I wouldn't let him. Joe never got sued with me."

He said the Wolfer case wasn't settled; "It was dropped. I paid out zero money. I spent $105,000 to win the case and protect my reputation."

Still, other court documents paint further unflattering pictures of Engelberg:

In a probate case involving Bertha Behrman, founder of the Madame Alexander doll company, Engelberg was accused of knowingly filing an invalid will. When Behrman died in Palm Beach, Florida, in October 1990, Engelberg immediately filed the will, complete with a clause stating he was unaware of any competing "wills or codicils."

But the court record reveals Engelberg's law firm not only was aware that Madame Alexander had filed a later will, but had prepared for a battle over the estate. Engelberg claims the

Madame was "in diapers" when the later will was drafted.

In the end, Engelberg was out as executor but not before receiving $100,000 in a settlement.

Florida Meeting

Engelberg, 59, grew up in Brooklyn and graduated from Brooklyn Law School in 1964. But he built his business in Florida.

One of his clients there, Cal Kovens, introduced Engelberg to DiMaggio in 1983, not long after DiMaggio had moved from San Francisco to Florida for tax reasons.

Shortly after he met Engelberg, DiMaggio had a falling out with Bert Padell, his business manager, over what Padell says was a mistake made by one of his employees.

By 1991, Engelberg was managing DiMaggio's affairs and making him money. Just as the market for sports memorabilia began to boom, Engelberg began negotiating deals for DiMaggio to appear at card shows and, later, for exclusive bat, ball and lithograph signing arrangements with collectibles companies.

"Morris turned Joe into a cash machine," said Padell. "He

made it a real major business for Joe."

Harry Bryant worked for Scoreboard, a company that paid DiMaggio $3 million to autograph 1,941 bats commemorating his hitting streak. "It was probably four times more money than he made his whole career as a player," Bryant said.

Meanwhile, Engelberg fulfilled the dream of many men of a certain age: He became Joe DiMaggio's friend. He named his office building Yankee Clipper Center. He left parking space No. 5 reserved for DiMaggio. Engelberg's custom license plates read DIMAG5. And three years ago, he moved his famous client next door in the gated community of Harbor Islands, into a house just like his own.

Despite the mutually enriching relationship, the last five years were tumultuous for both Engelberg and DiMaggio. Engelberg spent much of his time embroiled in litigation.

It's unclear how much, if any, of Engelberg's troubles were known to DiMaggio. But it is clear that by last year DiMaggio seemed to be looking for other counsel in his business affairs as his health deteriorated.

Condition Withheld

Brokaw recalled the last time he spoke with DiMaggio: last summer in a Hollywood, Florida, restaurant the night Mark McGwire hit his 62nd home run.

"He told me again there were some things he wanted my advice about, but he wasn't feeling well," Brokaw said. "Not long after, he went in the hospital, and we never talked again. Why did he come to me? Because he trusted me."

In the 99 days after DiMaggio entered Memorial Regional Hospital, the one adjacent to the children's hospital that bears his name, Engelberg misled the public about his client's condition.

"I never denied he had cancer," he said. "I just said I didn't want to address it."

DiMaggio's true disease wasn't revealed, not even to his family, for six weeks, Engelberg said.

Of the DiMaggio friends who were unable to get through to him during his illness, Barry Halper's case was one of the strangest.

Instead of a visit, Halper got a nasty letter. In it, Engelberg insinuated that DiMaggio's 1951 World Series ring, which Halper had purchased from another dealer, had been stolen.

Halper says he once offered to give the ring back to DiMaggio gratis, but Joltin' Joe declined, and instead gave Halper a handwritten note authenticating the ring as his. He told Halper that he'd given the ring away to a friend and that it was never stolen.

Engelberg's mention of the ring is interesting, since Engelberg himself has been publicly flaunting DiMaggio's 1936 World Series ring, the only one of nine Series rings still in DiMaggio's possession when he died.

"He gave me that ring on his deathbed," Engelberg said Friday. "I'm never taking it off my finger."

According to Richard Ben Cramer, the Pulitzer Prize-winning author who is preparing a biography of DiMaggio, a family member confronted Engelberg about the ring at the DiMaggio funeral in San Francisco, and was told by Engelberg, "Joe said I could have the ring for one year," and then it was to go back to the family.

When asked if he had offered to give it back to the family, Engelberg said, "I said 'If you want it back, it's yours.' No one wants to wear it."

"[DiMaggio] wore that ring every day of his life," said another longtime DiMaggio acquaintance, who added that he couldn't imagine Joe giving it to anyone other than someone in his family.

High Price

With many friends cut off, DiMaggio still had Engelberg to keep him company, although to hear Engelberg tell it, that was quite a sacrifice. Longtime DiMaggio friend Bernie Esser wrote a letter to Engelberg complaining about the lawyer's handling of the press during Joe's hospital stay. "Basically," Esser said, "I just told him to stop all the stupid statements, in fairness to Joe."

Engelberg fired a letter back, defending himself by saying Joe had become a full-time job. "I have walked away from a legal practice for the past 70 days to handle all of Mr. DiMaggio's affairs as well as the press at a cost of over $200,000 to our law firm," he wrote.

DiMaggio died a peaceful death with his dear friend Joe Nacchio at his side and Broward County Hospice workers comforting him.

But the days since have not been peaceful for Engelberg. Since Joe D's death, the attorney has been more combative in trying to protect his client's name.

He says he is going after counterfeiters and wrote the

hard-nosed letters to politicians because Joe wanted his name only on a park in Hollywood, Florida, the West Side Highway in New York and the Joe DiMaggio Children's Hospital, also in Hollywood.

"I had to stop his name from being all over the papers," Engelberg said. "It was just too much."

To a large extent, Engelberg's tactics have worked. Several DiMaggio confidants declined to be interviewed by *The News*, saying they feared Engelberg might tie them up in litigation.

But not everyone is afraid. Scott Roberts, a board member of the Hollywood Chamber of Commerce, wrote a letter to the Daily Business Review of Broward County excoriating Engelberg.

"If DiMaggio was alive, he may not have approved of Engelberg's exploitation of his memory," Roberts wrote. "Although he 'guards' the reputation and use of DiMaggio's name, he named his own office building 'The Yankee Clipper.'"

The letter goes on: "Engelberg should enjoy his current 15 minutes of fame...Engelberg's legacy will be his nastiness."

Legacy Questions

Engelberg disagrees. He says his legacy as DiMaggio's friend is pur, and will be reflected in projects such as a proposed museum of memorabilia at the Joe DiMaggio Children's Hospital.

He insists he "never made a dime off Joe, never sent Joe a bill in 15 years with him."

Engelberg did allow that his law firm charged a "couple of thousand dollars" for contract work on certain deals, although according to documents, on four separate memorabilia deals alone, a total of $28,000 was paid to the law office of Engelberg and Cantor.

Through it all, Engelberg says he did nothing wrong, but faithfully executed the wishes of his friend and client, Joe DiMaggio. He says DiMaggio's feelings for him could be seen in the number of gifts he got from him, like the autographed bats he received on his birthday every year. Or the fact that Joe was godfather to his children.

"All these stories you hear," he said, "are B.S."

With Luke Cyphers and Michael O'Keeffe

REAL DEAL:
PHILLIPS NO GENIUS

DECEMBER 23, 2001

Maybe this all works out. Maybe the Mets go get Mo Vaughn as the other big hitter they still so desperately need and maybe Vaughn shows up in Port St. Lucie a svelte 250 pounds with no after-effects of the torn biceps tendon that shelved him all of last season and starts hitting home runs right from the get-go.

And maybe Shawn Estes finds the pressures of pitching in New York much to his liking and reverts to the 19-5 form he had in his 1997 career season. And maybe, too, Roger Cedeno suddenly develops better baseball instincts and reverses his steadily declining walks and on-base percentage as their leadoff man.

Maybe all these things come to pass and Steve Phillips comes off as the genius he has been acclaimed in so many quarters during this whirlwind of trading over the past two weeks. I may well be proven wrong (believe it or not, it wouldn't be the first

time), but I think Phillips is on a losing streak since the Robbie Alomar trade, and I especially think this proposed Vaughn deal is nuts.

Let's start with the Vaughn trade as all the various reports have it going down. The Mets supposedly send Kevin Appier and possibly Todd Zeile, who are scheduled to earn a combined $16.5 million next year, to Anaheim for Vaughn, who is slated to earn $10 million. There have also been reports that the Angels don't want Zeile and, if so and the Mets have to keep him, the deal is even more insane. In any case, more payroll flexibility is the way Mets operatives are painting it, except that Vaughn is also owed an additional $8 million signing bonus which, I'm told, the Angels are insisting the Mets pick up as well. Then, after next year, Vaughn is owed $15 million in both 2002 and 2003 with an option of $15 million in

2003 that can be bought out for $2 million. Do the math. With the signing bonus and the buyout, that comes to an even $50 million Vaughn has guaranteed.

This, for a 34-year-old designated hitter-in-first-baseman's-clothing who didn't play a game last year. Not that I'm a big Juan Gonzalez fan either, but it is becoming increasingly clear that, because of his uninsurable back condition and the added perceived baggage of all his hangers-on, his market has been reduced to two years, $25 million—at most. So, conceivably, for half of what the Mets are prepared to owe Vaughn, they could have Gonzalez. Otherwise, they effectively block any chance of moving Mike Piazza to first base for the next three years and they still have a gaping hole in right field.

Meanwhile, the Estes trade was equally puzzling, especially since the word around baseball was the Giants were going to non-tender him if they couldn't move him. Facing the prospect of having to pay Estes at least $7 million in arbitration, the Giants have been actively shopping him since the end of the season. There was no way they could afford to pay a No. 4 starter that kind of money when they also had to factor in a $9 to 10 million raise

for Barry Bonds. So Phillips came to their rescue by taking Estes off their hands and giving them two very useful, productive and inexpensive semi-regulars in Tsuyoshi Shinjo and Desi Relaford. The added negating factor to this deal is Estes being an acknowledged head case who doesn't pitch well under pressure.

Assuming Phillips makes the Vaughn deal and it includes Appier, that would leave the Mets with four left-handers in their rotation, two of which, Estes and Glendon Rusch, have been proven to exasperate managers with their delicate psyches.

As for Cedeno, I'd be awfully leery of a guy whose on-base percentage has decreased gradually from .396 to .383 to .337 over the past three years and who, as a supposed speed guy, had only 14 doubles in 523 at-bats last year. Phillips gave him a four-year, $18 million deal with a no-trade clause. I know I'll get an argument on this, but until he lost his center field job to Marquis Grissom last year, the Dodgers' Tom Goodwin was essentially the same player as Cedeno and a far better outfielder. Goodwin averaged 45 stolen bases from 1997 to 2000 and had on-base percentages of .314, .378, .324 and .346. Because Goodwin is owed $3.25 million for each of the next two years and has been

Mets manager Bobby Valentine (left) and general manager Steve Phillips (right) present Mo Vaughn with his Mets jersey. (Dennis Clark/Daily News)

relegated to fourth outfielder status, the Dodgers are looking to give him away.

Taking nothing away from the job Phillips has done as GM—his trades for Mike Piazza, Al Leiter, Armando Benitez and even Rusch made the Mets a World Series team in 2000—he's shown himself to be a reckless trader as well. The minus side of his ledger is Terrence Long for Kenny Rogers, Jason Isringhausen for Billy Taylor and Bubba Trammell (whom he's supposedly been trying to reacquire all this winter) for Donne Wall. So pardon me if I don't anoint Phillips as Executive of the Year just yet. Maybe I'm wrong, maybe all of this will make a lot more sense nine months down the road. But for now anyway, it looks to me like Phillips, flush from all the accolades he got for the Alomar deal, has been dealing ever since like he's bulletproof.

CHAPTER 2

HEROES AND LEGENDS

I didn't know Mickey Mantle as a player, and the writers back then all said he was difficult, to say the least. But in his retirement years I got to know him fairly well, and, as is evident in this book, his life, particularly the end of it, became a frequent topic. New York could never get enough of The Mick. ...I've always likened the Hall of Fame induction ceremonies to baseball's "high holy day of obligation." You cover a guy his entire career and then you see him at the culmination of that career, the greatest moment of his professional life. Special. ...I was especially happy to have gotten one of the last interviews Clyde Sukeforth ever gave, as he was such a treasure chest of baseball history and lore. ...The Steve Dalkowski piece was something I'd wanted to do ever since reading about him in a book, *The Suitors of Spring*, by Pat Jordan. The problem was finding him, and then, to my good fortune, I got a tip he'd been brought home to Connecticut.

Baseball's Greatest Is Still a Young Kid

May 7, 1981

Willie Mays is 50. Pinch yourself when you say it, then dismiss it if you wish.

Somehow the mere thought of Willie Mays, everlasting symbol of exuberant youth, reaching middle age is simply not to be accepted. Mays understands.

"I'm still a young kid even at 50," Mays said Tuesday night, hours before reaching that one milestone no one wishes to believe he has achieved. "They never thought I would ever grow old. I understand that. It's just like people telling their kids how to play the game today the way I did. They never saw me play, but they know me."

Reclining on the sofa in his Riverdale penthouse apartment, Mays was watching his two old teams, the Mets and Giants, on TV with only a casual interest. He had just flown in from the West Coast to spend a couple of weeks here tending to his numerous business interests, including the Willie Mays Foundation for underprivileged kids and, of course, the much-ballyhooed Bally Connection in Atlantic City that has prompted Bowie Kuhn to keep him out of baseball.

"I'm busier now than I ever was, and I'm enjoying life," Mays said. "I really don't have time enough for myself anymore. But I don't fool nobody. I was happier as a ballplayer. People always ask me if I wish I were playing today, seeing all the money they're getting now. Sure, I'd like to be playing today. But I wouldn't take my 20 years and throw 'em away and start over. It's not the money. The money for me was *always* gonna be there. I played for the *game*."

And, oh, how he played the game. Who else but Mays supplied the memories from so many different dimensions of it? The four home runs in

Milwaukee in 1961. The spectacular catch off Vic Wertz in the '54 World Series. The throw that caught Billy Cox at home in 1951, prompting Dodger manager Charlie Dressen to remark, "I'd like to see him do that again."

"The most fun part of the game for me was playing the outfield," Mays said. "I loved running down a ball, then watching a guy rounding second base after the third base coach has told him to stop. There was something about that which gave me more satisfaction than any other part of the game."

And there was something about Willie Mays that gave the fans more satisfaction than probably any other player of his time. Charisma is the way some people would explain it. Mays has his own explanation as to why he is so beloved.

"It's because I love people," he said. "You can't fool people. They can tell if you're in a room and don't want to be there. I never shortchanged anybody, especially playing. I loved what I was doing. Everytime I went on that ballfield, I made something happen. I felt if people paid two or three dollars to be there, I had to do something. That's why I reversed the sweatband in my cap so it would fall off every time I

made a running catch. Wasn't anything wrong with that. I felt you got to do these things for the fans."

It is May of 1951. In baseball, which ruled the New York summers during that glorious era when at least one of our three teams inevitably wound up in the World Series, the Giants have lost 11 straight. Having reached his breaking point, manager Leo Durocher implored Giants owner Horace Stoneham to bring up the AA center fielder hitting .477 at Minneapolis.

Stoneham, fearful of a mass demonstration by the fans in Minneapolis, took an unprecedented step of placing ads in the local papers explaining the forthcoming move. "Willie Mays," said the ads, "is entitled to his promotion and the chance to prove he can play major league baseball."

As far as Durocher was concerned, the very first look at Mays was proof enough. A kind of eerie quiet came over Shibe Park in Philadelphia May 25 when the 20-year-old Mays stepped into the batting cage for the first time. The hometeam Phillies, as well as the Giants, watched, first with curiosity, then with genuine admiration as the young center fielder ripped one drive after another to the outfield walls and beyond.

"I swear I'm gonna marry him," Durocher said. And for the better part of the next five years, including two trips to the World Series, he did. But first there was the matter of building the shy and unassuming rookie's confidence.

In that initial three-game series with the Phillies, Mays went 0-for-12, and after the Giants returned home to the Polo Grounds, Durocher was summoned out of his office by Monte Irvin. "Willie's crying," Irvin said. Durocher immediately went out into the clubhouse and confronted Mays.

"What's this?" the manager demanded.

"Missuh Leo," Mays said, choking back his tears, "you better send me back to Minneapolis. They're too fast for me. I can't hit up here."

"Minneapolis?" Durocher said incredulously. "You're going to be up here the rest of your life. You'll be hitting balls out of here when all the rest of them are long gone. Tonight's a new game."

"I'll try, Missuh Leo," Willie said. "But I don't know."

"I do," said Durocher.

•

"He always called me 'Missuh Leo,'" Durocher recalled

by phone from Palm Springs Tuesday. "And I tell you, I wish I could have 10 sons like Willie Mays. I can't love a man any more than that. It isn't just because of what he did on the ballfield, either. Willie Mays is the only man I know who can walk into a room and make the chandelier shake!

"I remember this one time I took Willie to eat at Mike Romanoff's restaurant in Hollywood. Willie was very skeptical about going, but the late Spencer Tracy had invited me and he told me to bring Willie. Well, as it turned out, everybody in the restaurant who passed by our table stopped to shake Willie's hand, many of them passing right by Spencer Tracy."

Willie didn't understand then. He does now.

"I know now that people own me," Mays said. "I'm in a fish bowl. I can understand that and it doesn't bother me. But you can understand why I still don't like going out in public that much."

"Willie is wonderful," said Durocher. "The greatest ballplayer who ever lived as far as I'm concerned, and that's no knock on Musial or Aaron. There are only five ways to be great: Hit, hit with power, run, field and throw. A lot of players can do two, maybe three of 'em, Willie could do all five. It was God-given. Hell, he taught *me* how to play the game."

•

As Mays noted with pride, it was the fielding, more than any of the other four characteristics cited by Durocher, which gave him the most satisfaction.

"Willie always believed it was his solemn duty to catch any ball that wasn't hit in the stands," said Monte Irvin, a fellow Hall of Famer and Mays's first roommate. "Willie always plays down that catch in the '54 World Series off Vic Wertz and says he made a lot of others which were as good or better. But I'll tell, there's no *way* he knew he was going to get to that ball. I know because I was right there, running behind him to get the carom.

"The greatest catch he ever made, in my opinion, was a couple of years earlier in Pittsburgh. Rocky Nelson of the Pirates hit one of Sal Maglie's fastballs to deep right center in Forbes Field. Willie took off after it, and just as it looked like it was gonna go over his head, he reached up and grabbed it— *BAREHANDED*!

Mays cries as he says goodbye and retires. (Dan Farrell/Daily News)

"As he was coming in, Leo told us, 'Don't anybody say anything to him.' After a couple of minutes, Willie finally looked over at Leo and said: 'Damn, ain't nobody gonna say anything?'

"Leo said, 'Why, what happened?'

"'I made what I thought was a pretty good catch,' Willie said.

"'Geez, I was over at the water cooler; I guessed I missed it. You'll just have to make another one next inning.'"

•

April 30, 1961. Mays came about as close as a man can come to hitting five home runs in one game. He wound up settling for four, a feat accomplished by only six other men in history for a nine-inning game. Having already hit home runs off Braves starter Lou Burdette in the first and third innings, Mays hit a drive to deep center field off Moe Drabowsky in the fifth. But Hank Aaron, playing center field for the Braves, made the catch on the run a few feet from the fence.

Mays hit his third homer of the game off left-hander Seth Morehead in the sixth before coming to bat against right-hander Don McMahon in the eighth. Before McMahon pitched to Mays, however, Joe Adcock, who himself had hit four home runs in a game a couple of years earlier, strolled over to the mound.

"I called time and told Mac, 'Don't let this guy hit the ball this time,'" Adcock said. "He replied, 'Don't worry, I got him.' As soon as I got back to first base, Willie hit McMahon's first pitch for the darndest screaming line drive you ever saw—over the fence."

•

April of 1971. Willie Mays, now 40, is off to the hottest start of his career.

Hitting safely in his first 10 games, Mays smacked five home runs. By the end of April he was hitting .361. In late May, he was at .336 with 11 homers. Somewhere in that early summer of 1971, Mays suddenly began to act his age. He finished at .271 with 18 home runs, respectable figures, but hardly Mays-ian. His greatest achievements—3,000 hits, 600 home runs, two MVP awards, Rookie of the Year—were all behind him.

"I don't know if it was the extra doubleheaders I played that year at first base or what," Mays said. "I do know that then was the first time I knew it was coming to an end. I was really fatigued at the end of the year, and I knew something was happening. It wasn't until a couple of years later, though, that I began thinking seriously of a career after baseball. That's why I came back to New York to the Mets. I didn't want to leave San Francisco, but I knew the opportunities were here."

Mays played only two seasons with the Mets before retiring.

Later he joined the Bally organization and was promptly kicked out of baseball by Kuhn, who thought the game could in no way be connected to gambling, legal or otherwise. Mays wasn't bitter then and he isn't bitter now. He's leaving his future strictly up to Kuhn.

"I think he's beginning to see that what I do for Bally isn't dangerous or detrimental," Mays said. "I'd like to get back into baseball, but not as a coach or anything. Public relations. It's not that it's important to me as it is to baseball. Baseball needs me. Too much now, baseball is letting its people drift away."

In 1979, to the surprise of no one, Mays was elected to the Hall of Fame by the Baseball Writers Association of America his first time on the ballot. However, 23 voters somehow managed not to vote for Mays, causing an unbelievable furor among the voters. How could 23 writers not have voted for Willie?

Mays was typically unaffected by the slight, preferring to leave the outrage over the 23 know-nothings to others. When asked who he felt was the greatest player he ever saw, Willie, evoking the innocence of that long-ago day when he first reported to Durocher and the Giants, replied in complete candor: "I was the best ballplayer I ever saw. Nobody in the world could do things on the baseball field I could do."

"I guess I shouldn't have said that," Willie said, bursting into a sheepish grin. "A lot of people were really surprised. But I'll tell you, I said it for a reason. The writers, they needed a headline, and up until that point in the press conference, things had been dull."

Funny, but nobody seems to recall Willie Mays being dull that day...or any other day for that matter. Like the man said, he never shortchanged anybody. Happy Birthday, Willie.

Joe D Won't Get In Center of Fence Issue

August 3, 1982

COOPERSTOWN—As the car motored past the miles of cornfields lying along the winding two-lane highway that leads to the peaceful turn-of-the-century village that calls itself baseball's birthplace, the conversation turned to another of the game's shrines—Yankee Stadium.

The question raised was: "Isn't the mere thought of bringing in the Stadium's fences a sacrilege?"

Joe DiMaggio smiled.

"You're not gonna get me into that because it's none of my business," said the Yankee Clipper.

But, of course, it is Joe DiMaggio's business if George Steinbrenner decides to bring in the fences for Dave Winfield next year. It's DiMaggio's business because for 13 magnificent summers he made his living playing center field and hitting in Yankee Stadium—the old Yankee Stadium, where the fences were even harder to reach for a right-handed batter.

Whenever debates rage over the crimes perpetrated against right-handed hitters by the Stadium's vast playground in left-center, DiMaggio comes to mind as the man who best overcame the adversity. He hit 361 homers in his career, but there is no telling how many more he would have hit if Fenway Park had been his home stadium.

It seemed to one passenger that for the Yankees to consider bring in the fences now, some 31 years after his retirement, was an injustice to DiMaggio.

"All I can say is they should be thinking also about what it will do to help the visiting teams coming in that are stocked with right-handed hitters," said Joe D. "I can tell you, I wasn't the only one who paid a price. There were some pretty fair right-handed hitters—Hank   Greenberg,

DiMaggio greets fans and signs autographs. (Charles Hoff/Daily News)

Indian Bob Johnson, Rudy York to name a few—who had to deal with the Stadium 11 games a year. I know they felt cheated, and I felt for them, too."

The mention of Greenberg triggered one of DiMaggio's most vivid memories of how Yankee Stadium betrayed him. It was late in the 1937 season, and he and Greenberg were waging a tight battle for the RBI crown that Greenberg eventually won with 183.

"At the time, I was only about five or six behind," said DiMaggio. "Anyway, I came up twice in this game we were playing against the Red Sox, both times with the bases loaded. And both times I hit balls deep into the alley, 450 feet away. As they say, home runs in any other park. Well, each time, my own brother, Dom, robbed me by making catches on the warning track. Instead of a possible eight RBI— or at least five or six—I got nothing.

"That night, Dom came over to my place for dinner. I remember letting him in the door and then not speaking to him until we were almost through eating. I was that mad!"

There is no more lasting memory of DiMaggio's burden than the catch Al Gionfriddo of the Dodgers made off him in the 1947 World Series. As Gionfriddo raced to the fence in front of the bullpen in left center to make a backhanded grab of DiMaggio's line drive, the camera caught Joe in a rare show of public frustration, kicking his foot in the dirt as he rounded second.

"That winter, I was invited to attend a banquet up in Buffalo for Gionfriddo, and as a gift to him, they gave him some luggage. I remember joking on the dais that he would need these bags when the Dodgers sent him to Montreal. Wouldn't you know it—that's what happened. He never again played in the majors."

DiMaggio has no regrets. "I've been very lucky. I don't consider myself unfortunate to have played my whole career in Yankee Stadium. The way I look at it, the greatest thing in my career was the fact that I played on 10 American League champions and nine world champions in 13 years!"

"What about the 56-game hitting streak?" he was asked.

"It's probably what I'll be most remembered for," said DiMaggio. "But I'll tell you, Hank Aaron's home run record will be a lot harder to break. They take shots at my record every year. Each week you hear about someone else who has a streak going. But to break Aaron's record, it would simply take too many years of staying on top of the game and hitting for power. Hank was a very rare individual."

A few miles from the Hall of Fame, which DiMaggio would be visiting for only the second time since being inducted in 1955, the Yankee Clipper spotted a Dairy Queen.

"Let's get some ice cream," he suggested.

Inside, the waitress behind the counter blinked at the sight of DiMaggio strolling in, neatly attired in his blue suit, asking for a vanilla cone.

"Aren't you Joe DiMaggio?" she asked.

"Yes, I am," Joe replied.

"There's no charge for the cone," the waitress replied.

A few minutes later, DiMaggio, having finished his cone, stepped outside and shook his head, obviously unaware of the magnitude of his own presence in these rural surroundings.

"I wonder how this place makes any money if they give the ice cream away?"

CHEERS HUG SEAVER

AUGUST 3, 1992

COOPERSTOWN—What is normally a quiet green pasture of some 20 acres behind the A.C.C. gymnasium was now a sea of blue Mets caps, and at the mention of anything even remotely associated with Tom Seaver, the crowd erupted in spontaneous chants: "Let's Go Mets! Let's Go Mets! Sea-ver! Sea-ver! Sea-ver!"

Many of them had camped out overnight in order to get the choicest seats on the grass behind the picket fence that separates the masses from the Hall of Fame dignitaries. On this final leg of Tom Seaver's journey to baseball immortality, his most devoted fans—thousands of them—were feeling proud to be with him.

The ceremony began at 2:30 p.m. yesterday, and you could feel a restlessness among the blue caps as the preliminary speeches dragged on. It was not until an hour into the proceedings that the first of the four new Hall of Famers, Rollie Fingers, stepped to the podium to accept his plaque. The blue caps became quiet. The man of 341 saves and the most distinctive handlebar mustache this side of 1890 paid tribute to his fellow relief pitchers: "All of you who've sat in the bullpen, waited for the phone to ring and faced the pressure own a piece of this." Then he talked of his late father, the man who most influenced his life and his career.

"I was eight years old, playing with matches in my room, and I set the whole room on fire," Fingers related. "Later that night, my father came up to my room, but instead of scolding me, he took me out to the car and drove me down to the sheriff's office, where he had them put me in a jail cell. He left me there for three hours.

"I learned three things from that. One, it scared the hell out of me. Two, I never played with matches again. And three, I learned respect. It's ironic, though, that in my 17 years in the big leagues my job was putting fires out, not starting them."

Next up was the son of the late umpire Bill McGowan, who accepted his father's plaque. Then came Prince Hal Newhouser, the four-time 20-game winner of the '40s who thanked the Veteran's Committee "for finally making this my year."

It was now 4:15, and before the imperial commissioner of baseball, Fay Vincent, could even begin reading the words on Seaver's plaque, the blue caps had taken control of the afternoon. A huge blue and white flag with the number 41 was hoisted from behind the picket fence. And then the chants began again: "Let's Go Mets! Let's Go Mets! Let's Go Mets! Sea-ver! Sea-ver! Sea-ver!"

Tom Seaver, standing off to the side in a brown suit, waiting for Vincent to complete his task of reading the plaque, was visibly moved by the waves of affection echoing throughout the huge pasture. Upon accepting the facsimile plaque, he hoisted it over his head as if to say to the blue caps: "This is for you."

Rollie Fingers (left) and Tom Seaver acknowledge their acceptance into the Baseball Hall of Fame. (Pat Carroll/Daily News)

And then he spoke.

He began by talking about his life-long friend, Russ Scheidt, "who grew up on the same block as me and taught me how to wear a uniform." From there he thanked his three principal catchers, Jerry Grote, Johnny Bench and Carlton Fisk. When he got around to his long time roommate, Buddy Harrelson, who was seated in the audience, the blue caps erupted into an ovation so loud you would have thought last year at Shea never happened.

Now Seaver was getting down to the emotional part—his family. He introduced his father, then his two daughters, and finally his wife, Nancy. He had to pause for a moment before returning briefly to baseball and the late Gil Hodges.

"Gil Hodges was the most important person in my career," Seaver said. "Above all, he taught me how to be a professional. I know that God is letting him look down at me know."

The emotion of the moment was finally overtaking him, and with his voice breaking, he concluded: "And the other person who isn't here—my mom. God love her."

Later, at the press conference inside the gymnasium, Seaver confessed, "I knew I wouldn't last very long because I knew 'mom' was coming. That was my stopping point. I knew that five years ago [when she died]."

The blue caps understood. It didn't matter to them how long Seaver spoke. They just wanted to be a part of this. And as he walked off the stage with the rest of the Hall of Famers, a single sign hoisted by one of them said it all: "Thanks for the memories, Tom."

"Barber" Gave Hitters the Closest of Shaves

They called him "The Barber" because that, above all else, was what Sal Maglie was all about. An unyielding and unshaven old-school competitor, his calling cards were a fearsome stare and a wicked curveball that either paralyzed opposing batters or knocked them on their duffs.

Either way, Sal Maglie got his message across. Yesterday, the old Barber, who was given his nickname by the late *Daily News* Giants beat man Jim McCulley "because he shaved the plate and came so close to the batters," died at age 75 in Niagara Falls. In truth, Maglie had been at death's door for almost five years after suffering a stroke in May 1987. But you have to think that he regarded death in the same way as he regarded Carl Furillo, Roy Campanella, Jackie Robinson and Duke Snider—a formidable foe, to be sure, but one that would not be given in to.

"Sal was probably the one pitcher we least wanted to face," Pee Wee Reese said yesterday by phone from Louisville, Kentucky. "You always knew you were in for a battle when he was pitching. I remember in particular the last day of the 1951 season, when the Giants won to force a playoff with us, Campy said to me: 'Here we go again, having to face that damn Maglie. I guess I'm just going to have to get a football helmet.'"

As it was, the right-hander pitched the final game of the three-game National League playoff and actually stood to be the losing pitcher when he left the game, trailing 4-1, after the Dodgers rallied for three runs off him in the eighth inning. Of course, Bobby Thomson's three-run homer in the ninth inning rendered that as perhaps the least remembered Maglie pitching effort against the Dodgers ever.

"I was hated in Brooklyn," Maglie recalled in an interview in 1968. "At Ebbets Field, they booed me, yelled at me and I loved it. The first time Campanella would come to bat I'd put the ball about two feet over his head. Down he'd go, and the Dodgers would start screaming. They'd get so damn angry that they'd try to kill me with home runs and they'd break their backs swinging at bad balls. They didn't get anything. I had their number."

Back then, there was a saying in baseball, "If you can't beat him, buy him." Nevertheless, there were limitations to that, and nobody could possibly envision the Dodgers ever embracing Sal Maglie as one of their own. Then again, stranger things had happened—like Leo Durocher switching boroughs from Dodger to Giant manager in 1948.

"That," said Reese, "was about the most unbelievable thing I can think of that happened in my career. But Sal coming over to us in 1956 was hard to believe, too. He'd spent a lifetime brushing us back."

He had been released by the Giants the year before—despite a 9-5 record—and picked up by the Cleveland Indians, who had Bob Lemon, Early Wynn, Mike Garcia

Sal Maglie, a Brooklyn Dodger-killer with the N.Y. Giants. (Walter Kelleher/Daily News)

and Bob Feller on their staff and therefore about as much need for another starting pitcher as the Rockefellers had for a bank loan.

Sure enough, a couple of weeks into the 1956 season, the Indians sold Maglie to the Dodgers for the sum of $1,000. All that bought was 13 wins, including a no-hitter against the Phillies at age 39 in September, and two magnificently pitched games in the World Series against the Yankees.

I had the privilege of being at Yankee Stadium for the second of those two Series games Maglie pitched. It was October 8, 1956, and, by his own admission, The Barber pitched one of the greatest games of his life. Those who were there could hardly disagree. The only hard hit he gave up was Mickey Mantle's fourth-inning solo homer down the right field line. Unfortunately for Maglie, his opponent, Don Larsen, pitched the only perfect game in World Series history and is the only pitcher anyone remembers from that day.

"For four innings we were both no-hit," Maglie recalled years later. "Then Mantle hit a 2-2 pitch 310 feet down the right field line. A stupid hanging curveball. That was it right there. Every time Mantle saw me afterward, he'd joke: 'Did you see that tape-measure job I hit off you?' All I know is it would have been a double in Ebbets Field."

That was Sal Maglie, years later still unwilling to concede defeat, even to the greatest pitching performance in World Series history. He lasted only another half-season in Brooklyn, only to be released and signed by, of all teams, the Yankees! He thus became the 15th and last player with all three New York teams.

A few of the others—Waite Hoyt, Tony Lazzeri, Wee Willie Keeler and Burleigh Grimes— were Hall of Famers. Despite a 119-62 career record, Sal Maglie never will be elected to the Hall of Fame. Unless, that is, there's a Hall of Fame just for pitchers whom you wanted to have the ball in a game you had to win.

A PROUD YANKEE

On a cold, raw winter morning, a bunch of people gathered at a midtown hotel yesterday for the purpose of celebrating, of all things, *baseball!*

More precisely, they came to celebrate Reggie Jackson, the newest member of the Hall of Fame, who epitomized what baseball used to be all about. And for a couple of hours, how refreshing it was to hear people talking baseball in terms of home runs and strikeouts, fathers and sons, and all those not-so-long-ago sweet Octobers that were all so much a part of Reggie Jackson. Incredibly, the occasion was devoid of any mention of agents, strikes, lockouts, drugs, suspensions, Marge Schott or Kenesaw Molehill Selig.

Oh sure, somebody had to ask Reggie the obligatory question—what he thought he'd be worth in today's absurd market—and it got him to reflecting on the free agent contract he signed with the Yankees in November 1976. For the benefit of those who haven't realized just *how* absurd baseball salaries have become, Reggie's deal was five years for $2.66 million. That's a *total* of $2.66 million. To put it in better perspective, Matt Nokes earned only $100,000 less last year than Jackson earned in five years as a Yankee.

"The money was important to me, sure," Reggie said. "But when I signed with the Yankees it was for less than what I was offered from Montreal. I signed with the Yankees for a lot of reasons, but the most important was that I wanted to be with a winner. The fact was, I never wanted to leave any of the teams I played with. I didn't want to leave the A's, but [then A's owner] Charlie Finley was a tough guy and a tightwad. He knew

Reggie Jackson (left) and his father, Martinez, at the press conference. (Pat Carroll/Daily News)

a tailor in Philadelphia, played baseball, too, with the Newark Eagles of the long-defunct Negro National League. But he didn't raise his son to be a baseball player. He raised him to be a man.

"He was a 'no excuses' man," Reggie said, "just like George. I remember one time he gave me a quarter and sent me to the grocery store to get some Neapolitan ice cream. But when I got there, they were sold out. So I went across the street and borrowed another quarter from Uncle Bob, who had a gas station, and went down the street to another place called Kelso's and borrowed another quarter. Then I went back to the grocery store and bought a quart of vanilla, a quart of chocolate and a quart of strawberry and brought them home.

"When I got home, I presented my dad with the three quarts of ice cream and told him: 'You owe Uncle Bob and Kelso's a quarter each.' I was proud of my ingenuity, but he didn't say anything. It was understood. No

baseball, though, and I'd have to say part of the reason for my success in New York was that Charlie Finley taught me how to go about things."

As he reminisced about his Hall of Fame career and talked about Finley and George Steinbrenner and the influence both had on his career, his 88-year-old father, Martinez Jackson, sat off to the side listening. The old man, who was—and still is—

excuses. You were supposed to get the job done."

"Under no circumstances did I ever think he'd become a professional ballplayer," the elder Jackson said, "even though he came home every night at six or seven o'clock because he was playing either baseball, football, basketball or track. He'd do anything in sports to evade working. The deal was he had to be on the first team or else he had to come to work in the tailor shop after school."

So it was that Martinez Jackson's boy grew up to cut quite a swath—but as a baseball player, not a tailor. Of all his cuts, though, none will be quite as indelible as the three he took in the sixth and final game of the 1977 World Series against the Dodgers.

"I knew the scouting reports the Dodgers had on me were to pitch me inside," Reggie said. "So I decided to make a minor adjustment and back off the plate about six inches. The first pitcher I faced, Burt Hooten, walked me on four pitches, all around the plate, my first time up. The second time up, he threw me the first pitch inside and I hit it on a line into the right field seats.

"The next time up, they brought in [Elias] Sosa, and I'm saying to myself, 'He hasn't had time to talk to Hooten.' I was just praying he'd throw me another pitch inside, and he did. When I hit it, I hooked it and I wasn't sure it was going to go out until it did.

"Then they brought in [knuckleballer] Charlie Hough and I said, 'Man, I got eight or nine homers off Wilbur Wood, Eddie Fisher and Hoyt Wilhelm [all knuckleballers]. They *can't* be bringing *this* guy in!' The first pitch he threw to me was like room service. I mean the ball looked like a beach ball."

It was that last majestic homer, which landed in the black of straightaway center field in Yankee Stadium, that put Reggie Jackson on the same lofty pedestal as Babe Ruth—the only two players in baseball history to hit three home runs in one World Series game. Now, Jackson said with unconcealed pride, he will have a plaque in baseball's hallowed pantheon, alongside those of Ruth, Cobb, Speaker, DiMaggio, Williams and all the rest of the game's greats.

"I'm best remembered for what I did in New York," he said, "and being linked to Mantle, Ford, DiMaggio, Ruth, Gehrig is a good thing for Reggie Jackson. That's why I want to go into the Hall of Fame as a Yankee."

MR. HUMBLE HONORS GAME THAT BROUGHT FAME

AUGUST 2, 1993

COOPERSTOWN—For those who came expecting another dissertation on the "magnitude of me," Reggie Jackson threw them a curveball.

He could have chosen the occasion of his induction into the Baseball Hall of Fame to recite his accomplishments and remind us all why he was indeed the "straw that stirred the drink"—and not just during those five tumultuous seasons in New York. He could have talked of nothing other than October and how he owned it, or how they've once again named a candy bar after him because of the magnitude of him.

Instead, as the thousands stretched across the spacious cornfield saluted him with chants of "Reggie! Reggie! Reggie!" yesterday, he used his proudest moment in the summer sun to celebrate the magnitude of the game.

This was not about Reggie Jackson the presence, the supreme baseball being, or the straw. It was about Reggie Jackson the baseball historian and fan.

He saluted Jackie Robinson's widow, Rachel, whom he had invited to share the moment with him "because of Jackie, who opened the door for me" and "who was a role model we all needed whether we were black or white." But the historian in him made sure he didn't forget Larry Doby, the first American League black player, of whom he said, "I'm grateful you were there, too."

He could have said it was no accident that championships seemed to happen wherever he hung his cap and that was a measure of his greatness. Instead, the historian in him saluted Hank Aaron, who hit nearly 200 more homers.

"He taught me that greatness is measured over time," Reggie said, quickly adding that "Bob Gibson taught me the competitiveness."

George Steinbrenner (left) congratulates Reggie Jackson on his induction. (Pat Carroll/Daily News)

And when he got around to the World Series, he cited Mickey Mantle's unbreakable record of 18 homers.

"He was the original 'Mr. October.' I just thank God it didn't stick."

Oh sure, he talked about the road from the Philadelphia suburb of Wyncote, Pennsylvania, to Cooperstown and what it took to get here. But while we may have been led to believe otherwise all these years, it wasn't a mission accomplished through the sheer force of just being Reggie.

There was the time, for instance, in 1967, when he was

21 and the only black player on the A's Double-A team in Birmingham, Alabama. During an all-night bus ride, the team pulled into a truck stop to eat, only to file back onto the bus on orders from the manager, John McNamara.

"I brought Reggie in with me," McNamara recalled, "and the proprietor said: 'You can all eat, but he has to leave.' I just said, 'OK, we're all leaving.' That was it."

To McNamara, it was a very simple decision, but to Reggie, it was something he never forgot.

"He gave me dignity," Reggie said in telling the crowd why he invited McNamara here, "and he showed a sensitivity, stepping up like that at a time when very few did."

Later he would pay tribute to A's owner Charlie Finley, who signed him, and George Steinbrenner, to whom he said: "Thanks for the pinstripes, George." Above all though, it was the game Reggie Jackson wanted to see honored on his day.

"I'll continue to be reminded that, while this is my day, I'm just a link in the chain that makes the whole world go 'round," he said. "So too are today's players and those in the baseball community. So whether you're 'The Babe,' 'Stan the Man,' 'Say Hey' or 'Mr. October,' you're just a part of the long tradition of baseball and the game is owed our respect and gratitude."

It was a most un-Reggie-like Reggie, especially at the end, when, upon linking himself with the pride and tradition of the Yankees, he broke down briefly.

"In the words of Lou Gehrig," he said, his voice cracking, "today I feel like the luckiest man on the face of the earth. I had a dream and I was able to live it. Thank God, it's not done yet. I'm a real baseball fan."

After yesterday, nobody doubted that.

JORDAN FLUNKS CRASH COURSE

MARCH 4, 1994

SARASOTA—This was big.

Just in case the sight of people eagerly plunking down three dollars to watch a spring training intrasquad game in frigid, 40-mile-per-hour gales didn't tell you that, Ozzie Guillen made sure everyone knew it.

"I'm not playin'," shouted the White Sox' team captain and self-appointed three-ring master to the crowd, "but I'm sure stayin'! Michael gonna play a real game. Ain't no missin' this!"

The cynics will suggest Michael Jordan might have been better off missing yesterday's intrasquad game between the Hairstons and his team, the Nosseks. By his own admission, he made a lot of mistakes, not the least of which were dropping the first fly ball hit to him in right field and being struck out twice by a couple of minor-league pitchers who figure to spend most of this coming season at Nashville.

Another learning experience, His Airness said, but for all his philosophical offerings afterward, you couldn't help but wonder if he's finally beginning to realize there's a lot more to baseball than taking batting practice cuts against sandlot hacks.

His first time up, against hard-throwing rookie right-hander James Baldwin, a fellow North Carolinian, was about the only encouraging moment of Jordan's long afternoon in the March winds. After taking Baldwin's first pitch for a ball, he turned on a knee-high fastball and smoked it into left field. Warren Newson, running hard to his left and straining to follow the ball's flight in the tricky wind currents, made a spectacular diving catch.

"It was a tough day to play the outfield," Newson said. "After the inning was over, I kidded him about it. I told him you better hit the ball to right field from now on."

If only Jordan could hit the ball anywhere after that. And as he found out a couple innings later, playing right field was no day at the beach. The second pitcher he faced, right-hander Rod Bolton, couldn't get anybody out in the third inning—except him. Bolton had given up four singles and a home run before striking out Jordan looking on a fastball on the inside corner.

So much for the euphoria of that first hard-hit liner to Newson. As even the great hitters can tell him, baseball is a very humbling game. Further complicating it is the fact you have to catch the ball as well as hit it. And when Joe Hall, a right-handed-hitting non-roster outfielder for the Hairstons, hit an opposite field fly ball into the wind in right, you sensed a panic in Jordan as he raced in for it. Though he had been playing deep, almost to the warning track, his six-foot-six strides played to his advantage and enabled him to catch up to it—and then some.

The collective whoop that went up from the crowd as he positioned himself to make a Willie Mays basket catch turned into a gasp as the ball struck the heel of his glove and skittered away.

"I never thought I would get to it," he said. "[Outfield coach] Joe [Nossek] had told me to play everyone deep. Then, when I did get to it, I was fooled by the wind. I know the crowd was disappointed I didn't get it."

That would have been the third out of the inning and the end of a five-run rally. Instead, another run scored on the error, followed by a two-run single. The upside of it is that this was all part of Jordan's baseball education. If he didn't know before what constitutes an unearned run, he does now.

As luck would have it, atonement for his fielding lapse was in the offing in the bottom of the inning when he came to the plate with nobody out and two on. If only he could get around on one like the first time and get it into the air and the wind.

The pitcher this time was 22-year-old Scott Christman, the White Sox' No. 1 draft choice out of Oregon State last June, and he was having trouble throwing strikes. But after getting ahead in the count 2-1, Jordan fouled the fourth pitch off, then was completely fooled by a slow change down and away.

"I saw some good pitches I thought I could hit and I swung at them," he said. "I can't put doubts in my head now or else I can't improve. I look at today as being a crash course in the kind of pitches I'm gonna see. I saw three different pitchers out there. It's just one game and hard to judge me on that."

"He's gonna be swinging [at a lot more] for a while," said White Sox GM Ron Schueler.

He said it with a knowing grin that seemed to say, "Welcome to the big leagues, Michael. You ain't seen nothing yet."

Bobby O Finds Out Ending

April 26, 1994

This was supposed to be a much happier ending.

Anyone who knew of Bobby Ojeda and what he's been all about—both before and after he was the one who escaped death in that powerboat on Little Lake Nelly a year ago March—rooted for him to experience the ultimate triumph over tragedy. They rooted for one more World Series for him, for one more glorious autumn in New York, the place he has come to call his home.

But the Hollywood people and the literary agents who had approached him during the spring don't know about baseball reality. They couldn't see an ending such as the one that was reality on an overcast April afternoon yesterday; Bobby Ojeda getting into his van in the Yankee Stadium parking lot, saying goodbye, less than a month into the season, when he thought he should still be saying hello.

"I feel like Harrison Ford in that movie…what was it?… *The Fugitive*," he was saying. "The train has wrecked and it's off the track. I feel like I got derailed."

It was the kind of analogy you expected from an insightful guy such as Bobby Ojeda. He did get derailed once the games got serious. But he made the team this spring mostly because the Yankee high command wanted him to make the team, because they believed his guts and guile would be enough to overcome the loss of his skills—and whatever else—after Little Lake Nelly.

That explains why the Yankees so pointedly low-keyed the announcement that Ojeda had made the team that morning in Fort Lauderdale, March 28. As heartwarming a story as it was, they weren't at all convinced it was going to have a happy ending.

Then Ojeda made his final spring training start in New Orleans against the Red Sox and was awful, yielding five hits, five walks and seven earned runs in three innings. Ten days later in Columbus, in his final tuneup before his Yankee debut, he was roughed up again for seven hits and six earned runs in fivve and two-thirds innings by the Red Sox' Triple-A team.

Buck Showalter, who wasn't real crazy about the Ojeda gambit to begin with (if only because he knew it was going to be at the expense of Scott Kamieniecki), could only shrug when Bobby O couldn't get out of the first inning against the Tigers on April 16. Like everyone else, Showalter wanted Ojeda to show he still had something left from 1986, but the manager had seen only fleeting hints of it in the spring and now he was seeing none.

"It's no secret Bobby didn't pitch well in the big leagues," Showalter said evenly. "No one's ever sure how things will turn out, but you have to go with what you think."

As he leaned against the van in the parking lot, reflecting on everything that has happened in his brief tour of duty as a Yankee,

Ojeda did not seem sure of what *he* thought. One part of him seemed to be thinking that this was it.

"Everything in my life has become bigger than baseball now," he said. "My personal life and my professional life last year…the relevance of things in sports has changed for me."

At the same time, though, another part of him didn't seem to want to accept baseball finality just yet.

"I have to sort things out now. This is home. I've made a bunch of bids on houses. If they all come in, I'll have to work.

"People keep asking me about a book or a movie. I can't think about that. I don't know how to write the ending."

If he thinks about it, maybe he'll see that the Yankees provided the ending for him. And even if it wasn't an entirely happy one, it was at least a dignified one. As much as everyone wanted him to remind us of 1986, when he won 18 for the Mets in the regular season, then brought them back from an 0-2 World Series deficit by beating the Red Sox in Fenway in Game 3, reality was that this was 1994.

"Sending guys back to the minors in this job isn't so bad because it's not like the end for them. They have a chance to make their way back," said Yankee GM Gene Michael. "But this...this is like killing somebody. Bobby O is a tough guy, a class guy. I hated this day."

Hopefully Bobby O will see how painful it was for the Yankees to say goodbye to him so soon.

Like Michael said, you think of Bobby O, you think of guts and class and a night in Fenway Park.

Which is why just making the Yankees this spring should be considered a happy enough ending for a guy who didn't have anything else to prove to us.

MANTLE KEEPS BASEBALL ALIVE

FORT LAUDERDALE— Mickey Mantle is looking straight ahead into the October sunshine, his eyes fixed on a sixty-something guy playing first base.

It is World Series week, but this is the only place in the U.S. or Canada where you could find real World Series heroes playing baseball. Shouting instructions from a couple of feet away is Hank Bauer, Mantle's Yankee teammate throughout the 1950s whom he still likens to a "big brother."

Suddenly, the batter hits a high pop to first base and the aged first baseman is clearly not going to catch it because of the sun.

"Uh-oh," Mickey says. "Hey, Hank, remember when Casey taught me how to use sunglasses in the field when were in spring training in Arizona that year? Told me to flip 'em down as soon as the ball was hit?"

"Do I remember?" Bauer asks. "We was playin' the Indians and Ray Boone hit it. Ball about killed you, didn't it?"

"Hit me right square in the forehead," Mantle says. "And then you and [Gene] Woodling ran over and asked me if my glasses were all right. I got this big lump on my head and you guys are asking about my sunglasses."

All around Mickey Mantle's fantasy camp team, where grown men are fancying themselves as boys of summer, laughter abounds.

"I guess we're all boys at heart no matter how old or broken down we get," Mantle says. "Once this game gets a hold on you, it never lets go. I think in my case it goes all the way back to when I was a little boy and I used to watch my mother doing the ironing while she'd be listening to the Cardinal game on the radio with Harry Caray. She'd keep her own box score, which she gave to my dad when he got home from the mines at night.

"It was around that same time my father took me up to Joplin [Missouri] to see Stan Musial playing for the St. Joe Cardinals. He told me to watch this guy real close, that he was gonna be one of the greatest players there ever was."

There was, of course, a real romance to baseball then. On the professional level, it was the only game in town, and even when Mantle was a player and baseball had moved onto the television and into the jet age, there was an innocence about it.

"What I remember most," he says, "are all those Yankees I played with. We were like a family. After the games, guys would hang around in the clubhouse for hours. Nowadays you walk into a clubhouse after the game and everyone's gone. I can't keep track of who's playing for what team anymore.

"To be honest, though, I don't know what I would've done if Cleveland had offered me $5 million to leave the Yankees."

When it is suggested to him the Yankees would have matched or topped any offer, Mantle smiles.

"Maybe," he says, "but I'll always remember in the spring of 1957 when [Yankees GM George] Weiss wanted to cut me $5,000 after I'd won my second straight MVP award. I wound up getting a $10,000 raise, but only after he threatened to trade me to Cleveland for [Herb] Score if I didn't get my butt to spring training. I'd hate to think what would have happened if I ever had to leave the Yankees. If there's one record I'm most proud of, it's those 2,401 games I played for the Yankees."

What about the World Series, he is asked. With his name synonymous with October heroics (Mantle has a record 18 World Series homers), did he not feel the same void baseball fans are feeling this week?

"I feel awful about it," he says. "I miss turning on the TV and seeing the games. I don't pretend to know all that's going on with the strike. I just know it's terrible that there's no World Series."

So for this year, there are only memories.

"People ask me what I thought was my greatest World Series moment," he says. "It wasn't the homer I hit off Barney Schultz in the third game of the '64 Series. More than anything, looking back, I'd have to say it was the catch I made off Gil Hodges to help save [Don] Larsen's perfect game in '56. I hit

18 homers in the Series, but I didn't make many great catches. I didn't realize what a big deal that one was at the time."

To Mantle's campers, sitting around him on the bench, everything he ever did was a big deal. Now they are playing for him and listening to his stories and feeling a part of them.

There is no World Series this year. But in this place on this glorious October afternoon, Mickey Mantle and his memories are all any baseball junkie could ask for.

HAIL DOBY THE PIONEER

APRIL 26, 1995

When the call came from Gene Budig asking him to move down 11 floors to become the special assistant to the American League president, Larry Doby was caught by surprise. After all, he is 70 now. And he'd been quite content working part-time in baseball's Major League Properties division.

It is perhaps a measure of Larry Doby that he didn't immediately see where Budig was coming from, that he didn't see why, at whatever stage of his life, it makes perfect sense for Larry Doby to be a key representative of the American League in baseball's uphill effort to restore itself as America's pastime.

"It wasn't until everybody up here started coming up to me, shaking my hand and offering me congratulations, that I thought about 1947 and how this puts it all in a different perspective," Doby said yesterday. "I'd say it was just the opposite of when I walked into a major league clubhouse for the very first time. Nobody congratulated me that time, and not everybody shook my hand either."

He was sitting at a conference table on the 29th floor of 350 Park Ave. For the longest time, the commissioner of baseball also resided at this address, but with his ouster by the owner suits who run the game—followed closely by the exits of league presidents Bill White and Bobby Brown— it is hard to find any real baseball people wandering the hallways of 350 Park anymore.

It took Budig to find one and give him a higher, more important profile.

Although himself a product of academia, Budig brought with him a storehouse of baseball knowledge when he was hired as AL president last year. Among his many baseball acquaintances was Doby, whom he met about 25 years ago through Bill Veeck. At the time, Budig was president of Illinois State University and Veeck was running the White Sox for the second time.

The manager of the White Sox was Doby, who had followed Frank Robinson as the second black man to manage a big-league team. In 1947, when he walked into that Cleveland Indians clubhouse for the first time, Doby was only the second black man to *play* Major League Baseball— the first in the American League.

Because Jackie Robinson had been the first to break baseball's color line a few months earlier, there was always a myth attached to Doby and the others who immediately followed that they felt no pressure. As if it were any different for them finding a place in spring training, or just finding acceptance and respect in an all-white world.

"When Bill Veeck brought me up to his office for my signing with the Indians, they had a foot-high notebook that had everything I'd ever done in my life from the time I was born," Doby said. "Bill then went on to explain all the things you can and can't do. There were a lot more can't-dos.

"The hardest part was not being able to stay in the same hotel as my teammates in some

Larry Doby speaks about his life from the MLB offices.
(Linda Cataffo/Daily News)

places. And in spring training I couldn't even ride in the same buses with them."

It is sad so many of today's players have little or no knowledge of the indignities Robinson, Doby and so many of the first line of black major leaguers had to endure in the late '40s and early '50s. In Doby's case—because he always came second—it is especially sad he has not had his place in baseball history properly recognized.

His numbers alone—.283 average, 253 homers, two home run titles—aren't quite Hall of Fame caliber. However, when you consider the rest of Doby's dossier—an All-Star second baseman with the Newark Eagles in the Negro Leagues before he broke the AL color barrier, a pioneer for his race as a manager, scout and an executive—it is easy to see why one of the first questions Budig asked upon taking office was: why isn't Larry Doby in the Hall of Fame?

Maybe now that he is back in the game's forefront, enough minds will be jogged and Doby will get his due from the Veteran's Committee. (Until this year, he was not even on the ballot.) The Hall of Fame would be nice, Doby says, but right now he's just too busy to think about it.

"What I really want to do," he said, "is restore baseball at the grassroots level. The only way you see kids playing the game today is when it's organized."

Whatever happened to pick-up games, he asks. To the stickball games he played as a kid growing up on the streets of Paterson, N.J.

"Why can't we go into these communities and build walls for stickball?" he said. "I don't know if it would get the kids to play, but it sure wouldn't hurt. And how much would it cost?"

It seemed strange listening to Larry Doby talking about building walls for baseball. He's spent a lifetime tearing them down.

FOREVER WITHOUT EQUAL OR EGO

He came to us carrying a straw suitcase and a couple of bats, this shy and scared country boy out of the mining country of Oklahoma. Mickey Mantle was pure hush puppies and hominy grits and about as far removed from the big city's neon and glitz as a rookie could possibly be.

It is that Norman Rockwell image more than any other that came to mind yesterday morning after word came out of Baylor hospital in Dallas that Mantle was gone at age 63. From day one, he wasn't sure if he could even make it here, and every day after, right up until his dying day, he never understood the hold he had on this city...on all of America. In his own eyes, he was just a simple country boy who was blessed with the God-given ability of speed and power to hit a baseball great distances from both sides of the plate.

From the day he stepped off a bus from Kansas City and into the major leagues, we knew Mickey Mantle was special. We knew the story of how his dad, Mutt, had named him after Mickey Cochrane, the great Athletics catcher of the '20s and '30s, and how the old man would come home from the mines in the late afternoons and teach him how to switch hit.

Mickey Mantle was a legend *before* his time, and I still remember the rush every time I got his baseball card. That forever-young image of Mantle, bat cocked, peering over his left shoulder on his 1953 card, is the way I will always choose to remember him.

The shrunken and weak Mantle at Baylor the last time I was in his presence has been erased from memory, as has the jaundiced Mick I hung out with those few days at his fantasy camp in Fort Lauderdale last October. *His* last October. He told me he was really not feeling well, but

The Mick shows off one of his home run balls.
(Daily News)

once said: "Here's a boy who can bunt and run down to first base, and if he bunts 10 times he'll reach first five times, and that's a .500 average. And if he hits, he'll hit as many home runs as he would anyway because there isn't anyone in the world [who] can catch a ball in the upper stands."

He hit home runs farther than anyone in history, off the upper deck facade in the old Yankee Stadium in 1963; 565 feet into a parking lot beyond the fence of Washington's old Griffith Stadium in 1953; 530 feet over the scoreboard above the left field bleachers of Sportsman's Park in St. Louis is 1953…and on and on, higher and higher, farther and farther. "Whenever someone blasts a long one," Tony Kubek said, "veteran people will say it wasn't like the one Mantle hit, and they'll be right."

then we got into his memories and he was the boy out of 1950s Oklahoma again, in his eyes and mine.

He said: "I guess we're all boys at heart no matter how old or broken down we get. Once this game gets a hold on you, it never lets go."

He might as well have been talking about himself, because whether you were a Yankees fan or not in the '50s and '60s, Mantle got a hold on you early and never let go. He was The Natural of whom Casey Stengel

It was only in his retirement years that I really got to know him and understand why he was so beloved and revered by his teammates. Even though he had always been the one on whom they placed the expectations of breaking Babe Ruth's record of 60 homers in a season, he was the gracious and supporting teammate to Roger Maris in 1961. You would ask Mantle what mattered most to him about his career, and his answer would be: "Just being a good teammate."

It was Kubek again who probably best described the essence of Mantle yesterday in comparing him with Joe DiMaggio. "People have always placed Joe and Mickey on the pedestal," Kubek said. "The difference is Joe always liked being there and Mickey never felt he belonged there."

That was Mantle. You would ask him to talk about his accomplishments, his 536 homers, the record 18 he hit in World Series games, the 1956 Triple Crown, the three MVPs, and he would tell you how much more he could have done had he taken better care of himself. He never thought of himself as special, just one of the guys. He was a superstar without the ego, and although he

lit up every major league city for 18 seasons across the '50s and '60s, he was always a country boy.

In his autobiography, Bowie Kuhn summed up his own achievements as commissioner and concluded: "For all of our accomplishments, we managed to do it without ever finding another Mickey Mantle."

They never will.

Mantle acknowledges the cheers from fans at Old Timers' Day in Yankee Stadium in 1982. (Daily News)

A Song Touched Mick's Heart

"The taste of life is sweet as rain upon my tongue, I teased at life as if it were some foolish game…the way the evening breeze would tease a candle's flame…I ran so fast that time and youth at last ran out. I never stopped to think what life is all about…yesterday when I was young."

DALLAS—Under a scorching noontime sun, they began gathering in front of the Lovers Lane United Methodist Church in Dallas bearing their memories and their grief for their fallen hero. Old Yankees who knew Mickey Mantle when he was young, who watched him run so fast and shared the sweet taste of life with him. had come to say goodbye to him.

"He was my teammate for life," Bobby Murcer said. and that seemed to sum it up for all of them on the sad day that had brought them together again.

"Just being here today," said Joe Pepitone, "has made me a better person."

He was a hero to them, yes, but he was one of them, and if being a good teammate was all that Mickey Mantle ever wanted to be remembered for, he can rest in peace.

Maybe to his millions of fans he was about mythical home run power and blazing speed on the basepaths, but to these people who knew him, Mickey Mantle was about friendship and forgiven flaws.

"Never mind about his baseball greatness," said Jerry Coleman, the Yankees' second baseman who roomed with Mantle for two years in the '50s.

"What this is all about is a humble human being who never left his roots. Look at all the people around him. He was as close with the third-string catcher on the team as he was with the stars.

"He started out as a humble human being and he left as a humble human being."

"A thousand dreams I dreamed...the splendid things I planned...I only built to last on weak and shifting sands...I lived by night and shunned the naked light of day and only now I see how the years ran away..."

At exactly 1 p.m., the church bell began chiming and the long, gray hearse carrying Mantle's body pulled up to the church.

Coleman and the other '50s Yankees who had come early— Bobby Brown, Eddie Robinson, Andy Carey—stood respectfully to the side as the casket was lifted and rolled into the church.

"I've got to go in now," Coleman said. "I know so much has been said about how self-destructive Mickey was, but he never hurt anyone but himself. I guess the best thing about this was that it happened so quickly."

"So many happy songs were waiting to be sung...so many wayward pleasures lay in store for me and so much pain my dazzled eyes refused to see...yesterday when I was young..."

So often in the last year Mantle talked about his flaws and the abuse he inflicted on his body from all the long nights of boozing, and it was as if his had been a wasted life. It was left to Bob Costas in his eulogy to dispel that notion. "We wanted to tell him that it was OK, that what he had been was enough," Costas said. "And then in the end, something remarkable happened— the way it does for champions. Mickey Mantle rallied. His heart took over, and he had some innings as fine as any in 1956 or with his buddy, Roger, in 1961.

"But this time, he did it in the harsh and trying summer of '95. And what he did was stunning. The sheer grace of that ninth inning—the humility, the sense of humor, the total absence of self-pity, the simple eloquence and honesty of his pleas to others to take heed of his mistakes."

In the end, when there was only the pain, Mantle told his teammate friends who were at his bedside—Whitey Ford, Yogi Berra, Bobby Richardson, Hank Bauer, Moose Skowron and Johnny Blanchard—not to let on about his condition. He had found his God, Richardson said, and his pain was eased by the knowledge his demise from liver cancer had created a new awareness for organ transplants. If only, though, there were more time.

"There are so many songs in me that won't be sung...I feel the bitter taste upon my tongue...the time has come for me to pay for yesterday when I was young."

He always loved that song, so much so that he befriended Roy Clark, the country singer who made it a million-selling hit. They golfed together and partied together and every so often Mantle would say to Clark, "Promise me you'll sing that song at my funeral."

Other times he would simply say: "That song is me. Every time I hear it, it makes me cry."

"I didn't think this would be so soon," Clark said as he fulfilled that promise, and when Mickey Mantle was gone, it made everyone who knew him cry.

How About That Mel

Phil Rizzuto was regaling a bunch of strangers with old baseball stories at the Yogi Berra golf tournament yesterday—much the same way Mel Allen loved to do—when a 50-something guy approached and somberly shook his hand.

"I'm so sorry about Mel," the guy said. "You and he are synonymous with the Yankees. Now it's just you, Scooter, to carry on the tradition."

Rizzuto paused a moment from signing a baseball and, for a moment, seemed lost in thought. So many memories of the man he considered to be his mentor, so many stories forever recounted, so many valued critiques, so many kindnesses across the five and a half decades of camaraderie.

Mel Allen had been an inseperable part of Rizzuto's life since the day the Scooter arrived in the big leagues in 1941 until Sunday night, when he heard the news that the Voice of the Yankees had been stilled.

"You know," Rizzuto said, "I don't think I would have ever become a broadcaster were it not for Mel. He's the one who urged me into it during my last couple of years as a player. [Casey] Stengel was platooning me and three other shortstops those last two years, and I wasn't playing much when Mel came by one day and invited me upstairs to the booth. At first it was just to do little interviews, but then one day he let me do a half-inning with him.

"Once he saw that I was starting to get a little serious about it, he told me to go out and get a tape recorder and go home and practice, either off television or, if that was too hard, go to high school or college games."

There is, of course, nothing in his unique "Holy Cow, I don't believe it" style of play-by-play to

Casey Stengel (left) and Mel Allen talk baseball. (Daily News)

suggest Rizzuto ever took Allen's early coaching. However, in the years they worked together in the booth, from 1957 until '64 when Allen was summarily fired, Rizzuto had no choice but to learn from the master.

"He taught me everything about baseball broadcasting," Rizzuto said. "You have to remember as a player, I was always taught to anticipate. In broadcasting, it's just the opposite. 'Don't make the call until the umpire makes it!' Mel would constantly remind me. A lot of times he'd correct me right on the air and my mother would get really mad at him.

"But I mispronounced so many words. 'It's ath-LETics,' he'd say to me, 'not ath-EL-letics'. Same thing with Cuba, which I used to pronounce Cuber. He was just like Joe McCarthy was as a manager. McCarthy would chew you out right there in front of everybody because that was the only way you'd learn not to make the same mistake again. Mel was a perfectionist who just wanted me to get it right."

The legendary Mel Allen. (Daily News)

There was something else about Allen that Rizzuto quickly got to know. He was a workaholic whose whole life was the Yankees and the describing of their deeds. He surely had an ego, but you'd never have known it. To Mel Allen, the *game* was always the thing. In all the years of telling his baseball stories, the heroes were always the players, never the storyteller.

"The Yankees were his life," Rizzuto said. "When it came to

describing the games, he was an artist the way he'd build the excitement—like a boat nearing the Niagara Falls. And he had that great Southern voice which never grated on your nerves like mine.

"After the games were over he'd want to stay longer in the booth and talk about them. Being a ballplayer, I was used to just going home."

For Allen, home was always the ballpark, and even when they told him he'd have to leave in 1964, he never really did. Long after the departures of all the Yankees he so wonderfully nicknamed—Tommy "Old Reliable" Henrich, Hank "Man of the Hour" Bauer, Gene "Old Faithful" Woodling, Allie "Superchief" Reynolds, "Steady Eddie" Lopat, Vic "Springfield Rifle" Raschi—he remained as much a part of the stadium scene as the Reggie Jacksons and Don Mattinglys. And while he didn't feel it was his place to dub them, "Mr. October" and "Donnie Baseball" sure sounded like his.

And, happily, like Tony Bennett's MTV renaissance, Allen found a new generation of listeners on *This Week in Baseball.* But then the great ones have a way of transcending eras. If Bennett's singing of songs could have the same appeal to audiences four decades apart, so too did Allen's telling of stories.

Three years ago, Barry Cogan, an engineering services salesman who is one of the volunteer workers at Yogi's golf tournament for handicapped Boy Scouts, volunteered to pick up Allen at his Greenwich home and drive him to and from the outing.

"All the way down from Greenwich, I don't think I went over 45 miles per hour," Cogan said. "He was telling stories, and I didn't want to miss anything. If you're 40 or over as I am, that voice is the most identifiable voice you've ever heard."

It's silenced now, but it took 83 years of telling thousands of baseball stories, in action and remembered, before it could be. For such a gift of life, even Mel Allen would have to say: "How 'bout that."

SCOUT'S HONOR

JULY 28, 1996

WALDOBORO, Maine— Like Forrest Gump, his more famous fictional equivalent, Clyde Sukeforth didn't think it was any big deal to have been the source of all that baseball history going back to Jackie Robinson 50 years ago. Nevertheless, he said, he'd be glad to talk about it over a glass of fresh-squeezed lemonade and some of Grethel's homemade molasses cookies.

After a drive up the Maine Turnpike and across Route 1 to this rural oceanside community, a dog is barking furiously as the car pulls up to the yellow clapboard house. Out from the front porch emerges a white-haired man in khakis and a blue and white checkered long-sleeved shirt. His handshake is firm, belying his 95 years. The next thing that strikes you about him are his eyes, so clear and blue.

These are eyes that once looked straight into the midday haze at a Grover Cleveland Alexander fastball. So, too, they are the eyes of a scout who needed to see just one throw from the right arm of Roberto Clemente to know intuitively this was untapped greatness. And they are the eyes of the only remaining witness to Robinson's historic signing with the Dodgers in 1945.

"I guess there are days in your life you don't forget, and for me, that certainly was one of 'em," says Sukeforth. "I know this. I wouldn't have missed it. I was as interested as Robinson as to what was going to happen."

In August of 1945, Sukeforth was working for the Dodgers as a scout when his boss, Dodger president Branch Rickey, summoned him to his office at 215 Montague St. one morning.

"I want you to go to Chicago where the Kansas City Monarchs will be playing in Comiskey Park against the Lincoln Giants," Rickey said. "There's a particular player on the Monarchs named Robinson I want you to look at. He plays shortstop. Especially, I want you to look at his arm. Tell him who sent you, and if you like his arm, bring him back to Brooklyn with you if his schedule permits."

Having been an integral part of what Rickey had called "the great experiment" (in which, for two years, the Dodgers had been sending a pair of three-man crews across the country to specifically scout the Negro Leagues), Sukeforth surmised the time was at last at hand for monumental change in baseball.

He wasn't sure why Rickey was so interested in Robinson's arm, but he knew the wily Mahatma (as Rickey was called) wasn't summoning the young black shortstop to Brooklyn to talk about the working conditions in the Negro Leagues. The problem was, when he got to Chicago he discovered Robinson had a sore shoulder and wasn't playing.

"I got out to the park early and found an old scorecard lying on the ground which listed Robinson's uniform number as 8," Sukeforth recalls, sipping his lemonade. "As he came out of the dugout, I called him over and told him what Rickey had told me to tell him. He was thunderstruck. He told me he couldn't

understand why Rickey wanted to know about his arm, and I told him: 'I don't know either, Jack. I just work here.'

"He kept asking, 'Why does Rickey want to see me?' and I kept answering that all I knew was there was a lot of interest in him in Brooklyn."

Later that day, Sukeforth met with Robinson at the old Stevens Hotel in downtown Chicago in an effort to get a better feel about the man who was about to be tapped to break baseball's color barrier.

"I could see the determination all over him," Sukeforth says. "He'd have impressed anybody."

Most important to impress, of course, was Branch Rickey, who was waiting for them in the Dodgers' offices when they arrived from the train station the next morning.

"I introduced them," Sukeforth says, grinning. "I said: 'Mr. Rickey, this is Jack Roosevelt Robinson and I haven't seen his arm. He's going to be out of the lineup a few days.' That's when Rickey took over, and I just watched and listened. He said to Jack: 'All my life I've been looking for a great colored player, and I have reason to believe that player might be you.'

"He'd already gotten a lot of reports, even though he'd never seen Jack himself. That night we had dinner, and Rickey really drew a picture as to what Jack was going to face. He said: 'You have to take the worst kind of abuse that can be handed out to a man and there's nothing you can do about it. You can't even talk back. It's a condition that exists. You'd be justified, but you'd set the cause back 20 years.'"

There were only three people in Rickey's office when Robinson signed the contract that would pay him $3,500 to play for the Montreal Royals, the Dodgers' Triple A farm team, in 1946—and Rickey didn't announce it until two months later.

Such was the trust and bond he felt with Sukeforth. Theirs was a union that didn't get accorded near the notoriety of Rickey's and Robinson's. Nevertheless, it was one that would make both of them integral players in some of the most significant chapters in baseball lore.

•

Sukeforth leans back in his chair and gazes out the porch window at his dog, Belle, frolicking in the ocean. It is a moment of private reflection on the events that only he can talk about now as a first-hand witness. His wife, Grethel, who walks with a cane as a result of two recent hip transplants, interrupts his thought by depositing a plate of cookies on the table in front of him.

"Mmmmm," he says, turning back to his visitor and pointing to the cookies after grabbing one for himself. "You'll want to try these. They're molasses. Good for you, too."

He is asked how he came to forge a career in professional baseball having grown up in the backwoods of Maine. It wasn't until after the war—World War I—that he first got into it, he says, playing for industrial plant teams.

"Every little town in Maine had one," he explains. "Before that, my main connection to baseball was reading about the Red Sox in the *Boston Post,* which was brought into town every day on the stagecoach. In the fall of '25 I signed with Cincinnati, and two years later I was in the big leagues to stay. Then in 1929 I moved in as the Reds' No. 1 catcher. It started with a doubleheader in Sportsman's Park in St. Louis. I got one hit off Grover Cleveland Alexander in the first game and two more in the second and wound up hitting .354."

•

Sukeforth would like to think he'd have been a pretty fair

Jackie Robinson (left) and Branch Rickey discuss the contract that in 1950 made Robinson the highest-paid player in Dodgers history. (Daily News)

country catcher for a long time, too, but an off-season hunting accident in 1931—in which he was struck by a companion's errant shotgun fire—short-circuited his career.

"Feel this," he says, placing his visitor's hand on a tiny lump on his forehead. "Number six buckshot. Still there after all these years. It was a freak accident. Got some in my right eye, too, which is why I never saw the ball the same way again."

The Reds traded him to the Dodgers in a five-player deal that sent future Hall of Famer Ernie Lombardi to Cincinnati in the spring of 1932. After four seasons as the Dodgers' backup catcher, he accepted an offer to manage in their minor-league system. He had managed five years, the last three at Montreal, when Rickey took over as Dodgers front office chief and assigned him to one of those scouting crews.

Then, on April 9, 1947, the day before the Dodgers called up Robinson from Montreal, commissioner Happy Chandler announced he was suspending Dodger manager Leo Durocher for consorting with gamblers.

"Rickey asked me to manage the team," Sukeforth relates, "but by then I didn't want any part of managing. I did it for [the first] two games [of '47] before I went to him and suggested he talk to Barney Shotton about taking the job. Shotton had managed the Phillies and he was a proven guy."

Shotton agreed to take the job on the condition he could manage in his street clothes. That, in turn, inadvertently led to Sukeforth's next brush with baseball immortality.

In 1949, renowned American artist Norman Rockwell painted one of his most famous *Saturday Evening Post* covers—three umpires standing in the rain at home plate at Ebbets Field. Pittsburgh Pirates manager Billy Meyer is debating whether the game should continue, and from behind the back of one of the umpires peers a face with a Dodger cap that is unmistakably Sukeforth.

"I was asked about that a few years ago by the Hall of Fame," Sukeforth says, glancing at a small framed print of the painting that hangs on the wall of his porch. "The incident never happened. Rockwell was a big baseball fan, and I used to see him at Ebbets field a lot. I guess I'm in it because Shotton couldn't come on the field in his street clothes and I was the coach who usually represented him."

•

Four years later he was still a Dodger coach—only now in the bullpen—when destiny once again tapped him on the shoulder as one of the principals in the famous "shot heard 'round the world" that decided the Dodgers-Giants playoff game October 3, 1951. Sukeforth was on the receiving end of the phone call from Dodger manager Charlie Dressen asking which reliever, Ralph Branca or Carl Erskine, was ready to face Bobby Thomson.

"I should have said either one and let it be his decision, but Branca was throwing good and I was always a Branca man," Sukeforth relates. "Erskine had the best overhand curve in the league. If I'd have seen a couple of those I'd have told him Erskine could get the job done, but I didn't see it."

So on Sukeforth's recommendation, Branca got the call. "Only at the Polo Grounds was that a bad pitch," Sukeforth grumbles all these years later. "It was the only call I made all year. Of course, Charlie didn't make any bones about pointing the finger."

It soon became inevitable that Sukeforth was going to have to move on as the fall guy after the longest tenure—19 years—of anyone in the Dodger organization.

"At one point, the worm turned and [Dodger owner] Walter O'Malley himself called me to offer my job back. But I told him: 'You don't want me back and I don't want to come back.' Besides, I was already lined up to go to work for Mr. Rickey again in Pittsburgh."

Together again as Pirates, Rickey, the chief executive, and Sukeforth, his trusted scout, were just that in extracting the sweetest of all revenge against their former club. Late in the 1954 season, Rickey sent Sukeforth to Montreal to scout the Dodgers' farm club, particularly pitcher Joe Black, who was recovering from an arm injury. As with Robinson nine years earlier, Sukeforth got to the park early, but never did see Black. What he did see was a young Latin player in right field who could throw like no player he had ever seen before.

"Roberto Clemente," Sukeforth says. "Turns out, the Dodgers were trying to hide him because he was signed to a minor league contract and subject to the draft that winter in which we had first pick. I saw him throw and run and that was all I needed to see. I wrote Mr. Rickey and said, 'I haven't seen Joe Black, but I have your draft pick. For $4,000 you'll never get this kind of talent.'"

In having a hand in fostering the career of the first black player as well as the first great Latin player, Sukeforth shrugs. "I've seen this game grow up," he sayd, "and it just happened I was lucky to be in the right place at the right time a lot."

Or to paraphrase Gump, baseball has been kind of like that box of chocolates his visitor has brought for Grethel. He just never really knew what he was going to get.

LOVE STORY

As Don Mattingly stood addressing the media hordes yesterday, flanked by his wife, Kim, and his three sons in the Yankee Stadium Great Moments Room, it seemed like half my life was flashing before me.

Actually, it was *his* life Mattingly was recounting, but I was there for all of it, and in this day of transient baseball where even a Boston institution such as Roger Clemens takes his game to another team in another country, I wonder if that will ever happen again. I listened to Mattingly talking about how fortunate he felt to have been a Yankee his whole career and to have played as well as he did for as long as he did, every so often turning to Kim and smiling, and my thoughts drifted back to that first spring training in 1983.

They were just a couple of kids out of the farmlands of Indiana who barely had enough money to buy groceries. Every day they would arrive at the ballpark in Fort Lauderdale with their dog, Honey, driving their old Chevy Monte Carlo. You'd see them hugging and kissing like a couple of lovestruck teenagers, and it seemed obvious that even if Mattingly didn't make it, they would go back home to Indiana and, if nothing else, always have each other.

Of course, that spring Mattingly did make it, over the reservations of Billy Martin, the Yankee manager. As with every George Steinbrenner team, this was a ballclub loaded with high-salaried veterans with "no vacancy" and "rookies need not apply" signs posted at every position. But as the spring wore on and the lefty-swinging kid with the sloped shoulders kept wearing out opposing pitchers with his line drives, Martin slowly got won over. Or maybe he just got tired of hearing Yogi Berra, his top aide, telling him what a mistake it would be not to keep Mattingly.

"Being there, in that first camp around all those big-name players, yeah, we were kinda scared," Kim remembered. "I never really thought about getting there and then, all of a sudden, Donnie got to go north with the team. He played a couple of games, then sat around for the next 28 days before Billy sent him down. Thanks, Billy."

The tipoff that Mattingly was indeed a special player was when he went down to Columbus and showed no sign of rust from the long layoff, hitting .340 in 43 games, to earn another, permanent callup to the Yankees. The next year Berra had replaced Martin as Yankee manager, but Mattingly faced the same obstacle in spring training—too many high-priced veterans like Ken Griffey and Roy Smalley, whose best position was first base.

"That's okay," said Berra, "Mattingly will be my swing-man."

He meant swinging between the outfield and first base, but to Mattingly, the word swing had only one connotation. He would swing the bat—which he did from day one until the final game of the season, when he went four for five to edge Dave Winfield for the batting title.

The next three years were nothing short of phenomenal. The MVP season of '85 in which he batted .324 and knocked in 145 runs. The '86 season in

Don Mattingly and his wife Kim at a Knicks game at Madison Square Garden. (Vincent Riehl/Daily News)

which he hit .352 and broke the Yankee record for hits with 238. And '87, when he hit a record six grand slams and tied the record for most consecutive games (nine) hitting a homer.

If you didn't get a high watching him perform on the same level as the game's deities, then you were in the wrong profession. But there were low points, too.

In August 1991, Mattingly created a stir when he refused to cut his hair to conform with the Yankees' longtime regulations. He was the captain of the team, but he was defying the manager, Stump Merrill. I wrote a column saying he was out of line (not to mention out of character), and I suggested frequently the rest of that season he was acting like so many spoiled-brat ballplayers. That winter, Kim confronted me at a dinner. "Why are you getting on my Donnie?" she screamed. "Because," I replied, "he helped get a good man [Merrill] fired. He's the captain of the team. He should have gotten the haircut."

Mattingly and I didn't speak for the next couple of years. We had begun to make peace when another column I wrote, in response to a comment he made in 1995, the final year of his contract, touched off a firestorm of controversy. His back was aching and he was mired in another terrible slump when he

said defiantly, "I know I'm going to play somewhere next year, even if the Yankees don't want me."

I wrote how painful it was watch him swinging the bat the way he was now, with no more drive in it, and I urged him to retire with dignity and not to hang around for another payday. Unfortunately, the headline the guys in the office put on the column was "Done Don," which I knew wasn't going to go over real well in the Mattingly household.

Nevertheless, Mattingly did retire with dignity, even if it took him a year and a half to be able to say the word. When he finally did say it yesterday, he looked back at that day in Milwaukee in 1987, when his back went out and he instinctively knew he would never be the same player he was, and he said that was okay.

"From where I came from— a guy who couldn't run, couldn't throw and couldn't hit for power—to where I am today, it's been a long road and a real nice ride."

Sitting there with his three sons and the woman he married out of high school, Mattingly said he had no regrets the ride didn't last as long as it was supposed to. To him, it's good enough to be remembered as a pretty fair country ballplayer. Which is what he was.

SAFE AT HOME

NEW BRITAIN, Conn.— The field is empty and quiet on this day, in many ways a reflection of the man who once filled it with the buzzing sound of people—thousands of people—who came here to bear witness to a phenomenon.

The fields Steve Dalkowski would toil on years later in tattered jeans and a T-shirt picking fruit in the unrelenting summer heat of Bakersfield, California, are today nothing more than a blur in the recesses of his mind. But mention *this* field, or any of those other early fields where a baseball was his tool of trade and the pitcher's mound his own private bastion of peace, and a faint smile crosses his face.

"I know I could have won 15 games a year if I'd have ever made it," he says. "I was that good. There were nights after when I'd curse the gods for what happened to me. But I didn't drink to forget. I just drank."

It is no wonder Dalkowski can't or doesn't want to remember the bad times. To all of those who loved him throughout them, though, it is at least heartening that he can still hear the cheers. Because it doesn't really matter if he never made it to the big leagues, or how hard he tried to drink the pain and frustration of it all away. Steve Dalkowski could never run away from his legend of being the fastest pitcher of them all.

"It was truly a magical time back then when Stevie pitched his high school baseball games there," said Dalkowski's sister, Patti Cain, pointing to the field just beyond the ridge in Walnut Hill Park. She was standing in front of the Walnut Hill Care Center, where the man they called "the living legend" miraculously still lives.

"People would come from hundreds of miles away to see him pitch. You had to get to the park two hours ahead of time to get a good seat."

There was one particular day in 1957 when Dalkowski struck out 24 batters and basically left the multitude gasping. All the scouts were there, of course, as they had been for three years, watching in wonderment at this smallish (five foot 10, 175 pounds) bespectacled left-hander with the slingshot delivery who threw harder than anyone they had ever seen before. "They called it Stevie's 'radio pitch,'" Patti said. "You could hear it, but you couldn't see it."

A few weeks later, the man from the Baltimore Orioles, Frank McGowan, won the prize over 15 other clubs and signed Dalkowski to a $4,000 bonus—the major league limit at that time—and from there began the wildest, most unbelievable journey ever taken through the ranks of professional baseball.

The first stop was Kingsport, Tennessee, where Dalkowski quickly served notice to the Oriole high command of the project they had on their hands. He struck out 121 batters in 62 innings, but won only one game, losing eight and leading the Appalachian League in walks with 129. The next year, after similar bouts of untamed wildness at Knoxville and Wilson,

North Carolina, Dalkowski was assigned to Aberdeen, North Dakota. Despite all the horrific advance notices, his manager there, ex-major league shortstop Billy DeMars, took an immediate liking to the happy-go-lucky little lefty.

Watching Dalkowski throw in his first game at Aberdeen, DeMars spotted what he thought to be a likely source of the kid's wildness. "He never let his foot come off the rubber," DeMars, now a Phillies minor league instructor, recalled. "Essentially, he had no follow-through. It was unbelievable when you think about it. This kid was throwing 100 miles per hour with his arm alone. I told him 'Stevie, I'm gonna yell from the bench to let it go every time you don't follow through.' We worked on it, and in his next start he walked only five batters and struck out 20. They took our pictures together in the local paper, and I got quoted as saying he was the fastest pitcher I'd ever seen. I think that's how the 'fastest ever' legend got started."

And from there the legend merely grew to mythic proportions. There was the time when Cal Ripken Sr. was catching him in Aberdeen and got crossed up on a pitch. Instead of the slider Ripken had called for, Dalkowski threw a fastball that struck home plate umpire John Lupini in the face mask. The mask was shattered to bits and Lupini was momentarily knocked unconscious. Longtime National League umpire Doug Harvey, who crossed paths with Dalkowski a few times in the minors, once said: "I've umpired for Koufax, Gibson, Drysdale, Seaver, Maloney, Marichal and Gooden, and they could all bring it, but nobody could bring it like Dalkowski."

And it was Dalkowski whom director Ron Shelton used as the prototype for his "wild man" character "Nuke LaLoosh" in the movie *Bull Durham*.

To this day, the mere mention of Dalkowski's name to anyone who played, managed or umpired professional ball in that era, 1958-65, evokes one tale more unbelievable than the next.

"Only guy I ever saw bean a guy in a concession stand," remembered Hall of Famer Bob Lemon. "It was in Miami and Dalkowski was throwing batting practice. He let go of a pitch that sailed right over the backstop into the stands and hit a guy in the back of the head who was buying a hot dog."

"Dalkowski introduced the fear factor in baseball to me," said Cardinals manager Tony La Russa, who batted against him in the Eastern League in 1962. "He acted like he couldn't see and he seemed to relish being wild."

And then there is the most recounted chapter of all in the Dalkowski legend.

As the story goes, Dalkowski was throwing batting practice at Miami Stadium prior to an Orioles-Red Sox spring training game when Ted Williams ambled by the cage for a look. The "greatest of all hitters" had just retired and was working as a spring training instructor for the Red Sox. After watching the crowd stir with one crackling Dalkowski fastball after another, Williams could no longer resist the temptation to grab a bat and step into the cage. A hush came over the stadium as Dalkowski stood on the mound, squinting at the sight of his New England boyhood idol waiting to take his licks at him. Dalkowski went into his delivery, raising his right leg and, in an instant, the ball was in the catcher's glove, unseen, unheard and untouched.

Williams looked back and walked out of the cage. Afterward, the crowd of writers asked him how fast Dalkowski really was, and Williams reportedly confessed he never saw the pitch, adding that he'd be damned if he'd ever step into the cage against Dalkowski again. Thirty years later, Williams said he couldn't recall the incident. But even in his own limited capacity for recalling so many of the events of his life, Dalkowski remembers.

"I wasn't thinking about trying to strike him out," Dalkowski said. "I just didn't want to hit him. I threw him more than one pitch, and when one of them kinda took off, he put up his hand and yelled, 'I'm gettin' out.'"

For all the awe and fear Dalkowski's fastball may have engendered, however, the Orioles were still at a loss for how to harness it. The same could be said for Dalkowski's off-field behavior. There wasn't a minor league manager in the Oriole system back then who didn't have to bail Dalkowski out of jail. DeMars in particular felt like a father to him and even let him live with him

Pitching legend Steve Dalkowski with his sister Patti Cain in New Britain, Conn. (Mark Bonifacio/Daily News)

for a while in order to keep him straight.

"But one day after he got rained out of a start in Lewiston, Idaho, I told him he'd be starting the next day and not to stay out late," DeMars related. "I did a room check and found out he came in at 2 a.m. That was it for me. I'd hear from him periodically years later, usually a late-night call when he'd be drunk. The last time was about 10 years ago. He said, 'I'm sorry for everything. I love you, Billy.'"

"He wasn't a bad kid," said Cincinnati Reds coach Harry Dunlop, who managed Dalkowski at Stockton in 1964. "Everybody loved him. He was just easily led astray and he couldn't stop drinking."

Meanwhile, Paul Richards, the Orioles' general manager and acknowledged pitching guru, tried everything to get Dalkowski to throw strikes. One spring, Richards had a huge wooden target constructed with a strike zone painted on it. The experiment lasted for the 15 minutes it took Dalkowski to completely splinter it. Next, Richards had Dalkowski throw between 76 and 100 pitches before each start in order to tire his arm out. Finally, in the spring of 1962 at the Orioles' minor league camp in Daytona Beach,

Clyde King, one of Richards's pitching instructors, came up with the idea of having Dalkowski pitch to two batters on each side of the plate at the same time.

"I had to ask for volunteers," King said. "As I remember it took a couple of days to get two guys with guts enough to stand in there against him. But after watching Dalkowski at Richards's request, I couldn't see anything wrong with his mechanics. He just needed to take something off his fastball. And darned if his first six pitches didn't go right between the two batters. I impressed on him that you can still get people out throwing 94. He had taken a lot of pride at being wild and watching guys diving into the dirt, but it wasn't getting him to the major leagues."

Whether it was King's advice or simply a matter of maturity as a pitcher, Dalkowski began to put it all together under Earl Weaver at Elmira that '62 season. Although he still had a losing record (7-10), he had more strikeouts (192 in 160 innings) than walks (114) for the first time and his ERA (3.04) was two runs per game lower than he'd ever achieved.

When Dalkowski came to spring training the following February and continued throwing strikes, the Orioles thought at last they had something. In mid-March, Dalkowski had thrown six hitless innings of relief, and the Orioles decided he was going to be their closer. They told him he'd made the club. Then, on March 23, 1963, Dalkowski was called into a game against the Yankees in the sixth inning. He struck out Roger Maris and Elston Howard before Hector Lopez broke his spring hitless streak with a single. The next inning, facing Phil Linz, he broke off a slider and felt something pop in his elbow.

It was probably the ulnar nerve, but in those days they didn't have MRIs or arthroscopic surgery. All we know is, Dalkowski never threw with the same velocity again. Although he did compile his first winning season at Stockton under Dunlop in 1964, his off-the-field carousing finally wore out with the Orioles. In November of 1964, *The Sporting News* ran a small article with the headline: "Living Legend Released." His final record for nine minor league seasons: 46-80, 5.59 ERA, 1,396 strikeouts, 1,354 walks in 995 innings.

His dream shattered, Dalkowski embarked on a 30-year freefall to oblivion. He drank all day, every day now. He drifted to Bakersfield, picking fruit and chopping cotton as a migrant farm worker. It was there, staying in a rundown rooming house, that he met his wife, Virginia. She did her best to take care of him, but when Ray Youngdahl, a former teammate who's now a probation officer in San Mateo, offered to get him into a hospital, she welcomed the help.

"In 1973, I got him enrolled in the 'Project 90' drug and alcohol program," Youngdahl said. "When he got out, I took him in with me and set him up to get a landscaping job. But he wanted to go visit Virginia first, and on the bus ride to Oildale where they lived, he got off at San Jose and went to a bar. He never came back."

Some 18 years later, former Orioles catcher Frank Zupo, Dalkowski's batterymate at Stockton who works with BAT (the Baseball Assistance Team), drove to Oildale from his home in Anaheim along with a freelance TV producer, Tom Ciapetta. Zupo convinced Dalkowski to go to a hospital in Los Angeles, but after a few weeks there, he walked out. On Christmas Eve 1992, an Hispanic couple found Dalkowski, disoriented and incoherent, in a laundromat in Los Angeles.

Once they were able to determine who he was, Virginia

came and got him and took him to her family's home in Oklahoma. It was when Virginia died suddenly in January of 1994 that Patti, with the help of Zupo, got Dalkowski back to New Britain.

"For nearly 30 years I had lost my brother," she said, "and it was time for me to take care of him."

Sitting in a conference room at the Care Center, Dalkowski, now 58, strains to recall anything about those lost years. "Catching a bus at 3 a.m. to go out in the fields…building bonfires to keep warm before the sun came up…"

His eyes have a vacant look, the one visible scar from trying so long to drown his broken dreams in the companion of a whiskey or wine bottle. Otherwise, he is remarkably healthy. His high school coach, Bill Huber, comes by every Sunday to take him to church, and for DeMars, Dunlop, Youngdahl and all the others who shared his best of times and dreaded the worst, there is a happy ending after all.

Steve Dalkowski is safe at home.

FAREWELL TO PEE WEE

AUGUST 19, 1999

LOUISVILLE—Two by two—Duke Snider and Sandy Koufax, Carl Erskine and Don Zimmer, Ralph Branca and Clyde King—the old Dodgers strode solemnly into the Southeast Christian Church in Louisville, accompanying the casket carrying their captain, teammate and friend, Pee Wee Reese.

In front of them were Reese's family: Dottie, his wife of 57 years, son Mark and daughter Barbie, and right behind were former Dodgers owner Peter O'Malley, who came all the way from Hawaii, and Jackie Robinson's widow, Rachel, who took a red-eye flight from California. Snider also had made the cross-country overnight trek from California, while Koufax interrupted a Caribbean cruise and had his ship make a special stop in order for him to catch a flight to be here for a final farewell to the man who, he said simply, "was my captain for four years

and my friend for 45. What else can I say?"

In truth, their mere presence and the extremes to which so many of them went to be here said the most about their feelings toward Reese. Still, after learning of Reese's passing Saturday night at age 81 after a battle with cancer, Snider was moved to call him the greatest of all Dodgers.

"He was there whenever anybody needed help, whether it was a family problem or merely a slump," the ex-center fielder said. "You needed someone to talk to, you went to Pee Wee, or if he heard about your problem, he'd go to you. His availability was overwhelming."

And never more so than the day Reese, a native Kentuckian, unassumingly walked over to Jackie Robinson at second base and put his arm around the new Dodger, silencing the jeers of the opposing team and a ballpark of fans not ready to accept a black man playing in the major leagues. Robinson always said the incident occurred in Boston. Others insisted it was in Cincinnati. It doesn't matter. It happened. Probably in both places, and with it, the wall of racial prejudice and segregation in baseball as well as the nation was dealt a subtle but significant blow.

"That took such guts because Pee Wee had to go home and answer to his friends," said Erskine. "I told Jackie years later it helped my race more than his own."

And it certainly was never lost on Rachel Robinson.

"I wanted to hug him when I heard about it," she said. "That's why there was no way I wasn't going to be here today. It took 12 hours, but Pee Wee was a major person in my life and this is my last tribute to him."

At the request of Dottie Reese, there were no eulogies in the 45-minute service yesterday, just a warm and poignant soliloquy of Reese's life, delivered by senior minister Bob Russell, accompanied by some nostalgic film footage of the '50s Dodgers, shown on seven TV screens in the huge amphitheater of Southeast Christian Church. Among the more than 1,000 mourners were Paul Hornung and Denny Crum, luminaries from different sports

who were longtime friends of Reese.

They said that Dottie Reese wanted to keep the service as simple as possible, that eulogies would be too hard for her to bear. She had to know, though, that Pee Wee Reese simply meant too much to too many people not to be eulogized, even if the venue for it was the church foyer, where Zimmer, Snider, Erskine and Rachel Robinson put the captain's life in perspective.

"You want to know the kind of thing it was that made Pee Wee the captain?" Zimmer said. "A little thing like this: We're in spring training, playing against Kansas City, who had got Bob Cerv, one of the meanest guys ever on a ballclub. Always sliding spikes-first into people. A couple of years earlier, Cerv had spiked one of our guys, really hurt him. Now he's sliding into second and Pee Wee, covering the bag, takes the relay and throws it right at Cerv's head. Cerv jumps up and says, 'Did you throw that ball at me?' and Pee Wee says, 'You're [expletive] right I did.'"

"Clutch," said Erskine. "That's the word to sum him up. Everything significant Pee Wee did was when it counted. The incident with Jackie was a prime example. That gesture will be historic for civil rights."

Pee Wee Reese (left) and Jackie Robinson chat in the dugout at Yankee Stadium. (Ed Jackson/Daily News)

"What it did," said Rachel Robinson, "was change the dynamics of that whole team, showing them they had something dramatic to deal with. The dissidents were traded and those who were left had to adjust. Jack felt very close to Pee Wee the rest of his life. Each of them had a strong sense of their impact on social change."

Now they are both gone, the heart and soul of the rhapsodized Boys of Summer. Gil Hodges, Roy Campanella, Carl Furillo, Billy Cox, Junior Gilliam are all gone too. They were a special team in a special New York baseball era.

It was Reese, however, who was their captain, and many of those who are left will remember him for the leader he was.

"We grieve for the family," said Branca, "but we came here to celebrate a great life of a good man."

STAUB CHARITY AIDS KIN OF WTC VICTIMS

SEPTEMBER 23, 2001

Suddenly, the deficit now stands at three and a half games behind the Braves when as recently as August 18 it was 13 and a half. The surge continues, 22-5 since that low point of the season.

And so, from here on out, we are going to hear a lot about Met miracles now, miracles that can help lift the spirits of a terror-ravaged city, the sorts of miracles that inspired us in '73, a far different time—when the World Trade Center was still a work in progress.

And so, how strange the irony that Rusty Staub, an enduring symbol of that 1973 Mets miracle, has been such a visible figure in our city these past 11 days, as the Mets of the present do their best to imitate his team amid the backdrop of death and destruction a couple of blocks from where he lives in Battery Park City.

The night before the horrific events of September 11, Staub had dinner with a mutual friend of ours, Frank Brennan, a bond trader at Cantor Fitzgerald. They had first met about 15 years ago, became golfing buddies, and now they were the closest of friends, Brennan serving as a top aide in Staub's foundation for the widows of policemen and firefighters.

"We were going over plans for our dinner at the Hilton on November 19," Staub was saying. "You have to bear with me here. This is very hard for me. I would have lunch with Frank two or three times a week—and I don't even do lunch. We'd meet at the same place, equidistant from where he worked at the World Trade Center and where I live. We both ordered the same thing every time. We'd run in, sit down, eat and talk about foundation plans, all in about 25 minutes."

Rusty Staub pauses to remember his friend and the other victims of the WTC attack. (Howard Simmons/ Daily News)

For 16 years, Staub, through his foundation, has remained part of the fabric of this city, as well as the Mets, raising money to help the families of police and firefighters killed in the line of duty. There is the picnic he holds at Shea in June and the dinner in November. Last year, he raised $1.8 million. He thought that was a lot, until the Friday before last when suddenly the number of families in need of his help swelled by 350.

When the planes struck and the twin towers crumbled, then imploded into a mass of ash, twisted metal and granulated concrete, Staub was among the thousands fleeing lower Manhattan on foot through the enveloping clouds of dense, black smoke. It was only after he found refuge in the apartment of a friend some 40 blocks north that he began to collect his thoughts. Watching on TV the cops and firefighters desperately scouring through the wreckage in search of their lost and wounded brethren, Staub instinctively began marshaling his volunteers into action.

It was all he could do to take his mind off Frank Brennan, among the thousands he knew were missing.

"We've raised $7.5 million so far this week," Staub was saying yesterday. "Basically, we went out and told the world. The faxes and E-mails have just pyramided. It comes down to this: We're the purest vehicle there is in that everything we collect goes directly to the families. I don't have a staff of paid employees. Essentially, we're all volunteers—and we don't go away. Now we've got 350 additional families to take care of forever."

If you're wondering why Rusty Staub, after retiring from baseball, elected to devote so much of his life to charity work, it goes all the way back to his upbringing in New Orleans.

"My mother's brother, a man named Marvin Morton, was a policeman killed in the line of duty in New Orleans," Staub related. "I was just a little kid, but I remember sitting on the bed with my mom and my brother saying the rosary and how tough it was on the family. I never got over that. All through my life I've been friends with police and firemen and, in 1984, I was sitting in my old restaurant when a cop I knew was killed, leaving a wife and three kids, the oldest of whom was only five.

"I said, 'Someone needs to do something about this,' and I went to the PBA and, with their cooperation, I started this charity which began with just the picnic."

Friday night at Shea, Staub was on the field, mingling among all the players, uniformed personnel and media. His mission was to spread the word even further, although his presence could not help but serve as a baseball reminder of 1973, when the Mets won 20 of 28 games in September to climb from fifth place to first. Staub hit .279 with with 15 homers and led the team with 79 RBI that year.

"They dumped on us all year, but we just kept playing," he said. "You can't escape the similarities of that year and this Mets team. It would be a wonderful and uplifting thing if they pull it off, too. I'm with them. I'm still a part of the organization, but my priorities right now are with my 'other' family."

For this year only and, particularly, this incredible outpouring of generosity, Staub has amended his charter to include, as he said, "everyone who was working there."

Left unsaid, that meant all the other innocent and unknowing people like Frank Brennan who went to work Tuesday morning, September 11, and never came home.

CHAPTER 3

VILLAINS
AND
SCOUNDRELS

Even though the baseball memorabilia series ran in the *The News* in 1994, I'm sorry to report that nothing much has changed insofar as the hobby being proliferated with forgery and fraud as well as the same crooks and scam artists I thought I'd exposed here. ...The Billy Martin dial-a-victory caper was one of the more bizarre chapters in Yankee lore, even for them. ...As it turned out, Denny McLain did get himself another term in the slammer and is out again, still proclaiming his innocence. ...I always liked Pete Rose—if you're a reporter thirsting for a guy with great quotes, how could you not?—but, like McLain, he became a pathetic figure who probably will never get it.

MARTIN PHONES DIAL-A-VICTORY

JULY 30, 1985

CLEVELAND—There are those who swear the Cleveland Indians are so pathetic you can beat them blindfolded. Billy Martin is living, breathing (however impaired) testimony to this.

Last night, by long-distance telephone from his hospital bed in Arlington, Texas, Martin was able to direct an 8-2 Yankee victory over the Indians that he could not see. The game ball was presented to Lou Piniella, who managed the Yankees on the field while Billy lay recuperating from a punctured lung. But as Piniella, in his continuing role as George Steinbrenner's "manager-in-waiting" was oh-so-careful to point out, "this one was Billy's and the ball club's."

When you're managing against these last-place Indians, however, quite often it is simply a matter of biding your time until they find a way to beat themselves, which is precisely what happened last night.

While Billy was relaying instructions by phone to Piniella through Butch Wynegar, the Indians managed to give the game away by virtue of three unearned runs in the seventh inning that broke a 2-2 tie. With the bases loaded and two out in the seventh, Indians ace Bert Blyleven was already walking off the mound when Dave Winfield hit a routine grounder right at Tribe shortstop Julio Franco. Suddenly, Franco reached once, twice, three times for the ball in his glove only to come up empty as Mike Pagliarulo crossed the plate with the tie-breaking run.

"It had a little English on it," Winfield said, "but [Franco] knows it was a play that had to be made."

Unnerved by yet another betrayal from his teammates, Blyleven served up a two-run

Billy Martin looks haggard while smoking in his office. (AP/WWP)

single to right by Dan Pasqua that broke open the game and helped the Yanks stay within seven games of first-place Toronto.

"At that point," said Piniella, "Billy told me: 'All right, you guys are on your own now. I'll read about it in the papers tomorrow.'"

Piniella, though, still had to make one more managerial move on his own. That was the removal of Ed Whitson (6-7) after a leadoff double by Jerry Willard in the eighth. Strolling to the mound for the first time, Piniella raised his left arm and waved in Dave Righetti.

"It was really kind of funny," said Righetti, "although I was trying not to laugh out there because the situation was serious [still 5-2]. I'm so used to Lou talking about hitting and here he was suddenly talking about the situation and how to pitch. Finally, [catcher Ron] Hassey says: 'Just go at 'em,' and Lou says, 'Yeah, yeah that's right, just go at 'em.'"

That's what Righetti did, retiring the final six Indians to record his 18th save, which was made easier by Winfield's two-run homer in the ninth. By then, Billy was presumably fast asleep, having long since accomplished what may well be a baseball first—phoning in a victory.

"It was," said Wynegar, "a very interesting night. He called a pitchout once and at another point he wanted to make sure Pasqua wasn't playing too deep on [Tony] Bernazard. As for me, I did a great job on the play-by-play."

Indians president Peter Bavasi said he asked the switchboard operator to switch Martin's calls to the Cleveland dugout, "and let him give all his information to [Indians manager Pat] Corrales. I thought we'd have a little fun with Billy."

Bavasi later reported that Martin had indeed been switched to the Indians' dugout, but his reaction to the joke apparently was very un-Billy-like. "He simply called back and asked our operator very politely to be connected to the correct dugout." Bavasi said, "I guess he's resting comfortably. Either that or he was sedated."

Piniella, meanwhile, was asked if he was nervous or uncomfortable in his role as acting manager.

"Nah," he said, grinning, "not unless the visiting team doctor decides to give me a shot."

COLLECTOR CURVEBALL

MAY 29, 1994

Collecting baseball memorabilia—a hobby of kings fueled by the nation's romantic obsession with the national pastime—is often an exercise in misplaced trust.

A year-long *Daily News* investigation of the once burgeoning hobby/investment has revealed an industry rife with deception, secret deals, artificially inflated prices, and in some cases, outright fraud.

The villains are fly-by-night dealers who suddenly uncover a treasure trove of supposedly documented authentic memorabilia. But, as *The News* discovered, in all too many cases the documentation is unsubstantiated, erroneous or even fraudulent, and the memorabilia phony—undetectable to all except the trained eye.

And when someone does spot a uniform or glove as fake, the dealers have been known to turn around and offer it to someone else.

In the most egregious case, a tattered glove purportedly used and autographed by Ty Cobb, the Georgia Peach who banged out 4,191 career hits, sold at auction for $38,500. The glove was a fake.

Two other gloves, sold at the same auction, supposedly were used and signed by pitching great Cy Young and Negro League legend Josh Gibson. Both were fake, yet the Young mitt fetched $36,500 and the Gibson glove went for $28,000.

The gloves were sold by Richard Wolffers Auctions, a San Francisco auction house whose president is Duane Garrett—a prominent Democratic Party fund raiser with close ties to Vice President Gore and Sen. Diane Feinstein (D-California).

In November 1991, Wolffers offered a 1957 Brooks Robinson "rookie" road Baltimore Orioles jersey for $10,000 to $12,500. Before the auction, a Wolffers executive, having been informed by a Baltimore collector that the jersey "didn't look right," sent a picture of it to Phil Wood, a sports radio broadcaster in Baltimore who is an acknowledged expert on Orioles memorabilia.

Wrong Size, Too

"There were so many things wrong with that jersey," said Wood, "starting with the fact that it was a Rawlings jersey when Spalding was the company that manufactured Orioles jerseys that year.

"Also, in '57, the Orioles didn't use a front number on their jerseys, and this one had one," he said. "Plus, it was a size 44 and Robinson was a 42 for nearly his whole career."

Wood said that even the uniform's orange lettering looked different from the orange number on the back of the uniform. Despite the unanswered questions of authenticity, Wolffers sold the jersey, said Wood.

That same year, a 1941 Hank Greenberg Detroit Tigers home uniform, which knowledgeable collectors have said is a fake, was once sold at auction by Wolffers for $85,000.

"When I saw that jersey, with the rounded No. 5 on the back of it, I knew it was wrong," said Ed Budnick, a Detroit-based dealer and collector who is a respected authority on Tigers memorabilia.

"I wrote Garrett and showed him pictures of Greenberg from *Baseball Magazine* in May of 1941, hanging up his uniform to go into the service. The number 5 was a block letter. The Tigers have never had rounded numbers on their jerseys."

Three years later, in March 1994, the same Greenberg jersey turned up for sale by Sports Heroes, an Oradell, New Jersey, publicly traded sports memorabilia company, which has worked closely with Wolffers on the sale of numerous high-ticket items through auctions.

But this time it was sold by Sports Heroes to a private collector for a reported $28,000.

"I seem to recall there were some questions about that Brooks Robinson jersey, and I think we refunded the money on it," Garrett said. "I don't recall ever getting a letter from [Budnick] on the Greenberg jersey."

Sports Heroes, the first sports memorabilia company of its kind to go public, opened at $6 per share over the counter in 1989 and reached a high of $10 in 1992.

But the combination of a recession-depressed memorabilia market and what industry sources say were inflated prices paid for items that were later sold or traded at a loss resulted in the company's stock plummeting to a current low of less than $1 per share.

Three weeks ago, Jerome Zuckerman, the point man on most of Sports Heroes' acquisitions and transactions, resigned as president of the company.

Loaded Warehouse

"Zuckerman's involvement in the hobby coincided with the price of uniforms especially going berserk because he overpaid in so many cases," said one hobby insider. "They [Sports Heroes] still have a huge inventory of big-ticket items in their warehouse."

That inventory, however, no longer includes the gloves that supposedly belonged to Hall of Famers Cobb, Young and Gibson. They were among a parcel of circa 1920 mitts that was sold at auction by Wolffers on consignment from Sports Heroes.

A closer examination of how these gloves were sold—despite damning evidence that they were fake—reveals how unreliable the industry can be.

The gloves first surfaced in the hobby several years ago through a collector named Anthony Abbott, a quality controller for Amprobe Instruments in Lynbrook, New York.

Abbott said the gloves were given to him by the late sportswriter Fred Lieb. In selling the gloves to Sports Heroes, Abbott provided letters of authenticity from Lieb and the Hall of Fame, through a now-deceased library researcher named Jack Redding.

"Not only did [Redding] not write that letter, no one at the Hall of Fame has the authority to write letters of authenticity," said Hall of Fame president Ed Stack. "We will not do that. We could only get in trouble. If someone donates something to us, we can't even give them an appraisal."

Before selling the gloves to Sports Heroes, Abbott offered them to noted New Jersey collector Barry Halper, a limited partner in the Yankees whose baseball memorabilia collection is reputed to be the most extensive anywhere—including the Hall of Fame.

Halper passed on the gloves because he questioned their authenticity.

"Abbott called me and said he had these autographed gloves he had gotten from Fred Lieb," said Halper. "He sent me one of them, along with an 8-by-10 sheet of paper with autographs of Cobb, Cy Young, Honus Wagner and most of the others on the gloves.

"What he didn't know was that Fred Lieb had been a good friend of mine. I had asked Fred numerous times if he had any memorabilia, and always he told me how he never saved anything," said Halper. "So I instinctively knew something was wrong here, and I passed on the glove."

Too Perfect

Halper also rejected the autographed paper because it looked "too perfect." But Halper didn't return it, and Abbott has not asked for it back.

Abbott then went to another of the hobby's high rollers, Alan (Mr. Mint) Rosen—the self-acclaimed "million-dollar dealer" of baseball memorabilia—who bought two gloves, Kiki Cuyler and a Jimmie Foxx.

It was shortly after Rosen put up the gloves in his own auction that he learned the accompanying letters of authenticity from Abbott were frauds. Upon confronting Abbott, he got his money back.

"I then told Zuckerman the gloves were fake," Rosen said, "but he went ahead and put them in Wolffers anyway."

When asked by *The News* about the Abbott gloves transactions, Zuckerman would only say: "I have no comment about Anthony Abbott."

Abbott, reached at his Amprobe office, was equally abrupt. "I don't know what's going on. Why are you calling me? I refuse to talk about any things in the past I've done," he said before hanging up the phone.

Despite common knowledge of the phony Abbott gloves circulating the hobby, Garrett insisted this was the first he'd heard of it when contacted by *The News* last week. "To the best of my knowledge, no one asked for their money back," he said, adding: "We stand behind everything we sell."

The other problem perpetuated in the industry is an across-the-board inflation or exaggeration of prices for items supposedly sold—creating a fragile market based on fictional prices.

In October 1992, the hobby was abuzz with the announcement that a 1927 Lou Gehrig road flannel, consigned by Sports Heroes to Wolffers, had fetched a record $363,000.

The winning bidder, a South Jersey ophthalmologist who asked for anonymity, actually put up $74,000. The rest of the payment was made with a Ty Cobb uniform for which Garrett gave him an inflated $300,000 credit—only to trade the uniform back to him later. The highest documented dollar amount ever paid for a Cobb uniform is $176,000.

"I don't remember exactly what the trade was," Garrett said of what his firm billed as a record sale. "I only know the Cobb was a beautiful uniform."

Another questionable "sale" involved an 1889 S.F. Hoss baseball card of Tim Keefe, which was supposedly auctioned for $33,000.

"Nobody had ever heard of Wolffers until they announced they had sold that card for $33,000 in auction," said a collector who once owned the Keefe card. "Nobody believed anyone really paid that much for it, but you couldn't prove it because Garrett wouldn't say who bought it."

Big Price Cut

A few years after the Wolffers auction, the now-famous $33,000 card turned up at a national card convention on the table of a Miami-based memorabilia dealer, Bruce Matthews, who was asking $11,000 for it.

Matthews acknowledged he once had the card. But when asked where he got it, his memory went hazy. "I think I got it in a trade with Garrett," he said.

Dealers' Pitch Hits Collector

MAY 30, 1994

The scene was a long, narrow conference room with seats for more than 1,000 in Atlanta's Georgia World Congress Center in July 1992.

As one of the sidelights to the National Sports Collectors Convention, an auction was taking place on a grease-stained 1942 Boston Red Sox uniform of Hall of Famer Jimmie Foxx.

Word had circulated in the room that a wealthy collector from Connecticut named Howard Rosenkrantz wanted the uniform "at any cost." Rosenkrantz, it seemed, had uniforms of every member of baseball's elite "500 homer club" except Foxx.

To do his bidding, he commissioned Richard Russek, a partner in Grey Flannel Collectibles, a company that both authenticates and brokers old uniforms.

According to several witnesses, the bids on the Foxx uniform kept going higher and higher, but once it got into six figures the only bidder anyone could see was Russek. When Russek's winning bid of $220,000 was announced, gasps of shock erupted from the back of the room.

"It was mind-boggling," said long-time collector and dealer Rob Lifson, who conducts his own sports memorabilia auctions. "It just didn't make sense. For someone to pay that much for that uniform was idiotic."

Bill Mastro, a respected collector and dealer who has worked as a consultant for Sotheby's Auctions in New York, was equally stunned.

"For one thing, it [the uniform] looked like it had been run over by a truck," said Mastro. "I can't prove it, but I have my doubts legitimate bidding was going on...There was no way that uniform goes for that figure."

On what basis did Mastro reach that conclusion?

"At one of the auctions I did for Sotheby's, I had the last uniform Mickey Mantle ever wore," Mastro related. "It was in perfect condition with a letter of authenticity from Mantle. It sold for $60,000."

Contacted at his office at U.S. Surgical Corp. in Norwalk, Connecticut, Rosenkrantz conceded that it had been common knowledge he badly wanted the Foxx uniform. He also acknowledged that he bought the uniform without any knowledge of its origin "other than it had been kept in the trunk of a car by an elderly woman who didn't know what it was worth."

Although Russek and his Grey Flannel partner Andy Imperato authenticated the uniform, Rosenkrantz saw nothing irregular about that arrangement.

"Immediately after the auction [Russek] did tell me that he didn't feel good about the way the bidding went," Rosenkrantz said. "He said he didn't see hardly anyone else bidding against me. In retrospect, I guess that sounds a little flimsy...To be honest, I thought the highest I would have

to go for the uniform was $150,000."

According to Russek, the uniform was actually first offered to him for $80,000 by a woman in San Diego who later decided to let Superior Galleries of Beverly Hills, California, auction it for her.

And even though Grey Flannel was paid by Superior to authenticate the uniform, Russek felt something was amiss with the auction when he didn't see anyone bidding against him.

"But you just don't jump up in the middle of the auction and demand to know who's bidding against you," Russek said. "That's not the way it goes. All I can tell you is the truth will come out."

When presented by the *Daily News* with the many questions that have since been raised about the Foxx uniform auction, Steve Applebaum, a spokesman for Superior, said he was not permitted to reveal either the underbid or the consignor of the uniform.

"All I can say is [the bidding] was there," he said. "It was an entirely proper auction."

But Rosenkrantz wonders. "I have a bad taste in my mouth now about this thing," he said.

And he isn't alone. In the course of a year-long *News* investigation of the baseball memorabilia hobby, numerous collectors expressed dismay and outrage over the behind-the-scenes deals, artificially inflated prices and questionable authenticity involving uniforms.

It is an entirely unregulated hobby. More than anything, word of mouth, stemming from the numerous uniform trades and sales they had brokered, was what enabled Imperato and Russek to become the preeminent authenticators of uniforms.

Though Rosenkrantz calls Imperato "my friend," others view Grey Flannel's dual role as authenticators and brokers as a conflict of interest. They cite the twisted trail of a reputed 1937 Lou Gehrig road uniform as the most blatant example.

Sources say Imperato initially came into possession of the uniform from a sportswriter in the Midwest, wrote a letter of authenticity on it, and arranged its sale to a wealthy ophthalmologist in southern New Jersey. The ophthalmologist later traded the uniform—through Imperato—to Sports Heroes Inc., a publicly traded sports memorabilia company in Oradell, NEW JERSEY

The uniform was then put on consignment in the Christie's auction in New York on October 17, receiving no bids, in part because serious questions arose regarding its authenticity. Finally, Sports Heroes—again through Imperato—traded the uniform to New Jersey collector Barry Halper.

"Andy is like one of those Wild, Wild West sherrifs," observed Alan (Mr. Mint) Rosen, the self-acclaimed "million-dollar dealer" who was hired by Christie's to supervise the auction. "He's both the judge and the jury. All his uniforms are good, and nobody hangs in his courtroom as long as he gets his piece of the deal. I asked him to inspect that uniform after all the questions about it came up. I never knew he was the one who came up with it in the first place."

On numerous occasions, Grey Flannel has authenticated uniforms for the consignor to an auction house as well as the auction house itself.

This practice has raised questions about other uniforms.

In 1991, for instance, Grey Flannel authenticated a 1941 Hank Greenberg Detroit Tigers home jersey for an auction by Richard Wolffers Inc. of San Francisco. The jersey sold for $85,000, although several collectors pointed out to Wolffers that the Tigers always had block numbers on the backs of their uniform, not rounded numbers such as the "5" that appeared on this item.

In March, it turned up again, this time with Sports Heroes, which sold it for $28,000—with yet another letter of authenticity from Grey Flannel.

"There was nothing wrong with that jersey," insisted Dr. Jerome Zuckerman, who recently resigned as president of Sports Heroes. "The only reason it dropped so much in value was because of the market."

"I don't claim to be infallible; nobody can be in this business," said Imperato. "I could make a mistake, although I don't think I did."

Mastro takes a different view.

"The problem we have in this hobby," said Mastro, "is that so many dealers and collectors want this stuff to be good. I'm confident this hobby will thrive again because there are still plenty of legitimate people stepping up to the plate to buy things. But it's a bad market for uniforms right now because of a bunch of guys who decided to play games."

BELLE'S WORDS RING IN HIS EARS

FEBRUARY 26, 1996

WINTER HAVEN, Fla.— When word began spreading faster than a Florida twister that Albert Belle had decided to refurbish his surly, bad-boy image, I reluctantly moved Winter Haven to the top of my spring training itinerary.

I say "reluctantly" because I am no glutton for punishment. I had no great desire to be blown off by Bad Albert, especially if it meant driving to Winter Haven for this hardly unique experience.

I arrived around noontime, nearly an hour before the Indians were scheduled to finish their workout. I was encouraged by the fact that a couple of days earlier, Belle had taken the first step in what was believed to be a sincere effort at mending fences with the media when he entertained a group of Cleveland TV, radio and print types for nearly 45 minutes.

My initial encouragement, however, was quickly tempered by an ominous prediction from the longtime Indians beat man, Sheldon Ocker of the *Akron Beacon-Journal*. "His last words to us the other day," said Ocker, "were 'See you in October, guys.'"

Still, that day Belle talked about everything from Hannah Storm (whose camera crew he wanted to break at the World Series) to Roger Maris (whose home run record he expects to break this year or next).

There is also his contract, which is up after this year. Coming off a season in which he became the first player to hit 50 homers and 50 doubles, and a player who has routinely knocked in 100-plus runs over his first five seasons, is it any surprise his agent, Arn Tellum, is asking for Junior Griffey money?

Perhaps not. But for all of Belle's production on the field, his image off it—especially next to the effusive Griffey—would seem to diminish his overall value to an organization. I asked Indians GM John Hart if Belle's image was having a bearing in his negotiations with Tellum.

"We like Albert," Hart said. "We pay him to play and he plays every day. We pay him to produce and he produces. He's combative and he loves to win. We know he has an image problem. He's never going to be sitting down shooting the breeze with the media. What Albert has to decide is whether he wants to be surrounded by the same bunch of people he's been playing with into the year 2000. We know him better than the people around the league."

In other words, the Indians know Belle can be a jerk, but as least he's *their* jerk.

Before talking to Hart, I had asked Indians media chief Bart Swain if he could set up an interview with Belle. After a consultation with the Sullen One in the trainer's room, Swain said it looked okay. "I told Albert who you were and that you were from New York and everything," Swain said. "I think he'll do it."

But as I approached his locker, he shook his head.

"Sorry, man," he said pleasantly. "I changed by mind. I

Albert Belle at bat in Yankee Stadium.
(John Roca/Daily News)

don't want to talk to the *New York Times* today."

"That's cool," I said. "I don't want you to talk to the *New York Times* today, either."

Belle looked at me quizzically.

"I'm with the *New York Daily News.*"

"Oh," he said. "Well, it doesn't matter. I want to get out

of here. Come back tomorrow. I think I might want to talk again then."

Much as everyone around the Indians doubted this, Belle kept his half-promise. The Storm affair, he said, "has dragged on too long" and besides "there's been a lot of players who have done a lot worse than I have to reporters." Players like Deion Sanders, who dumped ice water over Tim McCarver.

"That died down after a week or so," he said. "This [cursing out Storm] happened. So what? We have to move on."

Obviously, his new teammate, Jack McDowell, hasn't been able to teach him how

obscene behavior can be forgiven and forgotten with an apology.

As for moving on, Belle said he hopes to sign a new deal with the Indians "because I want to play on one team my whole career, like [Cal] Ripken and [Kirby] Puckett." Presumably, those were pleasing words to Hart as well as Belle's prediction of eclipsing Maris's record of 61 homers in a season.

"I never thought about hitting 50," Belle said, "but I think [61] is reachable before the turn of the century if you get a full season. If Matt Williams or I don't do it, someone else will."

And for all we know that will be the next time Albert Belle decides to oblige the media again.

Cool Heat

The teeming streets of Detroit were rife with tension and fear that summer.

Al Kaline remembers seeing clusters of youths on every corner of Michigan Avenue and wondering as he drove to Tiger Stadium each day when the city was going to explode in gunfire and flames again. On most hot afternoons and nights you could still smell the charred hulks of burned-out buildings on 12th Street a mile away, and ominous accounts of increasing gun sales around the city became a daily staple of the news reports.

"It was really eerie," Kaline remembered. "We had had the riots in '67, and it was another hot summer and a lot of people thought it was going to erupt again. But as the summer wore on and we kept winning, it seemed like everybody in the city was all wrapped up in us. It gave people something to talk about, and that's what those kids were doing on the street corners. A year earlier they were probably full of unrest and anger. I can't prove it, but I really think we eased the city's tension."

The summer of 1968 is indelibly etched in history with the assassinations of Bobby Kennedy and Martin Luther King and the unrest that gripped a nation torn by Vietnam and racial injustice (as epitomized by the gloved-fist protests of Tommie Smith and John Carlos at the Mexico City Olympics).

And yet in Detroit, a city that in many ways symbolized the rage of black America in the '60s, the public figures around whom the populace ultimately rallied included not only the slain civil rights champions, but a bunch of ballplayers, many of them white, named Kaline, Stanley, Northrup, McAuliffe, Freehan, Horton and Wert. And of them all, none did more to distract Detroit and an entire nation from the blood on its streets than an irascible, organ-playing, jet-setting, free spirit pitcher named Dennis Dale McLain.

In a fast-lane lifestyle that included flying his private plane and playing the organ in nightspots into the wee hours of the morning amid a constant whirlwind of business deals, Denny McLain won 31 games for the Detroit Tigers. The day he won his 30th, Dizzy Dean, who 34 years earlier had been the last man to win 30 in a season, was on hand at Tiger Stadium to congratulate him.

Thirty years have passed, and despite assaults on just about every other sacred record, including this season's race to break Roger Maris's home-run standard, no one has even come close to winning 30 again. It is highly doubtful if McLain, now 54 and serving an eight-year sentence in a federal lockup in Pennsylvania for stealing $3 million from a Michigan meatpacking company's pension plan, finds much satisfaction in that. His pitching career always did take a back seat to his other flamboyant and more risky endeavors. Still, the most wins by any pitcher since '68 has been 27, and with every passing year, 30 wins loom as a far more imposing feat than hitting 61 homers.

"For a lot of reasons, I don't think you'll ever see another 30-game winner," asserts Yankee broadcaster Jim Kaat, who won 25 for the Minnesota Twins two years prior to McLain's 31-win season. "For one thing, we no longer have four-man rotations and guys don't get to start 40-45 games in a season. If a pitcher wins half his starts, that's a pretty good year. Look at [Greg] Maddux, [Roger] Clemens or any of the best pitchers today and they don't make more than 35-36 starts per year."

For the record, the last pitcher to make more than 40 starts in a season was Charlie Hough in 1987 with Texas, but he was a knuckleballer. To find the last conventional pitcher to do it you have to go back to Toronto's Jim Clancy, who made 40 in 1982. McLain made 41 starts in 1968, but what made his 31 victories all the more remarkable was the self-created atmosphere of conflict in which he managed to accomplish it.

The previous season McLain had won 17 games by September, but with the Tigers locked in a furious, down-to-the-last-day, four-team battle for the pennant, he won none of his last five starts and missed two weeks due to a mysterious foot injury. During the off season, his spending habits began to engulf him, and as his

Detroit Tigers pitcher Denny McLain takes questions from the media. (Gene Kappock/Daily News)

debts mounted and his checks began bouncing with increasing frequency, the Tigers felt compelled to get him a business manager. At the same time, they seriously considered trading him.

Were it not for the fact that he began winning...and winning...and winning from day one of the '68 season, and that the team followed suit (nine wins in the first 10 games), the Tigers might have intensified their efforts, because McLain hardly toned down his off-the-field act.

"I don't recall how much transgressing I did in 1968," McLain said in his 1988 autobiography *Strikeout*, "but I sure as hell was busy. Pitching on three days' rest for an entire summer might have been enough

for most guys. But most guys weren't Denny McLain. I always preferred life in the fast lane and in 1968 there weren't any speed limits in sight. Airline pilots probably spent less time in planes than I did that summer. I was anywhere and everywhere. Go to a shopping center and you'd see me behind the keyboard of a Hammond organ. Turn on your TV and you'd see me on everything from the *Today Show* to *Joey Bishop*. The only thing I wasn't doing much was sleeping."

"Denny was just a very self-centered guy," said Mickey Lolich, the left-handed half of the Tigers' 1-2 starting pitching punch who followed up a 17-win season in '68 with three complete-game victories over the

Cardinals in the World Series. "Our manager, Mayo Smith, had one set of rules for Denny and another set for the 24 other guys on the team. We weren't mortal enemies, but we weren't friends either, especially after he flew me and my wife to the 1969 All-Star game in Washington in his private plane and left us there after he got killed by a homer by Willie McCovey. It was a lousy way to treat a teammate.

"Denny was always saying things, and the thing I'll never forget was what he said as we were going to the World Series that 31-game winners drive Cadillacs and 17-game winners drive motorcycles."

But McLain never apologized for anything. Rather he pointed to his idol, Frank Sinatra. The Chairman of the Board, he said, "doesn't give a damn and neither do I."

There is probably no better proof that he lived that philosophy than an incident late in the '68 season when McLain fooled with the integrity of the game and risked tarnishing his 30-win season with a suspension. His sin: Deliberately grooving a home run pitch to an aging Mickey Mantle.

It was September 19 and the Tigers had clinched the AL pennant two days earlier. McLain was pitching with a big lead when Mantle came to bat in the eighth inning, tied with Jimmie Foxx for third place on the all-time homer list.

Summoning his catcher, Bill Freehan, to the mound, McLain said: "Tell Mickey it's coming right down the pipe."

"What do you mean?" Freehan replied, taken aback.

"Just what I said. Tell him he's going to get one just where he wants it."

But when McLain delivered on his promise, Mantle didn't budge as the home plate umpire called strike one on the room-service fastball. Calling Freehan to the mound again, McLain asked: "What happened? Why didn't he swing?"

"I don't think he believes you," Freehan said.

"Well, tell him again. I'm going to give him another one."

This time Mantle swung and connected for a homer over the right field fence just inside the foul screen. As he rounded third, he looked right at McLain and smiled and tipped his cap.

"Denny was pretty much in his own world," Kaline said. "One time in '68 Mayo called a bunch of the veterans on the team into his office and told us that Denny had some sort of a doctor's appointment and had to fly separately to the next city we were going to. He wanted to know what he should do. We told him,

'Just let him go as long as he keeps winning.' Mayo did and Denny did too. We could care less."

Eighty-year-old Johnny Sain, who was the Tigers' pitching coach in 1968, chuckled over the phone at the mention of all the tribulations that were a standard part of the total McLain package. "You have to first understand," he said, "I never met a pitcher I didn't like. I suppose Denny was a little wild off the field, but I just remember him as a super guy. It hurts me to see him with all these problems now.

"I remember when I first came to the Tigers, [GM Jim] Campbell was worried about Denny bowling so much and what it could do to his arm. That year he won 20 games, and I went to Campbell and said, 'Do you think we can arrange for all of our pitchers to take up bowling?'"

Sain agrees that 30 wins will probably remain an unreachable feat unless some team decides to go back to the four-man rotation. There's no reason pitchers can't pitch with three days' rest, he says, but it isn't likely to ever happen again. "The real gone-forever pitching number," Sain added, "is 300 innings [in a season]."

Seemingly gone forever as well is the downtown section of Detroit, which never recovered from the '67 riots despite the rallying effect the '68 Tigers'

world championship had. Just as sadly, McLain fared no better.

The fast-lane lifestyle and cavalier attitude about his pitching career finally caught up to him and kept on catching up. After leading the AL again in victories with 24 in 1969, he hurt his arm and won only 17 more games the rest of his career. The Tigers traded him to Washington after the 1970 season, and he was out of baseball two years later.

In April of 1985, he was sentenced to 23 years in prison for racketeering, extortion and conspiracy but wound up serving just two and a half because of a judicial error.

When he got out, he thanked God for giving him a second chance. "I'm a changed man," he said in the final page of his autobiography. "At age 44, it's the first inning of the rest of my life and this time I'll go the distance. Even I can bet on that."

A surer bet would have probably been a return visit to prison. But despite his legacy of self-destruction, he also accomplished something that may never be achieved again: He won 31 games and helped ease the pain of a city. And 30 years later, in this season of records, Denny McLain is worth being remembered for his winning as much as for ending up a two-time loser.

BEFORE THERE WAS ROCKER

FEBRUARY 3, 2000

Now that the world has found another reason for outrage in the John Rocker case, a bit of perspective is in order.

All of a sudden, Rocker isn't by himself in being pilloried. Commissioner Bud Selig is taking his shots for his two-month suspension of the Braves' lightning-rod reliever.

Keep in mind, the critics are many of the same ones who have been decrying the absence of a strong commissioner for years.

Despite Rocker's remarks that offended minorities, foreigners, homosexuals and New York City humankind in general, the Players Association contends that, "It is literally unprecedented to impose a penalty on a player for pure speech."

Not true.

Try the 1938 Jake Powell decision.

In that case, Powell, an outfielder with the Yankees, was suspended 10 days by the first-ever commissioner, Judge Kennesaw Mountain Landis, for a remark made about blacks.

In a July 29, 1938, radio interview with a Chicago broadcaster, Powell boasted that he was able to stay in good shape because of his off-season job as a Dayton, Ohio policeman, "cracking niggers over the head."

Although baseball didn't allow black players yet, Powell's remark drew cries of outrage, especially from the black press. Landis acted swiftly and decisively by suspending him.

In addition, the Yankees, fearful of alienating their black fan base, ordered Powell to tour the bars, businesses and black newspapers in Harlem, apologizing and asking for forgiveness.

Think of it, though. This was nearly two decades before the rise of the civil rights movement, when the major leagues didn't hesitate to show blacks what they thought of them with a very closed-door policy.

Judge Kenesaw Mountain Landis tosses out the first ball. (Daily News)

There were no howls of protest from the white press over Powell's remark, and even Yankees manager Joe McCarthy passed the comment off as a joke, saying, "He sure meant no harm."

Yet Landis still saw fit to impose one of the stiffest penalties on a player of his 24-year reign. Under the circumstances of the time, Powell's 10-day suspension (without pay) certainly could be considered comparable to, if not more severe than, Rocker's in this age of racial and social enlightenment.

It is worth noting, too, that Landis was perceived as being as instrumental as any in keeping blacks out of baseball.

After rendering the Powell decision, Landis was accused by one New York newspaper of "smug hypocrisy," while *Chicago Tribune* columnist Westbrook Pegler noted that baseball "treats Negroes as Adolf Hitler treats the Jews."

Like Landis, Selig is under attack after dealing with an offensively loose-lipped player.

Whether he has gone too far in sitting Rocker down for two months is debatable and ultimately will be decided by baseball's arbitrator, Shaym Das.

But what does Selig have to do to satisfy his incessant critics?

When considering that he sat down one of his own, Reds owner Marge Schott, for a year for her insensitive remarks about minorities, the Rocker penalty seems consistent. And where was the public outcry about Schott's penalty being excessive?

Selig was in a no-win situation with his critics. Some have erroneously compared his two-month sanction against Rocker to the five-game suspension Robbie Alomar got for spitting in umpire John Hirschbeck's face.

The Alomar decision was rendered by then-American League president Gene Budig in consultation with the Players Association. Budig didn't want to be embarrassed by the union

appealing his decision and winning.

But he wound up being embarrassed anyway, because the lightness of the penalty was laughable. Selig was even more embarrassed, but didn't want to usurp a league president's authority.

Now there are no league presidents and the commissioner is the sole authority when it comes to punishment.

Selig acted decisively on Rocker—the way his critics have implored him to act. He did not consult with the Players Association but instead made a statement as to how baseball regards racial and ethnic intolerance.

Judge Landis made the same statement for baseball 62 years ago, but it has been long forgotten.

If you're wondering whatever happened to Jake Powell, he played six more uneventful seasons in the major leagues, retiring just before Jackie Robinson broke baseball's color line.

He received none of the backlash Rocker can expect for the rest of his career.

In 1948, at age 40, Powell committed suicide in a Washington, D.C., police station while awaiting charges of cashing bad checks.

Just Charlie's Latest Hustle

January 6, 2004

So Pete Rose, in his third (by my count) autobiography, now tells us he bet on baseball after all. Not only that, he admits he bet on his own team, the Cincinnati Reds, during the time he was their manager. At least, he says, he always bet on them to win—a revelation, I'm sure, Bud Selig must have found most reassuring.

After lying to all of us—from the commissioners of baseball, to his former teammates and respected opponents, to the writers whose votes he would now seek for the Hall of Fame—Pete Rose says he's sorry and asks us for a second chance. "It's time to take responsibility," Rose says, "and I'm 14 years late."

He's right about that. But in the meantime what are we supposed to make of all this?

Rose says the reason he didn't come clean from the get-go was because, in his mind, he knew he'd broken the letter of the law, "but I didn't think I'd broken the spirit of the law, which was designed to prevent corruption. I never took an unfair advantage. I never bet more or less based on injuries or inside information. I never allowed my wagers to influence my baseball decisions. So in my mind, I wasn't corrupt."

Just dumb.

Of course, we'll never know what went into Rose's betting on baseball. For this, we have to take his word, which after all this is pretty much worthless. All we finally know is that, by his own admission, he did it. And as everyone in baseball knows—from the explicit language of Rule 21 which is posted in both English and Spanish on every clubhouse door—"Any player, umpire or club or league official or employee who shall bet any sum whatsoever upon any baseball games in connection with which the bettor has a duty to perform shall be declared permanently ineligible."

Here is the dilemma facing Selig as he wrestles with the decision as to whether to reinstate Rose. As Tom Seaver, one of Rose's former teammates, put it to me yesterday: "This has never been a Pete Rose issue. It's a rule issue. It falls into the lap of the commissioner, who must decide whether baseball is going to have this rule or change it.

"Where is the standard where the rule no longer applies? Three thousand hits? Three hundred wins? If the commissioner wants Pete in the Hall of Fame, then change the rule."

In other words, if this were some .220-hitting utility infielder who bet on baseball, we wouldn't be having this debate.

As for Rose, he's going to have a hard time convincing anyone this isn't just another of his grand hustles, a last-ditch effort for sympathy as the clock runs down on his years of eligibility on the Baseball Writers Association ballot. He sure didn't help his cause arranging this big book splash to coincide with the latest writers' Hall election. Nor is it easy to dismiss the fact that when he finally did fess up after all these years, he did it in a manner in which he would get a high six-figures payday out of it.

I do know that, even if Selig somehow finds a way to get past Rule 21, Rose faces another dicey situation if he somehow ever makes it onto the writers' ballot. Rule 5 on the ballot states: "Voting shall be based upon the player's record, playing ability, integrity, sportsmanship, character and contributions to the team."

Rose insists he's no longer a betting man, which is good, because I don't think he'd want to wager that 75 percent of the voting writers would not have problems with his character and integrity after being lied to by him for 14 years.

The writer Rose lied to most was Roger Kahn, who authored his last autobiography in 1989. In that one, *Pete Rose: My Story*, Rose devotes nearly 40 pages to his gambling, denying he ever bet on baseball while maintaining baseball investigator John Dowd's case against him was based on nothing but hearsay.

Bob Feller, the hardest of the Hall of Fame hardliners as far as Rose's reinstatement is concerned, had a rebuttal for that yesterday. Asked if Rose's admissions of guilt in his new book changed his thinking, Feller said: "As far as I'm concerned, the book Pete Rose wrote was the one John Dowd gave to the commissioner."

And Kahn is now equally hard-lined against his former friend and literary soul-mate.

"It's an embarrassment for me to have believed the lies of a semi-literate," Kahn said yesterday. "I thought it was my job to present his case. I felt a little like a criminal lawyer. I didn't ask: 'Did you do it?' I asked: 'How do you want to plead?'

"I wonder if in 10 years O.J. will write a book? If he does, I want to say right here and now I'm not interested in collaborating with him."

We can only presume that goes the same for Rose's next autobiography, in which the all-time hit king denies all the admissions of his betting on baseball made in his previous one.

CHAPTER 4

COLORFUL CHARACTERS

I covered Lou Piniella though all his foibles and triumphs as a player and as a manager, and we've had a 25-year friendship. In my opinion, he's one of the best there is, as a baseball man and a person. ...Bill Parcells and I grew up together in Oradell, New Jersey, and I had fun getting him together with Piniella. They were quite a pair. ...Scooter's speech at the Hall of Fame was one for the ages—a classic. ...Uncle Hughie Alexander was a dear friend. I only wish I'd gotten around to doing that book he wanted to do. ...Then again, in Don Zimmer's case, I got to do two books.

Lou: I'm Sick of Steinbrenner

MARCH 18, 1982

WEST PALM BEACH, Fla.—The weighty problems of Lou Piniella escalated into a fiery war of words with George Steinbrenner here yesterday when the Most Volatile Yankee, saying he was "tired of being treated like Little Orphan Annie," unleashed a torrent of anger over the fines being imposed on him by the Yankee high command.

"I am utterly disgusted with George Steinbrenner and his policies," Piniella told a small group of reporters who were assembled prior to the Yankees' "A" game against the Expos.

"All we have ever been told around here is that what happens within the Yankee family is supposed to stay there. It's a sad way for a player to learn he's getting fired—through the press. The manager should at least have the decency to tell the player first."

Piniella, who was actually informed by vice president Bill Bergesch that he had been fined $1,000 by manager Bob Lemon for leaving Tuesday's scheduled "A" game against the Rangers in Pompano Beach without permission, then revealed that Steinbrenner had fined him an additional $7,000 for failing to reach the prescribed weight of 200 pounds by February 22. Both Piniella and the Yankees now admit that this requirement was written into the three-year $1 million contract the 38-year-old outfielder was given by Steinbrenner last winter.

However, it was Piniella's contention that Steinbrenner had verbally agreed to extend the weight deadline until March 1, the official opening date of spring training, and that the $1,000 per day fines would be forgotten if that deadline was met. Piniella did make the weight by March

1, but he claims the Yankees have continued to weigh him daily and, in the wake of Tuesday's fine, he was informed that other fines still stand.

"I'm sick and tired of this," Piniella went on. "I was invited here early and I end up getting fined $1,000 a day. I could have stayed home and saved myself $7,000.

"I have been playing baseball for 20 years and I have never conducted myself in any other way but professionally for the New York Yankees. Now I am being treated like a 19-year-old, and I find that insulting."

It was a vintage Piniella blow-up, and though hurt and upset, the famed Spanish temper was also tinged with some genuine humor.

"I'm not happy with the damn fines," Piniella continued. "I'm like Smith Barney. I've worked hard for my money. To be treated suddenly like Little Orphan Annie is ridiculous!"

Steinbrenner, upon being informed of Piniella's comments, was predictably unsympathetic as well as being equally caustic.

In regard to Piniella's contention that he was given until March 1 to lose seven pounds, the Yankee Boss snapped: "He was not told that verbally by me, and I don't believe

he was told by anyone else either. Let him tell you who.

"Sometimes Lou Piniella needs to be treated like a 19-year old," Steinbrenner shot back. "Everybody in Tampa will tell you that. I've got it [the February 22 weight requirement] in black and white. He knew what he was signing. If I'm a man and my employer is paying me $350,000 a year, which is more than the President of the United States is making, and there are 10 million unemployed people earning nothing in this country, I'd sure as hell take seven pounds off and honor that contract!

"Someday soon Lou Piniella will be out of baseball and in business. Boy, he'd last five days in business!"

Steinbrenner went on to say that Piniella "should keep his mouth shut because he's only making it worse." But Piniella did not sound like he would pay the fines without a fight.

"We lose a couple of games in spring training and suddenly they're looking for someone to blame, a scapegoat, someone to be picked on," Piniella said. "I want no part of that. I'm gonna appeal the first fines. I think $1,000 a day is too steep. To be fined $1,000 a day when you don't even have to be here is ridiculous."

SWEET LOU GETS HIS DUE

OCTOBER 14, 1990

CINCINNATI—It was 3 a.m., in a place called The Waterfront, just across the Ohio River from the still-glowing lights of Riverfront Stadium.

Lou Piniella hoisted a glass of Dom Perignon and proposed a toast to a table of family and friends.

"Free at last!" he exclaimed. "Free at last! At long last I have gotten the monkey off my back!"

It seemed, on the surface anyway, a curious expression of joy coming from a man who had just managed the Cincinnati Reds to their first National League pennant in 14 years. After all, most people would agree it was the Reds, a team of perennial underachievers under Piniella's predecessor Pete Rose, who were the ones with a monkey to shed this year.

But then, you had to know what it was that had driven Piniella to this city, nearly 1,000 miles from his home in Allendale, New Jersey, and ultimately to this moment of personal triumph at a little bistro in Covington, Kentucky at three o'clock in the morning.

A nation full of baseball fans watching the National League Championship Series play itself out across six exhilarating ballgames saw Piniella managing against Jimmy Leyland. Leyland, however, was merely the guy who happened to be in the other dugout. In truth, for seven long months, Lou Piniella has been managing against George Steinbrenner.

"I came here for one reason and one reason alone," Piniella said. "To win and prove George wrong. That man hurt me. Not just because he fired me, but because I had been successful in everything I ever did for him— as a player, a coach and a manager. Even as a general manager I made good deals for him. I gave my all for him, and it was never enough."

Once, of course, they had been as close as any owner-player relationship could ever be. Steinbrenner may have paid Reggie, Catfish and Goose more money, but he never made much secret of the fact that Piniella was his favorite. And when in 1986 he tapped Piniella to manage the Yankees, despite Piniella's having no previous managerial experience, it seemed almost like a father's bequest to his son.

Instead, what it was was the beginning of the end of a beautiful friendship.

"I loved that guy like a father," Piniella said, "and I was grateful to him for giving me the opportunity to manage in the big leagues without any experience. He showed confidence in me. But once he gave me the job, he never allowed me to do it. Nothing was ever right for him…the lineups, the pitching. And always there were the problems from upstairs compounding everything.

"When he brought out all that stuff about Rickey [Henderson] and cut my legs out from under me in 1987, I should have learned. My biggest mistake as Yankee manager was not firing back at him in the papers.

"No, I take that back. My biggest mistake was taking the job a second time. I believed George when he promised he wasn't going to interfere and that he was going to let me do the job. Two weeks into it, I knew I had made a terrible mistake. He was second-guessing me all over again. And, by the end of the [1988] season, he was accusing me of stealing furniture from him."

The furniture business, it turned out, was a typical Steinbrenner-Yankees fiasco in which Piniella had been promised by a high-level Yankee official to be compensated for a pregame radio show in sponsor merchandise. Steinbrenner claimed he knew nothing of the deal, and when he discovered on the Yankee ledgers a payment of Scandinavian Furniture to Piniella, he decided to make that an issue to fire him. All the while that 1988 season, however, he had been secretly negotiating with Dallas Green to take over the team the following year.

So now it was two years later, and Piniella was savoring his first trip to the World Series as a manager, at the same time Steinbrenner was back home in Tampa in disgrace and the Yankees he left behind were coming off their worst season since 1913. The fact that Marge

Schott, the penurious and egotistical owner of the Reds, is no panacea either, prompted the question: Could Piniella have won in Cincinnati if Steinbrenner were the owner?

"No way," Piniella said. "When we were banged up and I was resting guys through July and August and we were playing .500 baseball, George would have been hammering me to crack the whip. I admit there were times I got exasperated with these kids. But they were in first place. How could I whip them? I had to hand ride them. George could never understand that, and he's a horse man."

In all probability, a telegram of congratulations from Steinbrenner will be forthcoming to Piniella. The painful part of this victory is that it didn't happen in New York, where Lou Piniella really wanted to be at 3 a.m. yesterday morning.

"Managing," Piniella said, "is really a horsebleep job. People don't know what a mental strain it puts on you. Why do you think I lost 30 pounds this year? But I had to go back on the field one more time because I had something to prove to myself and something to prove to him. No matter what happens now, I feel vindicated."

PARCELLS 'BAILS OUT' PINIELLA

MAY 25, 1992

PHILADELPHIA—For the first quarter of the season, the Cincinnati Reds have been nothing but black and blue. And, we might add, blah.

All those best-laid plans of the winter—when they were widely acclaimed as dealmakers par excellence—were at least temporarily scuttled by injuries that claimed the core of their team—Barry Larkin, Chris Sabo, Hal Morris and Rob Dibble— almost from the get-go. Those players are all back, but the rookie sensation, Reggie Sanders, is down with a hamstring injury and takes with him a team-leading .330 average.

So tired was Lou Piniella of listening to the question, "Whatsamatta with Larkin?" or "Whatsamatta with Sabo?" he was about to suggest his top guns change their first names to "Whatsamattawith."

Finally, when he woke up the other day to see the Reds ranked 11th out of 12 in ERA, 11th in homers, eighth in runs and fourth in runners left on base, Piniella decided it was time to bring in some outside help. So to the City of Brotherly Love this weekend he summoned his pal, Bill Parcells, another blue-collar Jersey guy who has had nothing much more to do with his time these days than to polish his Super Bowl rings.

"My head-butting coach," Piniella proclaimed as he introduced Parcells around the clubhouse Saturday night.

Later, again answering the "whatsamatta with" questions from the press, Piniella looked at Parcells, sitting on the other side of his office.

"Larkin and Sabo have been hurt," Piniella said, "and even after they came back, you can't expect players to just turn it right

Bill Parcells's coaching magic still works—for manager Lou Piniella and the Reds. (Harry Hamburg/Daily News)

on again. When your players are hurt, what can you do, Bill?"

"If one of my guys was hurt, I just ran somebody else out there," Parcells replied. "In football, that's all you can do. If he can't block for the quarterback, the quarterback gets killed and your season's over, that's all."

Everyone, Piniella especially, broke up. But then Parcells offered his friend some serious advice.

"Sometimes," he said, "you have to get on one of your best guys to get things juiced up. I used to pick on [Lawrence]

Taylor. I could always count on ticking him off enough to have a monster game to throw it back in my face."

Piniella hardly had time to think about that when, by sheer coincidence, that very situation presented itself Saturday night. With the Reds clinging to a 1-0 lead, Paul O'Neill, their principal left-handed power hitter, led off the sixth inning and gave a less-than-all-out run to first on a grounder to short. The Phillies' rookie shortstop Kim Batiste had difficulty getting the ball out of his glove, then double-pumped on his throw but still got O'Neill by a good three feet.

"I don't like that," Parcells muttered in the press box.

Neither, it turned out, did Piniella, who jerked O'Neill from the game for his failure to hustle. The Reds scored three runs that inning and went on to rout the Phillies, 10-0, for their first laugher of the season.

"My runs coach," Piniella said, re-introducing Parcells. "Thanks for coming by, Coach," said Greg Swindell, the winning pitcher. "You coming to Cincinnati next Friday for my next start?"

"I don't know," Parcells replied. "I'll at least be around tomorrow. How many runs you gonna need, Skip?"

"I'll take five," said Piniella.

For a while yesterday it didn't look as if Parcells was going to deliver for his friend. The Reds went into the seventh inning trailing 2-1 and looking like they were once again afflicted by the blahs. But then Morris led off with a wake-up call triple and, about 25 minutes later, the Reds had batted around for seven runs.

When the inning ended, Piniella came out of the dugout, looked up at the press box and waved at Parcells. Parcells waved back and motioned as if to ask: "Is that enough?"

In the clubhouse later, baseball superstition as it is, the Reds were half-kiddingly asking if Parcells would be coming out to Shea Stadium these next three nights.

"If it takes dumping Gatorade on Lou every time we win to make [Parcells] feel at home, we'll do it," Bill Doran said.

"Geez, Bill," Piniella said. "Ten runs yesterday, eight more today. That's equivalent to about 11 touchdowns, isn't it?"

"This is an easy game," Parcells said with a smile of satisfaction.

THE FINE ART OF CHEATING

JUNE 24, 1992

Now that the evidence has been scrutinized and presumably digested, two things are certain about this Tim Leary cheating tempest: He needs to change his eating habits and he needs a new cheating coach.

George Bamberger, an admitted practitioner of the fine art of cheating, was thinking the same thing the other night. He watched Leary's apparent devouring act with amusement from his home in Redington Beach, Florida. The former Mets manager still isn't sure of Leary actually was cheating, but, if not, then what *was* he doing?

"If I were Leary," said Bambi, "I'd start practicing a little in front of the mirror. I hope he was just decoying. Otherwise, he needs to learn."

Still, Bamberger understands. There are any number of retired pitchers who, if the truth were told, could attest to extending their careers with Bamberger's notorious "Staten Island sinker." Baseball people often tell the story of when Bamberger, then pitching with the Baltimore Orioles, went to the mound to console Ross Grimsley, who was getting rocked.

"Do you know how to cheat?" Bamberger asked Grimsley, who shook his head.

"Well, in that case," Bamberger said, "I suggest you start learning right now."

Perhaps there wouldn't have been such a furor the other night had Leary's pitches not hit two Orioles in succession and knocked one of them, catcher Chris Hoiles, out of commission for six weeks. Baltimore manager Johnny Oates as much as conceded that spitballs and scuffballs are part of the game but maintained the reason they have been outlawed is as much for safety as for honesty or even sanitary reasons.

"A lot of time pitchers can't control them," Oates said. "We lost our catcher for six weeks because a pitcher couldn't control where the ball was going."

Hogwash, says Bamberger.

"I'd say if I threw 300 spitballs, 299 of 'em went where I wanted 'em to go," Bamberger said. "I didn't scuff the ball because it didn't do anything for me. I used to use slippery elm. It's a little piece of wood that you'd chew like bubblegum. Sometimes you'd almost start throwing up because your saliva would get so gummy. I'd get a good load on, then go to the resin bag to satisfy the umpires I was clean, but I'd still have plenty to throw on my 'sinker.' I was accused of having stuff on my shirt, my hat, everywhere, but I was getting it right from the resin."

It is Bamberger's contention—and Leary may be on to this—that the most successful cheaters are those everyone suspects of cheating. "That's the secret," Bamberger said. "When the other team is sure you're cheating, they're looking at your every pitch. Gaylord Perry was a master at psyching out the other team before the game even started."

"Never go out there on stage alone," said the late comic Joe E. Lewis, whose "prop" for success was usually a fifth of bourbon. Perry admits he forged a Hall of Fame career out of petroleum jelly. And Cubs coach Chuck Cottier, who managed Perry in Seattle at the end of his career, said it was no secret where the renowned "grease man" hid his stuff.

"Everywhere," said Cottier. "He had this routine he went through in the clubhouse before the game where he'd rub Vaseline on his cap, his collar, his arm, his right leg and on his neck and face."

According to Cubs announcer and former Cy Young winner Steve Stone, Perry was willing to teach his cheating secrets, too—for a price.

"He'll probably deny this today," said Stone, "but when I was a rookie with the Giants in 1971, making the major league minimum, Gaylord comes up to me and offers to teach me the spitter. 'But it'll cost you $3,000,' he says. I told him, 'Gaylord, that's 40 percent of my salary. I can't afford that.' You know what he said? 'It may seem like a lot now, but in the long run, think how much it'll be worth to your career.'"

Perry may have had a point. Some of the most revered pitchers in the game—Whitey Ford, Tommy John, Don Sutton, even Nolan Ryan—have been accused of extending their careers through illegal means.

A few years ago, John and Sutton were dueling when WPIX cameras caught Sutton putting something in his glove between innings, prompting George Steinbrenner to phone manager Lou Piniella in the Yankees dugout from Tampa.

"Damn it, Lou," Steinbrenner screamed. "Sutton's cheating and everyone in the ballpark knows it. Why aren't you out there getting him thrown out of the game?"

"What's the score of the game, George?" Piniella asked calmly.

"It's 2-0. We're winning. What's that got to do with anything?"

"What it means, George," said Piniella, "is that our guy is cheating better than their guy."

RIZZUTO SCOOTS INTO HALL

AUGUST 1, 1994

COOPERSTOWN—He began with a hoarse "Holy Cow!" and for the next 35 minutes Phil Rizzuto took us on a fly-swatting, side-splitting, magical mystery tour of his life that filled the hills with the sound of laughter.

If you were listening carefully yesterday you might have even been able to tell this was his Hall of Fame acceptance speech.

Then again, if the 76-year-old Yankee shortstop great did mention what it meant to finally be elected to the Hall after 32 years of waiting, it somehow got lost in translation, much like the score of the game in any of his Yankee broadcasts.

No, this was pure, uninhibited Rizzuto delivering an audience participation joke-a-thon—you have to wonder if this staid institution was really ready for it.

He started out thanking his Richmond Hill High School coach, Al Kunitz, but before we knew it he was talking about the price of girdles in the '30s and how his wife, Cora, didn't need one "because she was pretty well built."

For a brief moment—very brief—he got back onto his baseball career and his first professional assignment to Bassett, Virginia

"My father pinned a $20 bill to my undershirt and told me to watch out for the guys on the train," he said.

It was just then that a fly began distracting him, and as he continued to talk he began swatting the podium.

"Got it," he said triumphantly. "Now where was I?"

Bassett, Virginia. Oh, yeah, the South and his first taste of southern-fried chicken. Looking around the audience, Rizzuto spotted his old broadcast partner Bill White, who immediately covered his face at the mention of his name.

"Hey, White? What's the name of that stuff they serve with the eggs down there that tastes like oatmeal? That's it, grits. I remember I didn't know what to do with 'em so I put 'em in my pocket."

Behind him, the Hall of Famers on the dais were now convulsed with laughter, as were the 10,000 fans sprawled across the rolling hills countryside where the ceremonies were taking place. If this speech was going nowhere—as Rizzuto assured us it was—nobody cared.

"If anyone is understanding this, please raise your hand," he implored.

When nobody did, he shrugged and plugged on, now taking us with him into the navy.

"You know, I'd get seasick on a ferry boat," he said. "So what do I do but wind up in the navy.

"I was aboard ship for 30 days and sick for every one of 'em. Finally, they put me off the ship. But it was in New Guinea. I thought I'd see a lot of Italians there."

The record shows Rizzuto got out of the navy and rejoined the Yankees in 1946, although we still don't know how he got out of New Guinea.

He did say he loved playing for Joe McCarthy, the Hall of Fame Yankee manager, and that he was lucky to have been on a team of stars "where all I had to do was make a couple of double plays, get a couple of hits and pick up a World Series check every year."

And speaking of the World Series, there were all those Subway Series against the Dodgers in which the Yankees almost always won.

"It was unfortunate we beat them every year," he said. "But that one year [1955],

Phil Rizzuto speaks at a Yankee press conference.
(AP/WWP)

they lucked out. We figured we'd better let 'em win one or they'd leave town. But they left town anyway!"

By then, it was nearly 20 minutes into the speech and Rizzuto hadn't even begun his usual restaurant plugs and celebration of loyal fans' birthdays.

"Why don't all you huckleberries go back to the hotel and I'll just stay here and talk to the kids?" he said to the Hall of Famers behind him.

As if on cue, Yogi Berra and Johnny Bench got up and began walking out.

"They took too many balls to the mask," Rizzuto reasoned, referring to the former catchers, Berra for the Yanks and Bench for Cincinnati.

Before him, Lefty Steve Carlton, author of 329 wins and 4,136 strikeouts, delivered a long, rambling acceptance speech highlighted only by his chiding of the baseball writers whom he wouldn't talk to for most of his career.

"For me to be elected to the Hall of Fame by the baseball writers is kind of like Rush Limbaugh being elected by the Clintons," Carlton said.

And in the most poignant moment of the afternoon, Chris Durocher, son of the late Leo Durocher, broke down in tears as he accepted his father's plaque posthumously.

"After my dad's lifetime in baseball, I felt he survived the illness that plagued him in his last five years by waiting for the day when his call to the Hall of Fame would come," said the son of the former skipper of the Brooklyn Dodgers and New York Giants.

"At first I thought what a shame he could not have lived to receive it himself, but now I know my father stands here with us. He got time off for good behavior."

Even Rizzuto finally got serious—after wishing happy birthday to Ruby Sabatino and plugging his other former broadcast partner, Tom Seaver, for baseball commissioner "and president of whatever league he wants."

"When I first started as a broadcaster," Rizzuto said, "Howard Cosell told me: 'You'll never last. You look like George Burns and sound like Groucho Marx.'

"So, 38 years later, I'm doing it my way and I'm still here."

Yesterday, the Hall of Fame and 10,000 baseball fans could only be grateful for that.

THE SCOUT

BROOKSVILLE, Fla.— Blackie, a 10-month-old black and white hound, is barking frantically and pacing across the porch as the car approaches the farmhouse nestled in the rolling hills of Florida's horse country. Behind the screen door, Uncle Hughie is still in his nightshirt and drawers, a grin splitting his craggy face like a jack-o-lantern.

It is a face that tells you everything about a man who has traveled more than two million miles of lonely roads, smoked four and a half packs of cigarettes a day for more than 50 years, consumed untold gallons of whiskey and been married four times.

Well, the face tells you *almost* everything.

"C'mon in," he says. "I'm just cookin' some breakfast. Got a little bit of a late start 'cause I had some house guests and we stayed up pretty late tellin' stories. I finally kicked 'em out to the golf course this morning."

A week earlier, word had filtered north that Uncle Hughie wasn't feeling well and was undergoing some tests to determine why he'd lost 20 pounds over the summer. But if he had, it wasn't evident to an old friend.

He look weather-beaten and a little hobbled, which for Hugh Alexander, six-decade baseball scout and tireless raconteur, was nothing short of terrific. He has lived every one of his 77 years to the fullest, going all the way back to his youth when he watched his father, Harry, beat two men to death in separate street fights in rural Oklahoma. Some years later, Hughie's oldest brother died in his arms when the pickup truck in which they were both passengers flipped at a high speed while careening down a hill in the dark of the oil fields.

Of course, nothing was nearly so traumatic as the horrible accident at one of the rigs, when the sleeve of his shirt got caught

Allie Reynolds was Hughie Jennings's first find. (Hank Olen/Daily News)

No doubt about it, Uncle Hughie was The Natural in real life, or as he likes to put it, "I was Mickey Mantle before there *was* Mickey Mantle."

Staying Power

"I see they finally got around to making a movie about a scout," he says as he stirs some sausage in a frying pan. "It's *about* damn time. We're a different breed from most folks."

And none of them quite as different as Uncle Hughie, who, unlike the movie, has shown considerable staying power. By all accounts, no current baseball man has been in the game longer.

There's no telling what anyone else with Hugh Alexander's future might have done after losing a hand. Cy Slapnicka, the scout who signed him, cried when he heard the news. Alexander had to console *him*.

"What nobody could ever understand was that my daddy made me tough mentally," Uncle Hughie says. "When they cut my hand off, they didn't have any anesthetic. The doctor told me

in the gears, pulling his left hand into the teeth and grinding it up like a piece of beef.

He was only 19 and a month earlier had been promoted to the Cleveland Indians after hitting .344 with 31 homers in 79 games for the Class-A Springfield, Ohio, team of the Middle Atlantic League. Two years before that, he had run a 9.7 100-yard dash in the Oklahoma high school state meet at Norman, and had he not signed a pro baseball contract, he would have probably joined Jesse Owens on the U.S. sprint team at the 1936 Berlin Olympics.

he'd give me as much morphine and whiskey as he could without killing me. After they cut it off, I never looked back.

"All I wanted was a job in baseball because that's all I knew. Ol' Cy had no children and he loved me like a son. He always told me he signed the greatest pitcher he ever saw in Bob Feller and the greatest hitter he ever saw in me. He didn't want to lose me, so he made me a scout. I told him I'd be the greatest scout there ever was."

And, just maybe, he was.

After he was tutored by Slapnicka on how to "break down" a player's skills, Alexander was sent back home to Oklahoma and told to "go find some players."

The first player he found was Allie Reynolds.

First Time Lucky

"I was roaming around south Texas when I decided to go to Stillwater [Oklahoma] to see Hank Iba, the legendary basketball coach," says Alexander. "He'd tried to recruit me as a three-sport athlete at Oklahoma A&M, and I asked him if he knew of any good baseball players. He told me he's got a pitcher I've got to see, but that he's a *football* player.

"Because Reynolds was a senior, though, he didn't have to play spring football, and he was pitching for the baseball team. I saw five him times that spring. He struck out 19, 19, 20, 21 and 22 batters, and I signed him for $1,000.

"Two and a half years later, he led the American League in strikeouts."

It never hurts to have your first sign make it big right away. Reynolds, who may yet make it to the Hall of Fame, was traded by the Indians to the Yankees and anchored Casey Stengel's pitching staffs from 1948-54, pitching two no-hitters and winning seven World Series games along the way. Alexander's second sign, Dale Mitchell, didn't fare too badly, either. He hit .312 in his 11 seasons in the majors.

Slapnicka was so impressed, he increased Alexander's territory. Gave him six states across the southwest from New Mexico to Mississippi. Alexander would spend his springs and summers backtracking across the dusty Oklahoma prairies, where his father had taught him the ways of life with lasting images of blood in the dusty street. Scouting, he soon discovered, took only a good eye and two good legs. He didn't miss too many of the good players.

There was one, though.

"One day in Oklahoma City in 1947 I ran across an old friend who said to me: 'Hughie, you got to get up to Commerce to see a hell of a player at Commerce High School. The kid got hurt playing football, but he'll be all right.' I wrote the name down on a piece of paper—'Mickey Mantle.' Well, the following spring, I drove up there to check him out. But when I went in to visit the principal of the school, he told me they didn't have a baseball team and that Mantle might have osteomylitis in his leg anyway.

"It's a hazy memory now, maybe deliberately hazy, but I seem to recall tossing that piece of paper out the window of my car as I drove out of town without ever seeing Mickey Mantle."

One Slips Away

The one that got away will always haunt Alexander, but it would have been much worse had he actually seen Mantle and deemed him not a prospect. Besides, there were plenty after him who didn't get away.

In 1951, Alexander left the Indians to work for the White Sox. A few years later, he moved on again to the Dodgers. He was given the whole country to roam, which was like turning a hound loose in field full of foxes.

One of the first players he signed for the Dodgers wasn't hard to miss. At six foot seven, 250 pounds, Frank Howard attracted quite a bit of attention in the Rapid City, South Dakota, college summer league, where Alexander first saw him in 1957. Howard, who had been an All-America basketball player at Ohio State, was a free-swinging slugger in baseball, which scared off a lot of teams.

"He hit two home runs over a light tower the first game I saw him," Alexander said. "After that, Bert Wells, my partner, and I spent two weeks watching him, every day. He was raw, but he showed me intelligence and an ability to adjust as a hitter. We knew he was gonna command a lot of money, though, 'cause of his basketball ability. After we offered him $100,000, the Orioles called and wouldn't leave him alone until he would tell them what he wanted.

"Finally, at two o'clock in the morning, Frank called my room and said, 'I'll sign with you right now if you'll kick in an extra $8,000 as a down payment on a house for my mom and dad.' I wasn't supposed to go over $100,000, but once we'd gone that high I figured what the hell's an extra $8,000 for a kid who can hit like this?"

Scouting the same league a few years later, Alexander came upon Don Sutton, who impressed him immediately with his curveball, if not his velocity. "He didn't throw real hard," Alexander remembers, "and that was a problem. It seemed our area scout in Florida, where Sutton played high school ball, had him rated as a non-prospect and [then-Dodger farm director] Al Campanis wouldn't let me sign him.

"I arranged for Sutton to pitch in another semipro league on his way home to Florida, and when I saw him that time, he threw much harder. I wound up having to beg [Dodgers GM] Buzzie Bavasi to let me sign him. I told him: 'This kid's got a great curve that will get him through the minors, and if he can learn to throw harder, he can be a great one.'"

That curveball, of course, was not only good enough to get Sutton through the minors. It got

him 23 years, 324 victories and 3,574 strikeouts in the majors.

Dusk is settling on the farm now, and Uncle Hughie hasn't even gotten halfway through his life story. He is still beating a lonely path to sagebrush and prairie towns to look at 17-year-old kids when, in reality, he hasn't had to do that in 20 years. He's a major-league scout now, a trademaker, who served as the eyes and legs for Phillies GM Paul Owens and then three GMs with the Cubs.

A Lucky SOB

But there's another new regime at Wrigley Field this off-season, and Uncle Hughie doesn't know if Andy MacPhail, 41, and Eddie Lynch, 38, will need a 77-year-old baseball relic.

"I've been a lucky SOB," he says, waving his stump of a left arm. "All my life I've been outside at a ballpark. I've got enough money, but I'll never see enough ballplayers or ballparks."

MICK AND HIS MANIACS

OCTOBER 30, 1994

So I'm at Mickey Mantle's eatery a few weeks ago, contemplating my Moose Skowron salad with no-vaseline dressing and an October with no baseball when Bill Liederman, the proprietor of the place, approached my table.

"Have you thought about going to Mickey's fantasy camp?" he asked. "It could be good therapy for you as well as some fun. Besides Mickey, there'll be plenty of World Series heroes to talk to…Hank Bauer, Enos Slaughter, Catfish, Gator, even Moose."

I glanced at my salad and then at the TV screen, which was showing Mickey hitting that dramatic homer off Barney Schultz in the 1964 World Series, and I made a mental note to call my travel agent in the morning. Last weekend, I found myself at Fort Lauderdale, checking into the Yankees' spring hotel, which was also the official headquarters for Mickey Mantle's Week of Dreams fantasy campers.

I had reservations, but not just for my hotel room. I wondered just what kind of people go to these camps. At $4,000, Mickey's is on the high end of the price spectrum of 20-odd camps in operation, but definitely not the most expensive. So I figured this had to be a one-shot deal for self-indulging yuppies to hang out with The Mick for a week and play a little softcore baseball until they pulled or broke something.

It soon dawned on me that I had it all wrong.

The first camper I encountered was Marvin, a state legislator from Cedar Falls, Iowa, who was swimming laps in the hotel pool.

"I'm 70 years old," he said proudly. "I'm pretty sure I'm the oldest camper here. You're a first-timer, aren't you?"

I informed him that while, yes, this was my first time at the camp, I was here as an observer, not a participant.

"Oh, you'll be back," Marvin said assuredly, making a point to tell me this was his fourth camp. "You really have to put a uniform on."

That night, I went to the hotel bar, where I figured I'd find a bunch of raucous guys playing baseball trivia. There were a half-dozen or so campers at the bar drinking beers, but the mood was decidedly mellow. One of them, Steve, a burly vending service executive from High Point, North Carolina, offered to buy me a drink. Sitting next to him was Mike, who owned a card store in Kernersville, North Carolina.

Southern Yankees

At first, I figured Steve and Mike must be longtime friends. But I soon discovered they had just met that afternoon. Mike, it seemed, was here for the first time as a 50th birthday present from his wife. For Steve, it was camp No. 5. Besides both being from North Carolina, they had another link: They were rabid Yankee fans and lifelong devotees of Mickey Mantle.

"You're surprised we'd be Yankee fans, living in North Carolina all our lives?" Steve drawled. "They were the team I'd listen to on the radio when I was a kid growing up in Thomasville, North Carolina. As far as I'm concerned, the two most traumatic days of my childhood were the day Kennedy was shot and Bill Mazer-bleeping-roski."

Mike nodded in agreement.

"I live and breathe the Yankees and Mickey Mantle," he said. "Before I went in the army, I cut out every one of the box scores in which he hit a home run, from about 1954 to 1962. I wanted to come here and meet him before he dies. My wife paid, but already I know I'll be coming back next year and *I'll* pay."

When I pointed out that camp hadn't even officially begun, he motioned to all the campers sitting at the bar.

"The first year you come for Mickey," interjected Steve. "After that, you come for the experience. Mike's already seeing that. Ask Roy over there. He got *married* his first year here."

Roy is an orthopedic surgeon from Neptune, New Jersey, now in his fourth camp. His first one, he brought along his girlfriend. A couple of days into it, they decided to get married. So Mickey and all the campers arranged a baseball wedding with all the fixings. It took place at home plate before the final game. Catfish Hunter, Bauer and a few other old Yankees held bats aloft as the bride and groom walked under them to the plate. The ceremony was preformed by one of the campers, who conveniently happened to be a justice of the peace.

"Mickey was the best man and Whitey [Ford] was, I guess, the maid of honor since he gave the bride away," Roy said. "How many guys can say Mickey Mantle was his best man? The only problem is, we're getting divorced now. You'd think if she came here for the marriage, she'd come back here for the divorce."

The more I talked to Roy, though, the more I began to sense something much deeper about this camp than just hero worship and the search for lost youth. Like Steve said, the fantasy part wears off almost as soon as you meet Mickey and the other old Yankees. After that, it evolves into a near-spiritual experience, a retreat where men come to bond in Yankee pinstripes.

"I work 60 hours a week doing a lot of complicated operations," Roy said. "When I came here the first time and met Moose and Hank, I got chills. And when I met Mickey, I was like Ralph Kramden doing his 'homma-homma-homma.' I couldn't talk. Then, that first day, I put on the uniform and I began to cry.

"You're going to suit up, aren't you?"

A Clean Start

The welcoming get-together in the hotel conference room was different from all the previous ones, I was told, mostly because Mickey was sober. Even he apologized for his inebriated past.

"If I act like I don't recognize some of you guys who've been coming for years, it's only because I feel like one of the rookies here," Mickey joked. "This is my first camp, if you know what I mean. You guys are gonna have to teach me the rules. I didn't even know I was supposed to speak."

Take a Number

Walking into the Yankee clubhouse at Fort Lauderdale Stadium on Monday morning, I was immediately taken aback by the plethora of No. 7s wandering about. Then I remembered you got to choose your own uniform number, and who among these guys—especially the rookies— wouldn't want to emulate their spiritual leader? Even Bob Costas, broadcasting's resident baseball purist who was here as Mickey's celebrity guest, was wearing No. 7. Other than that, there were a few 49s (for Guidry), and a sprinkling of the other revered Yankee numbers. Then there was the No. 63 worn by a balding guy in locker No. 1.

"That's Al," said Roy. "He's a real legend here. You've really got to talk to him."

Al, it turns out, is the all-time fantasy camper. In 1979, he sold the toy company he and his brother had founded in Philadelphia. The sale price was rumored at $55 million. So, with his future secured, Al decided he was going to play baseball for the rest of his life. Or, as he said: "Baseball came along at just the right time for me."

Al is the only one who's been to every one of Mickey's camps. He's also gone to 75 other camps and will soon be acclaimed in the *Guinness Book of World Records*.

"The 63 is for my age," he said, "but I don't feel it. Besides, if anything ever happened, I've got lots of guys here to take care of any emergency. Doctor Jim over there is the most prominent heart surgeon in Florida. And then, of course, there's Roy. We all knew she wasn't the right girl for him."

"Don't you think you should put on a uniform?"

The Games Begin

As everyone began assembling on the field—they in pinstripes, me in street clothes—this thing about the uniform began to gnaw at me. Why did they all keep pushing it, as if it were some kind of drug to get me hooked? Then I noticed a big bald guy with a bushy beard who looked like a refugee from an old House of David team. He was the only guy on the field with a cellular phone. Actually two of them.

"That's Stan," said Al. "He's…a little different."

Upon further investigation, I learned Stan owned a trucking business in Southern Carolina and a lot of real estate in Manhattan. This was his fifth camp, and he planned to stay a second week. His first camp, he passed out drunk at the welcoming get-together. Some campers said he was usually on something else besides his cellular phone most of the day. Still, everybody liked him, even Bauer, the crew-cutted ex-marine who grabbed him by the beard as soon as he saw him.

"Baseball may be on strike, Stanley," Bauer growled playfully, "but them barbers in New York ain't."

Once everyone was split into six squads for three games, I gravitated to one of the back fields where Stan, Roy, Marvin and Doctor Jim were all playing. Marvin, one of the first up, hit a grounder to short—too hard for his 70-year-old legs to beat out.

I felt a poke from Jim, an attorney from Larchmont. "Not bad, huh?" he said. "I guess that says something for living in Iowa. By the way, when are you gonna suit up?"

But the cheering for old Marvin's hustle was nothing compared to what happened next when Doctor Jim's 22-year-old son, Mickey, came to the plate. The doctor, who has squeezed in 10 of these camps around all his heart transplants, had brought his son for the first time. You didn't have to ask who Doctor Jim named the kid after. And on the very first pitch, the young Mick slammed it over the left field wall for a home run.

As I watched in sheer disbelief as the ball disappeared, I had just one thought: These guys will stop at nothing to get me in a uniform.

HAPPY 70TH

Yogi Berra is 70 years old today, but if that seems as unthinkable as it is unacceptable, despair not. "It's not how old you are," Yogi assures us, "it's the age that counts."

Well, actually it wasn't Yogi who said that. It was his lifelong friend Joe Garagiola who said it for him in a patented Yogi "happy birthday" message. But as everyone knows by now, Yogi didn't really say a lot of those wonderfully goofy truisms of life attributed to him over the past five-plus decades. He just never denied them, and we were only too eager to add to his legend.

And what a legend his is. Is there anyone in America who is more recognizable or more

---

"You can observe a lot by watching."

---

beloved than Yogi Berra? Is there anyone more quoted? Hell, is there anyone more truly American?

"I dunno," Yogi said when I asked him that yesterday during his daily morning workout at South Mountain Arena in West Orange, New Jersey. "A lot of people were born here."

On the treadmill next to him, Yogi's pal and Montclair neighbor, Devils owner John McMullen, shook his head at the mention of the legend turning 70. "Look at him," McMullen marveled, "he looks better now than when he was a player. He's certainly in better shape. And I always tell him there's nobody more loved by the media than him and nobody more hated by the media than me."

Even Yogi, who as we know has never been awed by anything, finds his exalted status as an American icon and our favorite

American philosopher as hard to fathom as turning 70. You are where you were, Yogi was saying,

> "Baseball is 90 percent mental, the other half is physical."

and that was a squat, funny-looking, funny-walking kid, the youngest of four brothers who grew up in the Italian section of St. Louis known as "The Hill" in the 1930s. They didn't have a lot of money, which was why Papa Berra wouldn't permit the three older brothers to pursue their dreams of professional baseball careers.

"I always told Pop if he'd have let us all play he would have been a millionaire," Yogi said. "Tony, my oldest brother, was the best player of anyone who ever came off The Hill. But they all had good jobs when I came along, and that's why he let me play."

His first contract was for $90 a month, plus a $500 bonus from the Yankees that was conditional upon his making their Class D Norfolk Tars farm team. Who knew what fame and fortune would come from such humble beginnings?

"Yeah," said Garagiola. "Who knew? Certainly none of us. I always believed that [Cardinals GM] Branch Rickey wanted to sign Yogi along with me. I told him he was the best on the block. But the magnanimous Yankees got in there first and signed him for a bonus they wouldn't even guarantee.

"I guess if there's one word to describe Yogi it's 'underestimated.' All his life people have underestimated him, much to their embarrassment. They said he didn't look like a ballplayer, and he went to the Hall of Fame. They said he didn't have the intellect to be a manager, and he won two pennants. They said he didn't know how to speak, and he's become America's most quoted philosopher."

> "A nickel ain't worth a dime any more."

More than anything now, he just likes being one of baseball's elder statesmen. His only connection to the game any more is as a member of the Hall of Fame Veteran's Committee. But he buys four newspapers every morning and reads every box score. ("He's the only man in

America who knows what the Seattle Mariners and California Angels *drew*," says Garagiola.) As for the players of his era, he sees the Mantles, Bauers, Fords, McDougalds and Skowrons et al. nearly once a month on the charity/celebrity golf circuit.

Of course, being Yogi, he can play golf anywhere he wants to—even on courses that are so crowded nobody plays there any more. At the most recent Bob Hope Classic in Palm Springs,

> *"I want to thank you for making this day necessary."*

President Clinton agreed to make an appearance but insisted on being in Yogi's foursome. And you wondered why his approval rating went up six percent?

"Last month I got to play with Sinatra," said Yogi, who probably will never realize that it is the *other way around*. "But as much as I love golf, baseball will always be first with me. I don't go to the ballparks much anymore, but I follow the game every day in the papers, especially my guys—Mattingly, Craig Biggio and Jeff Bagwell. I had them all [as Yankee manager and Astros coach] when they all came up. They play the game the way it's supposed to be played."

Today, he will celebrate his birthday at home with his wife, Carmen, sons Larry, Tim and Dale, and their seven grandchildren. They are going to need more than one birthday cake for all those candles and all those people. Not to worry, though. Yogi has instructed them to cut the cakes in 10 pieces instead of 12 because nobody would be able to eat that much.

Happy birthday, Yogi. And thanks for making those 70 years and all those memories necessary.

WHAT A LIFER!

On the evening of June 6, in the fifth inning of the Colorado Rockies-St. Louis Cardinals game, Don Zimmer quietly got up from the Rockies' bench, tossed aside his last chaw of Red Man, grabbed his fungo bats and walked away from the only life he has known for 47 years.

His wife, Soot, whom he married at home plate as a minor leaguer in Elmira, New York in 1951, was waiting at the apartment for him, bags packed, gas tank filled for the 2,100-mile cross-country drive home to Treasure Island, Florida. They were halfway to Tulsa when the news got out that Zimmer had retired from baseball...in the middle of a game...with no announcement, no advance warning and sure-as-hell no damn fanfare.

"I told [Rockies owner Jerry] McMorris on May 22 what I wanted to do," Zimmer said, "and he said they had to have a night for me at Coors Field. I told him, 'No way, that's like giving me something when I've been given something all my life.' Who in the hell gives a night for a .235 hitter?"

It was a typical self-effacing statement from a guy who really did hit only .235 over 12 seasons in the majors. The way Zimmer always saw it, .235 was what should have dictated his baseball career. He had no more reason to expect anything more than a bus ticket home when the Washington Senators told him .199 just wasn't getting it done in 1965. But 30 years later, there he was, leaving the game on his own terms, a wealthy man in memories and friendships if not necessarily in dog-track earnings.

Actually, even the .235 shouldn't have dictated his career. The plate in his head should have. He was hitting .300 for the

Dodgers' Triple A farm, the St. Paul Saints, in July of 1953 when a right handed pitcher named Jim Kirk unleashed an overhand curve that struck him in the side of the head and knocked him unconscious. When he woke up 13 days later, the doctor told him a lot of things happen after brain surgery and there was a strong likelihood he would never be the same player.

"He was right," Zimmer said, "but I still think hitters are born, not made. I think Ted Williams was born to hit .340 and Don Zimmer was born to hit .240."

Nevertheless, .235 took him a long way—through every one of baseball's most exalted shrines and to a front-row seat for a good many of baseball's most enduring moments.

As a Dodger rookie in 1955, he played a pivotal role as Brooklyn won its only World Series: He left the seventh game so Sandy Amoros could be inserted in left field to make the game-saving catch off Yogi Berra.

In 1962, he was an Original Met—and the first of them to be traded. In 1978, he was the manager in the wrong dugout of the Yankees-Red Sox playoff game when Bucky Dent's home run sailed over Fenway Park's left field green monster to lift the Yankees to the AL East pennant.

"There isn't one regret about anything—even that," Zimmer said. "Oh, sure, I wish we'd have won, but I've often told people that 1978 was both my biggest thrill in baseball as well as my most disappointing moment. I laugh when people say, 'You choked that year.' Choked? Yeah, we stopped hitting and blew a 13-game lead, but it was without a doubt my biggest thrill when we won our 99th game on the last day of the season and I was going to the park on Monday for a playoff. We were dead and had to go on a nine-game winning streak to force the playoff."

The man they called "Popeye" because of his bulging forearms and matching jowls has two world championship rings as a player with the Dodgers in '55 and '59. It was those Dodger teams that were most special to him, he says, even though they were too good for a .235-hitting utility infielder with a plate in his head.

"I got to start the seventh game [of the '55 Series] at second base," he recalled, "and then I got to be part of the most famous managerial decision in history when [Dodger manager Walt] Alston moved Junior Gilliam from left field to second so he could get Amoros into the game for defense. I always said the

Dodgers couldn't win without me.

"But after that first World Series, I knew I wasn't gonna play much on that team. I only got to play that year because Pee Wee [Reese] hurt his back in spring training. We won 10 in a row at the start of the season with me at short, but I knew he'd be back. I never told [Dodger GM] Buzzie [Bavasi] to play me or trade me. I just told him to trade me because I knew I wasn't good enough to play for the Dodgers."

Turns out he outlasted Reese, only to be beaten out for the job in 1959 when another shortstop came along to give the Dodgers another dimension—Maury Wills. But it wasn't until April of 1960 that Bavasi finally agreed with Zimmer and traded him to the Cubs for three players (including future relief ace Ron Perranoski), plus $25,000. Not a bad return for a .235 hitter, but what a bad place to go.

Making of a Met

The 1960 Cubs lost 94 games and so exasperated their normally detached owner, Phil Wrigley, that after he fired two managers, he named a "college of coaches" to pilot the Cubs by committee in 1961.

It was an experiment doomed to failure, but not before it got Zimmer a guaranteed exit visa to the expansion Mets.

"The nine revolving coaches was a joke," Zimmer said. "It was a real mess, and I was the captain of the team. On the last day of the season, Lou Boudreau, who had managed the team the year before but was now in the broadcast booth, came to me and asked me on the air what I thought of it. I told him it was nothing more than a popularity contest and helluva way to run a ballclub.

"Well, as I was walking to the dugout after popping off, Charlie Grimm, the general manager, said to me: 'I just heard your interview, and I can assure you, you *will* be gone.'"

But, once again, the .235 hitter wound up departing in superstar fashion—as a "premium" $125,000 expansion pick. The Mets, with an eye on hidden Brooklyn roots, grabbed Zimmer to be their first third baseman. He lasted 14 games.

"I had a helluva spring for Casey [Stengel]," he related. "He thought he had another Mickey [Mantle]. I had a lot of fun with him, too. During the spring, after he'd been up all night talking baseball with the writers, he'd sit by the fence in Al Lang Field

THE ZIMMER FILE

Built like a fireplug and fitted with a metal plate in his head, Don Zimmer was one of baseball's endearing characters. He was called "Popeye" for his strength and resemblance to the cartoon character "Chipmunk" for his distended jaw caused by his chaw of tobacco, and "Gerbil" by eccentric pitcher Bill Lee, whom he managed in Boston. Now he calls himself "retired." A glance through the years with Zimmer the lifer:

- 1953—Remained unconscious for three weeks and nearly died after beaning while playing for the Dodgers' St. Paul farm team.
- 1955—Was Brooklyn's second baseman in World Series.
- 1956—Was nearly blinded after getting beaned by Cincinnati's Hal Jeffcoat.
- 1958—Was the L.A. Dodgers' starting shortstop, before losing job to Maury Wills the next year.
- 1960-61—Played for Chicago Cubs, under experimental "College of Coaches."
- 1962—Went 0-for-34 with Original Mets, traded to Cincinnati after 14 games.
- 1963—Traded to Washington Senators, managed by old Brooklyn pal Gil Hodges.
- 1965—Finished major league career with Senators, hitting .199.
- 1966-67—Played in Japan.
- 1971—Coached for Montreal Expos under Gene Mauch.
- 1972—Named manager of San Diego Padres, replacing Preston Gomez.
- 1973—Fired as manager of Padres after compiling 114-190 record in two years.
- 1974-75—Coached the Boston Red Sox under Darrell Johnson.
- 1976—Named manager of Red Sox.
- 1978—Led Red Sox to 99-victory season, but blew 14-game lead and pennant to Yankees in one-game playoff.
- 1980—Fired as manager of Red Sox.
- 1981—Named manager of Texas Rangers.
- 1982—Fired as manager of Rangers, replaced by Darrell Johnson.
- 1983—Coached for Yankees under Billy Martin.
- 1984-85—Coached for Chicago Cubs under high school pal Jim Frey.
- 1987—Coached for San Francisco under old Brooklyn Dodgers pal Roger Craig.
- 1988—Named manager of Cubs by GM Frey.
- 1989—Named Manager of the Year, leading Cubs to NL East title.
- 1990—Fired as manager of Cubs after 18-19 record.
- 1992—Bench coach for Red Sox under manager Butch Hobson, his former third baseman.
- 1994—Named bench coach for Colorado Rockies under Don Baylor.
- 1995—Retired from baseball on June 16.
- 1996-2003—Bench coach for New York Yankees.
- 2004—Senior advisor for Tampa Bay Devil Rays.

during the games and every so often his head would start to drop. Well, the third time it dropped, I knew he was asleep and I'd let out a whistle and scare the hell out of him. But always he'd look down at me and just wink.

"I only wish I'd have done better for him, but after 14 games I was hitting .077 and as I'm coming out of the shower Casey starts screaming at me, 'This is the greatest thing to ever happen' and I don't know what the hell he's talking about. Then he says, 'You've been traded to the Reds,' and I say 'Oh, I'm going home.'"

He grew up in Cincinnati and attended Western Hills High School, where his teammate on the basketball and baseball teams was Jim Frey. They became lifelong friends who played together, worked together and even got fired together.

When Frey was named manager of the Cubs in 1984, the first person he hired on his coaching staff was Zimmer, who had spent the previous summer coaching for the Yankees under Billy Martin. Together Frey and Zimmer won a division championship that year, but two years later it had all fallen apart and in midseason, Dallas Green, the team president, called the two of them to his office.

"Jimmy went in first," Zimmer recalled, "and when he came out he walked right by me without saying anything. I figured he got fired and that Dallas wanted me to take over the team. Instead, Dallas tells me because I was so close to Jimmy I was being let go, too. All I could say was, this ain't baseball. I always thought the coaches were *supposed* to be close to the manager.

"Anyway, I get home and my wife is all upset. She says: 'I heard on the radio they fired poor Jimmy. Isn't that awful?'

"I say: 'Yeah, it sure is. They got me, too. It's a quinella.'"

Life seems to always smile on some guys, though, and four years later, Don Zimmer, baseball lifer, was back at Wrigley Field, and this time he *was* the manager. Frey, it seemed, had been brought back, too—as GM after Green resigned—and his first move was to install his friend as manager. In the spring of '89 both of them wondered if they might again be a quinella.

"We went 9-23 in the Cactus League, and I've got to say we were the worst-looking ballclub I'd ever seen," Zimmer said. "Jimmy comes to me and says: 'Do you think we can win 81 games?' I said: 'If we do, you and

I will dance down Michigan Avenue together.'"

They almost did dance.

The Sweet Time

A funny thing happened after the Cubs broke camp. It all suddenly came together, and not only did they win 81 games, they won 93 and the NL East division title in the process. And the .235-hitting baseball lifer who got soaked with champagne was named Manager of the Year.

"To win that title, there will never be anything to top that," Zimmer said.

And maybe nothing will. It has, after all, been a 47-year ride of one thrill topping another.

"I can't imagine anyone being as lucky as I've been," Zimmer said. "I mean, I've played or managed in all the great ballparks—Ebbets Field...Polo Grounds...Fenway...Wrigley. I've been to the World Series. I was a '55 Dodger and a '62 Met. I wore Yankee pinstripes. I managed Hall of Famers and I made a million friends."

Bon voyage, Popeye. Who would've ever thought .235 could go such a long way?

THE ODD COUPLE

COOPERSTOWN—They are cut from vastly different cloth, Earl Weaver, the hard-living, peppery and often crude baseball lifer, and Jim Bunning, college-educated baseball activist-turned-U.S. congressman. So it therefore stood to reason that on the occasion of their joint enshrinement in baseball's Hall of Fame yesterday, they would express their gratitude in their own vastly different ways.

Earl Weaver made us laugh and Jim Bunning made us think.

The Earl of Baltimore, who managed the Orioles to five 100-victory seasons, four American League pennants and one world championship, had his legions of fans who bused up from America's crabcake capital laughing from the outset when he implored them to stop applauding: "It's hot out there, people, and we want to get out of here and get a beer."

Before he could, though, there were all those players to thank, especially his new fellow Oriole Hall of Famers Frank and Brooks Robinson, "and Jim Palmer, who I had more arguments with than my wife, Marianna." He went on to talk about the Oriole bosses, Harry Dalton, Frank Cashen and owner Jerry Hoffberger, who gave a career minor-leaguer the opportunity to manage in 1968 and add in typical brash Earl style: "I feel I justified their confidence in me."

And, of course, it wouldn't have been Weaver without a word about the umpires, whom he scorned and scourged with across 17 turbulent seasons. By his count, he was ejected some 92 times—which is very likely a record for career umpire abuse.

"I would be remiss if I didn't recognize the umpires of the American and National Leagues,"

Earl Weaver tries on his Hall of Fame jersey. (AP/WWP)

Weaver said, grinning. "Their integrity and honesty is and must be beyond reproach. They must have made a million calls in my career, and except for the 92 times I disagreed with them, they got the other ones right."

That had them really laughing, and then he left them with one final reminder of what he was to them. "I'm proud of my record," he said, "and I'm proud that I was even considered for the Hall of Fame. But I'm most proud of the fact that I spent my whole career in one city. Thank you, Baltimore fans, for letting me stay!"

By contrast, Bunning spent considerable time in both leagues, with four teams, mostly the Tigers and Phillies. And if Weaver was the consummate company man who did what his bosses told him and played the players they gave him, Bunning was the independent thinker who poked swords at management suits at the same time he was winning 224 games for them. It was not surprising, then, that among the Bunning well-wishers in the audience (neither of whom was introduced) were former union chief Marvin Miller and his longtime aide, player agent Dick Moss.

It took Bunning nearly 20 minutes to get to the real crux of his message, mostly because he had a lot of people to thank, starting with his wife, Mary, and their nine kids and 28 grandchildren. When he did, though, he minced no words.

"To the fans today, I would like to say, 'You made baseball our national sport. Don't give up on it now,'" Bunning said, "To the owners, I would like to say, 'Get your house in order! Figure out how you want to share your revenues without going to the players and asking them to foot the bill.'"

At that juncture, Miller and Moss applauded enthusiastically, but they seemed to be alone. It was when Bunning addressed

what all baseball fans can agree on—a game that has seemingly lost its way in recent years—that he got them cheering…and thinking.

"To the owners and players alike, I say: 'Get a commissioner! A real commissioner! Come up with a way to mutually share the cost of a commissioner's office and mutually hire—if necessary through a third party—a real commissioner with the restored powers of the commissioner's office prior to the year 1950.'

"For more than four years, baseball has been rudderless. For God's sake, find a rudder! Pick a course and stick to it and get your internal problems resolved before the Congress of the United States gives up on you and intervenes.

"The only thing that could be worse is if the fans give up on you."

As Bunning the congressman spoke so passionately, Earl Weaver, career baseball man, sitting to his right, nodded affirmatively and applauded. Everyone was hot, although not as hot as Bunning, and in this time and this place, what he had to say seemed a whole lot more important than a cold beer.

Niekro a Hit at Hall

August 4, 1997

COOPERSTOWN—Tommy Lasorda was finished working the biggest room he will ever work, telling his funny stories and preaching the gospel of baseball in and around introductions of his entourage of Italian-American celebrity pals, and now a nervous Phil Niekro stepped to the podium to accept his plaque of induction into the Hall of Fame.

As everyone had surely told him, when it comes to public speaking, there may be no tougher act to follow in this land than Tommy Pasta. But Niekro, perhaps reinforced by the advice of Tom Seaver, proved equal to the task.

The night before at a private reception in the Hall of Fame plaques room, Seaver was recounting his own induction speech experience. "I knew it was going to be tough when I started thanking all the people in my life, from my high school and college coaches, to my wife and my dad," Seaver said. "But the toughest part of it would be trying not to think about my mom, who was no longer with me. I saved her for last because I knew that was when I was gonna lose it. Once I got to her, I was out of there."

And so Niekro, the classy coal miner's son who, across three decades, baffled thousands of batters with the knuckleball his dad taught him in their back yard in Lansing, Ohio, started out with Bill Maughn, the scout who signed him for $500 all those years ago. Even then, though, he couldn't help making reference to the elder Phil Niekro, who passed away two months after both his sons, Phil and Joe, retired from the baseball in 1988.

"Bill Maughn offered me $275 a month," Niekro recalled, "and my dad said, 'It's nice you want my son to play professional baseball, but before he does, we have to sit down here and make a little deal.' I got $500, which was more money than my father ever made in the coal mines."

Phil Niekro on the mound in 1985.
(Vincent Riehl/Daily News)

If there was one common thread that ran through Niekro and his fellow Hall of Fame inductees, Lasorda and the late Nellie Fox and Negro Leaguer Willie Wells, yesterday, it is that none of them was looked upon as a "can't miss" prospect by the scouts who came to scrutinize them on the dusty sandlots of their youth. (In Wells's case, you'd have to say he was a "sure miss" prospect since he was 38 years old and well past his shortstop prime when Jackie Robinson broke the baseball color line in 1947.)

In her eloquent speech, Fox's widow, JoAnn, made note of the day in 1944 when Fox's parents drove their pint-sized 16-year-old son in the family pickup truck from Chambersburg, Pennsylvania, to a Philadelphia Athletics' tryout and Connie Mack, the A's patriarch, signed the scrappy infielder for $100. She would later cite nearly a dozen or so former managers, coaches and teammates who helped Fox become the self-made All-Star second baseman he was, conspicuously omitting Al Lopez, his manager with the 1959 AL champion "Go-Go" White Sox who kept him out of the Hall for so many years as an influential member of the Veterans Committee.

If Wells got here through the perseverance of his peers and Fox through grit and determination, Lasorda, who never did attain much degree of success as a big-league pitcher, used the sheer force of his personality to become a Hall of Fame manager. It has taken all these years for the Hall to get its first con man and standup comic, and Lasorda couldn't resist telling a story to verify both those parts of him. "One time when I was managing against the Reds in Cincinnati," he related, "I went to Mass one Sunday morning and who do I see sitting on the other side of the church but [Reds manager] John McNamara. I knew why he was there, and when the service was over, I watched him stay back and light a candle. Well, I knew that wasn't for some dead relative, so after he left, I went back in the church, knelt down in front of the altar and blew that candle out! Then, during the game, I kept yelling over at him, 'It ain't gonna work, Mac! I blew your candle out.'

"We killed them that day, 13-2, but then a couple of years ago I got a postcard from Mac from Rome. All it said was 'Blow *this* candle out!'"

Those were the jokes. It was left to Niekro to provide the tears.

With his brother sitting right in front of him clutching a picture of their dad, you knew this was going to get around to fathers and sons playing catch in the backyard. And so as he began to feel that welling sensation Seaver had been talking about the night before, Niekro evoked the movie *Field of Dreams* and a fantasy game being played "up there" among a bunch of Polish coal miners.

"I can see them all now," Niekro said, "and [looking skyward] I say to you, Dad: 'Play ball, Dad. Play ball.'"

And with that, he was out of there.

Niekro shows off his knuckleball grip. (Dan Farrell/Daily News)

FOR THIS GAME, HE WAS A WHIZ

SEPTEMBER 10, 1997

At around 5 a.m. yesterday, Eddie Ferenz, the longtime traveling secretary of the Philadelphia Phillies, was awakened by the phone in his room at the Grand Hyatt. On the other end was Richie Ashburn, who was having a heart attack and calling for help.

Ferenz immediately alerted the front desk and the Phillies' team trainer, but by the time the emergency medical people got to the room, Ashburn, 70, was gone. And along with him, a whole lot of laughter suddenly went out of baseball, too.

There wasn't a funnier guy anywhere in the game than Philadelphia's "Whitey," who ran and singled his way into the Hall of Fame and then made a second career for himself in the broadcast booth with his homespun wit and blunt observations of today's ballplayers and umpires. Born and raised on the plains of Nebraska, Ashburn won two batting titles and led the National League in hits three times in 12 seasons with the Phillies before finishing his career by earning the dubious distinction of being voted the MVP on the '62 Mets, losers of a record 120 games.

It therefore seemed eerily ironic that in his final broadcast, the Phillies clobbered the Mets, 13-4, and Ashburn got to call Nebraska U. product Kevin Jordan's 15-pitch "Richie Ashburn" at-bat—in and around railing about home plate umpire Frank Pulli's generous strike zone.

"In that respect, I'm sure Whitey couldn't have asked for a better game to go out on," said Chris Wheeler, Ashburn's broadcast mate for the last two decades. "All he kept saying to me during Jordan's at-bat was, 'You realize this kid is a *Cornhusker!* And then, of course, he was getting on Pulli all night. What can you say about him? He was truly a unique guy, a kind of a wise old sage as well as the nutty professor."

Such was surely the case when it came to retelling all the tales of the misbegotten '62 Mets. Ashburn hit .306 that year, his last as a player. His reward was a boat. "Just what a guy from Nebraska needed," he said. "But even worse, when I docked it at a yacht basin in Ocean City, New Jersey, it sank. It took nearly five days to go down and then I had to drag it up, so I just sold it. Problem was, when I cashed the check the guy gave me, it bounced."

Another story he loved to tell about himself was of the day he hit a woman in the stands with a foul ball. Then, as they were carrying her out on a stretcher, he hit her *again*. He was a pesky singles hitter and proud of it. Bunting, running and fouling off pitches until he got the one he wanted were what his game was all about. Russ Meyer, the hot-headed Dodger pitcher of the '50s, once got so infuriated with Ashburn's fouling off of pitch after pitch, he finally hit him in the behind with one. "You want to get on first?" Meyer screamed. "There!"

Years after his retirement, Ashburn openly complained about being snubbed for the Hall of Fame by the Baseball Writers Association. His misfortune was to have been a singles-hitting center fielder in the same era as Mickey Mantle, Duke Snider and Willie Mays. "Hell," he grumped, "they wrote a damn song about them. How am I supposed to compete with that?"

But in 1995 the Veterans Committee saw fit to elect him into the Hall, largely on the presentation made in his behalf by retired *Philadelphia Inquirer* sportswriter Allen Lewis. "It was true a lot of Whitey's accomplishments got overlooked because he played in the shadow of Mays, Mantle and Snider," Lewis said. "Besides winning two batting titles and finishing in the top 10 seven times, you could make a case for him being the greatest defensive center fielder ever. He's the only outfielder in history to have 500 putouts in two different seasons. Of course, he had to make them because he played between two real slowpokes in Del Ennis and Dick Sisler."

Though his arm was always regarded as the least of his physical tools, the defensive play for which Ashburn is most remembered ias throwing out the Dodgers' Cal Abrams at home in the last game of the 1950 season, which clinched the pennant for the Phillies.

Because he took such pride in playing the game right and

Richie Ashburn as a Philadelphia Phillie in 1959.
(Daily News)

baseball. These Phillies, he said, had a lot more things going for them than those Mets did, Rookie of the Year lock Scott Rolen and pitching ace Curt Schilling, to name two.

"He's sort of like I am," said Ralph Kiner last night. "You live the baseball life and it's a great life. It's hard to walk away from this game. I'm just glad for Richie's sake he lived to see himself get elected to the Hall. He was a terrific ballplayer, and as a broadcaster he had that great, caustic wit. He was the one who made those Mets legendary."

None, of course, more legendary than Ashburn himself. In Philadelphia, he was bigger than Ben Franklin, which you'd have to agree says a lot for a guy who made a career of hitting singles, assailing umpires and telling funny stories. As a player or a broadcaster, Richie Ashburn was a joy.

executing all the little things that separate winning teams from losers, Ashburn had little patience for players who didn't. That was one of the primary reasons why he decided to retire after the '62 Mets season. "I just didn't think I could go through another year like that," he said, and he didn't have to until about a month ago when the Phillies were making a serious run on the '62 Mets futility.

Still, when I made the obligatory call to him awhile back to ask him to compare the two teams, he didn't sound like someone who'd had his fill of

EL DUQUE GOES TO WASHINGTON

JUNE 10, 1999

PHILADELPHIA—It is now on to the White House for the Yankee bus caravan. Good riddance to the City of Brotherly Love, where the Phillies' brooms were happily dispatched to the closet by an eight-run Yankees haymaker last night. We say happily only because the idea was to still be a first-place team when it came time for Bill Clinton to meet Hideki Irabu.

Meanwhile, the reception-line possibilities defy imagination.

"Mr. President, this is Orlando [El Duque] Hernandez. He heard about your love of cigars and brought some nice Cuban Cohebas for you. He also says, 'What a country, America.'"

"Derek Jeter, Mr. President. Just a suggestion: When in doubt, arbitrate."

"Nice to have you, Derek. By the way, do you still have Mariah's number?"

They were all trying to make light of it last night, mostly because, given their druthers, they probably would prefer spending the off day on the beach in Florida. But the President calls, and it isn't every day that happens. As David Cone, who doubtless will want to talk hitting with Clinton today, summed it up: "It's an honor to go down there. How many chances do you get to go to the White House as a world champion?"

For reasons never explained, the '96 Yankees never got an invite, but then that was long before Hillary ever had any designs on running for the Senate from New York. "I don't have anything to say about politics," said Jeter when asked if he knew why the Yankees didn't go in '96. "I just wish we were flying there instead of taking this long bus trip."

There are a few Yankees, Paul O'Neill ('90 Reds), Chili Davis and Chuck Knoblauch ('91 Twins), for whom this White House world champion reception is not a first. And even though he was never invited with a world championship team until now, Don Zimmer was there on a number of occasions. (What else would you expect of Zim, who has been everywhere?)

"I finished my career playing in Washington, for Gil Hodges," he said, beginning another recitation of his baseball travelogue. "Then when I managed the Red Sox, I got to go to the White House a bunch of times 'cause Yaz (Carl Yastrzemski) was best friends with that House guy."

Say who? What House guy?

"You know, that Tip O'Neill guy," Zim said, referring to the former Speaker of the House.

To hear the rest of the Yankees' White House veterans tell it, though, the experience is quite benign. "It's not like we got into the Oval Office or anything," O'Neill said.

He won't want to this time either.

"In '91, Bush was involved with Desert Storm, and we barely

First lady Hillary Clinton demonstrates her Yankee spirit.
(Harry Hamburg/Daily News)

got to see him," said Davis. "It wasn't at all like I expected it to be. I probably should have realized the President has more important things to do than meeting with a World Series championship team. He flew in on a helicopter from a meeting, greeted us in the Rose Garden and took right off again."

With the war in Kosovo winding down and his war at home put to, er, bed, Clinton is expected to have a little more time for the Yankees. For one thing, Hillary isn't about to let him deny her that that all-important one-up photo op on Giuliani. The President ought to know, however, if he gives some of these Yankees the opportunity to talk about something other than baseball, they might just take him up on it.

"Back in January of 1993, when Clinton first took office, my wife and I had gone through a miscarriage and I picked up the Grand Rapids [Michigan] newspaper, and it had his picture with a pen in his hand signing the abortion bill," said the religiously conservative Chad Curtis. "I don't think it's any secret about my personal beliefs. That was his first act in office, and I really took it personal."

George Steinbrenner actually is scheduled to speak, as is Cone. What do you think, Mr. President? Any chance of a pardon for Darryl Strawberry? As for El Duque, the mention of cigars evoked a waving of his arms and shriek of protest. "I'm not going there," he said through interpreter Jose Cardenal. "You [media] guys crazy. You pretty heavy today."

"You've got to understand," Cardenal cautioned later, "Duque is still trying to get his [citizenship] papers. He can't say anything, even as a joke."

So instead, El Duque was asked a much more innocuous question.

"What do you think about going to the White House?"

"I don't know," he replied, "what the White House is."

VALENTINE WILLING TO TAKE THE HEAT

AUGUST 15, 2002

A welcome breeze managed to cut its way through the oppressive 95-degree heat in the Mets' dugout, where Bobby Valentine was sitting and enduring the baseball version of hell last night.

About the only thing that isn't so hot around the city these days is Valentine's Mets (who were about to lose their fourth in a row and second straight to the last-place Padres), and now here he was being asked to explain how it all came to this: how this $102 million team of so many much-ballyhooed, off-season acquisitions could be under .500, out of viewing range of first place and seemingly out of postseason hope in mid-August. While it was surely an unwelcome and uncomfortable hot seat Bobby V. was asked to assume, at least he didn't cop out.

"So what sort of controversy do you want to stir up today?" he asked.

"The controversy," I replied, "has pretty much run its course. I was just wondering if, in your private moments, you've thought about how it all came to this."

Valentine crossed his arms, looked straight ahead for a moment, and heaved one of his patented sighs.

"It's not over," he said softly but with conviction. "But if you're asking me if I know what's happened, all I can say is we haven't played well; our best players haven't played up to expectations and I haven't done a very good job on my part."

We would get back to that in more depth a few minutes later. When I broached the subject of team chemistry—and the perceived lack of it on this Mets team—Valentine bristled. In particular, he was annoyed by a feature story on Mike Piazza in last week's *New York Times Magazine* that was written by a freelance journalist who spent two months with the team. The general tenor of the piece was that the Mets are a team of detached, big-name players who have little or nothing to do with each other away from the ballpark.

"That story," Valentine said, pursing his lips, "was written by a guy who wouldn't know a locker room from a powder room. People who write those things are people who don't see Armando Benitez bringing cartons of stone crabs into the clubhouse, or guys all going to the Mike Tyson fight together. They haven't seen all the pitchers going out to dinner together.

"I can't say for sure…I may be wrong…but I suspect Greg Maddux and Rafael Furcal don't go out to dinner together."

"Okay," I said, "so maybe the chemistry thing has been overblown, but how else to explain the lack of cohesiveness on the field and the sloppy fielding all season? On any given night this year, you've had five players on the field, not counting the pitcher, who were on different teams last year."

"Early on," Valentine said, "my challenge was to make everyone as comfortable as possible. But from the very beginning, even when we were in first place, there was no joy in

Mudville. We weren't blowing people out like people expected…we weren't playing good defense. So we were in first place and we were getting booed.

"Then Mo [Vaughn] got hurt [broken bone in his hand] at the worst possible time, just as the season was beginning, and it set him back almost until the All-Star break. There was also the contract thing with [Al] Leiter. I know it upset him when we broke off negotiations with him. The guy bleeds orange and blue and now he was talking about going to the Yankees.

"But the worst thing was probably all that Piazza gay nonsense. With all my experience, I should have seen that coming, how it was going to blow up into the thing it did. It was a catch-up process for me. Like I said, I don't think I did a good job. I missed beats."

That said, was it possible this Mets team was overrated? Were the high expectations based on the comparable high salaries of the players GM Steve Phillips brought in? Where is it said that Roger Cedeno is a $6 million per year player?

Valentine deftly deflected those questions.

"All I know is," he said, "there's no way I would have ever believed Jeromy Burnitz would

Manager Bobby Valentine (left) hangs his head during a game the Mets lost to the Padres. (Keith Torrie/Daily News)

go nearly three months hitting just two homers. I just don't believe that."

But, of course, it has happened, just as Cedeno has been a total bust, and two of the three starting pitchers Phillips added to the rotation over the winter, Shawn Estes and Jeff D'Amico, have been largely inconsistent.

"We still haven't put together a long winning streak," Valentine said wistfully. "If it comes now, at the end, it'll justify all the other stuff."

Only Valentine believes it will, because he has no choice but to believe. Despite it all, his job is probably secure, but that didn't seem to be any consolation for him in the heat of Shea last night.

"Otherwise," I said, "I have to believe this has probably been the worst season of your baseball life—at least the managing part of it."

"Without a doubt," said Bobby Valentine.

CHAPTER 5

REMEMBERED FRIENDS

Bob Lemon was like a second father to me, and I'll never forget the night in 1982 we were riding in a taxicab in Chicago and I talked him out of quitting as Yankees manager. He was fired the next week when we got back to New York, but at least he got his money. ...Eddie Lopat lived a few miles away from me in northern New Jersey and had been a golfing pal of my dad's. In his last year, I'd take him to lunch and he'd regale me with all his stories of the Yankees' golden age. I really miss him. ...Catfish Hunter's funeral was probably the toughest assignment I ever had at *The News*. Anyone who knew him loved him for the down-home, unassuming guy he was. His death was tragic and vividly brought to mind the old adage about the good dying young.

Bob Lemon: A Man of Integrity, by George

September 11, 1981

They tell this behind-the-scenes story about Bob Lemon's first day back as Yankee manager with a certain affection for the man. The coaches, pitchers and scouts were huddled in the manager's office, going over the hitters in the Brewers' lineup. As you might expect from an organization that answers to George M. Steinbrenner, the scouting reports were a model of infinite detail.

The scouts began to discuss the first hitter, reciting chapter and verse on the half-dozen ways *not* to pitch to this man when Lemon suddenly raised his hand and asked for the report.

"I don't see where it says here that this guy is Cobb or Ted Williams," Lemon said calmly after studying the report for a few seconds. "What's he hitting?"

"Two-fifty four," the scout said somewhat sheepishly.

"Just throw the bleeping ball over the plate," Lemon said, and not much later the scouting report session was over.

He has never been a man of great detail, never been one to make anything more out of something than it is. He has never taken himself too seriously, and his baseball philosophy could not be more simple. "Baseball," says Bob Lemon, "is a fun game for children that we grownups have managed to bleep up."

When the phone rang in his Long Beach, California, home last week, Lemon could not have been more surprised to discover the voice on the other end belonged to Steinbrenner. ("It was kind of far-fetched, don't you think?" Lemon would say later.) What made it far-fetched, though, was not just the fact that Steinbrenner had not spoken to him since the previous October. What made it so stunning is that, as Lemon himself would concede, he probably does not fit the mold of Steinbrenner's kind of manager.

In almost every way you can imagine, the two of them are a different breed. You will not likely ever see Lemon and Steinbrenner dining together at "21." If invited, Lemon would go, but he is most comfortable in the casual atmosphere of a "shot-and-beer" joint where the small talk is about baseball and horses, not stocks and bonds.

And while Steinbrenner has never left any doubt as to "whose circus this is," it is also the nature of this beast to have relished those spicy acts of impudence from Messrs. Martin, Howser and Michael. Sure Steinbrenner fired every one of them for their indiscretions, but just as certainly he would hire every one of them back if the opportunity presented itself. Steinbrenner is not happy without a good fight to keep his adrenaline flowing and the presses rolling, but it is not in Lemon's nature to provide him with that forum. They will have their differences, but we will doubtless never know how many or how severe.

"He's a decent man," says Steinbrenner. "If there is one word to describe Bob Lemon, it's decent."

Lemon's father, Earl, was an ice man in Long Beach and a semipro player who turned down a pro contract because he was making more money selling ice. Rather than furthering his own career, Earl Lemon chose to help others pursue theirs. He coached other kids in the neighborhood, including his own. Back then, Bob Lemon was a shortstop as well as a pitcher, and after graduating from Wilson High School, he took the step his dad had chosen to pass up. He signed a $300 bonus to play for the Cleveland Indians.

In the minor leagues, he was a pretty fair hitter and might have even made it to the major leagues as a third baseman had the Indians not had Ken Keltner at the time of his promotion in 1946. It was apparent that Lemon wasn't going to stick with the club unless he could find another position, and although he opened the season in center, the word had already been passed to Indians manager Lou Boudreau that he could pitch. Boudreau, in need of another right-hander, asked him to try it.

"I never liked sitting around waiting to play," Lemon recalled. "I wanted to play every day, but I didn't want to be sent down, either."

Bob Lemon shrugs on the dugout steps as he takes the Yankee helm
for the second time. (AP/WWP)

Lemon's closest friend, Jim Hegan, who coached for him with the Yankees, roomed with him on the Indians and was his batterymate for almost all of those 207 wins that took him to the Hall of Fame.

"We've been together since high school," said Hegan, "and he hasn't changed one iota. He would blame himself if he lost a game. It just wasn't in his nature to get ripped at someone else. I remember so many times he'd say to me, 'If you call a pitch, don't ever let me shake you off.'

"I don't think he feels he's a genius as a manager. He makes out the lineup and lets the players play. He's not a hunch manager. He played for [Al] Lopez and patterned himself after him."

That is not to say, however, that he does not take pride in his accomplishments or isn't hurt when others don't appreciate them.

Three times now in his managerial career, Bob Lemon has been fired. And all three times he has been wounded by it for good reason. In 1971, he led the Kansas City Royals to 85 victories, the most in their history to that point, and the following year owner Ewing Kauffman fired him over the protest of general manager Cedric Tallis.

"Yeah," the 61-year-old Lemon says today, "that was because they said I was too old."

A few years later he got his second chance with the White Sox, and in 1977 he directed them to their most exciting and successful season since 1959. But the following year, the White Sox, unable to pay the price of keeping Richie Zisk and Oscar Gamble over the winter, could not hold up, and once again Lemon was fired. That one hurt, too, because the man who lowered the ax was

one of his best friends and drinking companions, Bill Veeck.

"I don't hold any grudges against Bill," Lemon said the other day, "because I know he hated to do it. I also think he was pressured into it. There were about 20 other stockholders he had to answer to."

Similarly, two years later, Lemon agrees that Steinbrenner had to fire him less than six months after he had led the Yankees to the most miraculous of their 22 world championships. The circumstances of that firing have been well documented. A few weeks after the '78 World Series triumph over the Dodgers, Lemon's youngest son, Jerry, was killed in an automobile crash.

In the words of one of his close friends, "Lem just seemed to withdraw into himself after that. He lost that wonderful wit about him, the smile was gone and he just kind of lost interest in everything else."

Lorn Brown, the Chicago broadcaster who traveled with Lemon during the White Sox years, put a perspective on the Bob Lemon others had never known up to then.

"It was during the World Series out in Los Angeles," Brown recalled. "When Lem was in Chicago, I had been going through a divorce, and I hadn't seen him until the first day of the Series. He was in his office surrounded by reporters, and I just poked my head in to say hello. He looked up and said, 'How's everything, especially that family situation? Everything okay now?' I mean here's a guy in the middle of a World Series and he still remembers—and cares about—my family problems. That's the kind of man Bob Lemon is."

•

You see Lemon today and you see how the two years away from the game, the two years back home with his wife, Jane, and the more frequent visits with his other two boys have revitalized him. He admits candidly that being fired by Steinbrenner was possibly the best thing that could have happened to him. The two years allowed him time to heal.

And when the time comes for Steinbrenner to fire him again, Lemon will go back to Long Beach, quietly, with dignity, like the good soldier and company man that he is. He has come to learn there are far worse things in life than being fired.

"I've had a hell of a life," he once said. "I've had everything in baseball a man could ask—All-Star Games, World Series, the Hall of Fame. So you don't win the World Series. Who gives a damn? Twenty years from now who will give a damn? But I'll remember Jerry."

True, Lemon probably does not fit the mold of a Steinbrenner manager, since intensity and occasional impudence are principal criteria. But better, say Lorn Brown, Jim Hegan, Charlie Lau and the others who know Lemon best, that we could all fit the mold of integrity Bob Lemon has set as a man.

A Glorious Mourning

One by one, they filed into St. Mary's Roman Catholic Church in Greenwich, Connecticut, yesterday morning: Bowie Kuhn, Yogi Berra, Phil Rizzuto, Gil McDougald, Mel Allen, Ralph Branca, Don Dunphy, Buddy Hassett, Tom Ferrick, Joe Pignatano, Sal Yvars, Jim Fanning, Fay Vincent and George Steinbrenner.

Yes, Vincent *and* Steinbrenner. In the same place. At the same time.

They came for the purpose of saying a final goodbye and laying to rest Steady Eddie Lopat, but maybe, just maybe, they left in the spirit of laying to rest their personal animosities.

For when it was over, there was Steinbrenner shaking hands with, first, Carmen Berra and, later, Vincent on the front steps of the church. They spoke only briefly, but the fact that they had come together unexpectedly at this place for this occasion—to pay their respects to a magnificent, if unassuming, Yankee who was a hero to both of them—brought out the best in them.

Heaven knows we have not seen much of that in recent days. Steinbrenner, of course, has been a villain to Yankee fans for quite a while, as far back as 1980 when he fired Dick Howser and on through the '80s when he fired Yogi and Lou Piniella (twice) and kept firing Billy Martin and basically took the Yankees out of the Yankees. Perhaps the final "out"—though it got little notice at the time—was when he allowed his appointed Tampa hatchetman, George Bradley, to fire Eddie Lopat as a scout a few years ago without so much as an explanation.

You wanted to believe yesterday that Steinbrenner's flying all the way up from Tampa for Eddie Lopat's funeral was an act of genuine love and respect for

Steady Eddie Lopat in 1951. (Daily News)

a friend he regretted having wronged, and that his seeking out of Carmen Berra, Yogi's wife, was an act of contrition, however small, for a Yankee legend he regrets having humiliated.

At the same time, as you listened to Vincent's reading of Corinthians 13, you hoped that the commissioner of baseball was listening to his own words and would make peace with Steinbrenner for the good of the game.

This witch hunt he is conducting on Steinbrenner's alleged contacts with Yankee officials during his 22 months of exile is most unbecoming to baseball—especially the mean-spirited, Gestapo-like tactics his underlings used the other day on Gene Michael, an innocent pawn in all of this.

"And though I have the power of prophecy to penetrate all mysteries and knowledge and though I have all the faith necessary to move mountains—if I am without love I am nothing."

Certainly, as Eddie Lopat looked down on this gathering of commissioners, Hall of Famers and sports dignitaries, he had to feel a great sense of warmth and pride at what his passing had wrought on this day. Buddy Hassett, a Yankee before Lopat's time but a close friend in later years, seemed to set the mood for everyone with his reading of Ecclesiastes 3:5:

"To everything there is a season and a time to every purpose under the heaven...a time to cast away stones and a time to gather stones together."

But it was Lopat's son, John, who reminded everyone—Vincent, Steinbrenner, Yogi, Bowie Kuhn—of the common bond and common love that had brought them all together on this day with a moving, historical eulogy of his father. In concluding, the younger Lopat said: "My father had a 54-year romance with ballparks that could not have been more joyous."

Steinbrenner, sitting in the aisle across from the Berras, wiped a tear from his eye, as did Vincent, sitting off to the left of the altar. Ralph Branca, Lopat's closest friend and distinguished Dodger baritone, sang "Amazing Grace" and "The Lord's Prayer" and the throng filed out into the street to tell Eddie Lopat stories.

"There was no way I wasn't going to be here," said Tom Ferrick, who caught a commuter "puddle jumper" from Philadelphia to White Plains and drove from there to Greenwich. "When Eddie managed the [Kansas City] Athletics, I was his pitching coach. Jimmy Dykes and Luke Appling were his other coaches, and boy, did we have laughs. We had more laughs than wins."

"I gave Eddie his name, Steady Eddie," recounted Mel Allen. "That was about the easiest nickname I ever gave a guy. It rhymed and it was *him*—steady. I remember one time we were in Cleveland and Eddie was walking under the stands before the game when he saw a bunch of the Indians' hitters taking batting practice against a left-handed pitcher who was throwing nothing but soft curves and the off-speed junk that Eddie threw. So what did he do? He came out in the first inning and threw nothing but fastballs and completely baffled them."

Rizzuto joined in the reminiscing, recalling how he and Lopat (who was then a left-handed-hitting first baseman) tried out together for the Dodgers in the late '30s. Lopat got signed, but Rizzuto was sent away because he was "too small."

Looking around at the crowd, Rizzuto said: "You know, I couldn't help notice all the people here who haven't been able to get along with each other and I wanted to get up in the middle of the service and shout, 'Hey, all you people, make up!' I just didn't have the guts."

Maybe he didn't have to. Steady Eddie Lopat may have done it for all of them.

A Baseball Voice is Silenced

They say that good things eventually come to those who persevere, which is why you have to believe Rex Barney already is rediscovering his long-lost strike zone on some heavenly field of dreams today.

Barney, who was truly one of baseball's sweethearts, was found dead yesterday at his home in Baltimore. He was 72. Cause of death was not immediately determined, but—suffice to say—it was the culmination of Barney's long and painful battle with diabetes that resulted in a stroke, a heart attack and eventually the amputation of a leg a few years ago.

Yes, you could say Rex Barney persevered, all right, from the beginning to the end of his 54 years in baseball. And while he never made it to the Hall of Fame with a fastball they compared with Bob Feller's, he achieved legend status in both Brooklyn and Baltimore three decades apart.

If you are the product of '40s Brooklyn, then you know Rex Barney, the legendary right hander who threw harder than any Dodger from Ebbets Field to Chavez Ravine with the possible exception of Sandy Koufax. If only he could have thrown straighter.

Of his six big-league seasons, only once did Barney strike out more batters than he walked. That was in 1948, the year he finally put it all together for one magnificent summer, winning 15 games including his crowning baseball moment, a no-hitter against the Giants on September 9.

Two years later he was back in the minor leagues, an eternal enigma to all who tried to help him find the strike zone, especially Dodger president Branch Rickey, who went so far

*Rex Barney (left) and catcher Bruce Edwards hold the ball
that became the final out of a no-hitter against the Giants
on September 9, 1948. (Tom Watson/Daily News)*

as to send him to a psychiatrist long before "head shrinks" became fashionable in baseball.

He might have become a "why me?" sulker the rest of his life or turned to booze or drugs, as so many before and after him did, but that wasn't Rex Barney.

Once he reached the painful conclusion that he never again was going to be able to throw strikes with any consistency, he put away his glove and determined to make a career for himself in baseball as a broadcaster and public address announcer.

For the last 23 years he was a Baltimore institution, regaling Oriole fans with his classic PA style. "Give that fan a contract!" was the Barney trademark call every time a fan would make a catch of a foul ball, and always each announcement would be punctuated by the definitive Barney "Thank yooooooou."

I never saw Barney pitch; I only heard about him from those who did, and whenever he would talk about himself, it was in his typical self-effacing way.

"I saw Jim Palmer his whole career, and I threw harder than him," he said. "Warren Spahn was the best I ever saw, and I had the same kind of stuff and threw harder. It bugged me I had the same kind of abilities as they did except one. But boy, how you have to have that one—the ability to put the pitch where you want it."

Just as typical of Barney was a remark he made a few years ago to Tom Villante, the longtime major league TV exec who produced the Dodger games in the '50s. Shortly after Barney's leg had been partially amputated,

Villante called him in the hospital to wish him well.

"Don't worry about me," Barney said. "Hopefully with my leg shortened, this will help me get my control back."

Such was Barney's wonderful, irreverent sense of humor. Years after his stroke in 1983, he loved to joke that Billy Martin caused it. "I was up all night with Billy the night before. I should have known better than to try to keep up with him."

Similarly, when by pure chance he came face to face with his all-time idol, General George Patton, while roaming the advance positions in Germany drawing enemy fire as a tank commander in World War II, he was not without a quip.

Patton, who came riding up in a Jeep from the rear of the tank brigade, shouted to Barney: "Where's the front, Sergeant?"

"General," replied Barney, "the front of this *tank* is the front." To which Patton, according to Barney, abruptly turned his Jeep around and retorted: "That's too goddamn close for me! Carry on!"

To those of us who only knew the Baltimore segment of Barney's life and legend, his storytelling and just plain kindness were as much to appreciate about him as was his blazing fastball to a kid at the Polo Grounds that rainy Friday night in 1948 when he survived a bases-loaded jam in the first inning (thanks to two walks) and went on to retire the final 22 Giants in order, throwing 75 of his 116 pitches for strikes. In recent years, the ravages of diabetes had really taken a toll on him, but it couldn't remove the smile from his face whenever he spotted a familiar face among the visiting media corps from his accustomed perch in the Orioles press box.

"I'll never forget last year when he came up to me on our last trip into Baltimore and asked me if I was all right," recalled Suzyn Waldman, who had missed the first Yankees-Orioles series at Camden Yards because of her cancer treatment.

"He was so concerned, and all I could think of was here was this dear, sweet man who was on crutches caring only about how I was feeling."

So if you can take a moment from throwing to Campy up there, Rex, consider this a final appreciation from all of us who watched you persevere all those years with such grace and good humor.

Thank yooooooooou.

All-Star Farewell to Catfish Hunter

September 13, 1999

HERTFORD, N.C.—The high-noon sun was beaming down on the modest brick farmhouse where Jim (Catfish) Hunter surrendered to the ravages of Lou Gehrig's disease at age 53 last Thursday. Now, the pitching great's Yankees and Athletics teammates were gathering on the terrace, sharing their grief.

They came from all over the country: Ron Guidry, who drove from Lafayette, Louisiana; Reggie Jackson, Graig Nettles and Vida Blue, each of whom flew in from California; Lou Piniella, who let someone else manage his Seattle ballclub in Baltimore. Dick Williams, Gene Tenace, Ray Fosse, Gaylord Perry, Blue Moon Odom, and the Yankees' front office contingent of Brian Cashman, Gene Michael, Arthur Richman and Stump Merrill.

"We've all lost a good man," said Merrill, who had made many a visit to the farmhouse on Grubb Road while manager of the Yankees' Columbus farm club, when Hunter would visit him when the team played Norfolk and even pitch batting practice.

"The thing about Catfish was, it didn't matter if you were the most important person in the world or a nobody. I'm the perfect example."

Inside the home, Hunter's wife, Helen, was greeting mourners, her three children Todd, Paul and Kim at her side. In the corner was a huge floral wreath from George Steinbrenner and the Yankees.

"He was never right again after the fall," Todd Hunter said, referring to the fall his father took at home on August 8, putting him in the hospital for a month. "I'm just glad he was able to come home, but the ALS had really progressed in the month he was in the hospital.

"He just couldn't fight it anymore."

As the funeral cortege proceeded onto Main St., several townsfolk stood on almost every corner, heads bowed in silent prayer for one of their own. Befitting the simple country boy who happened to go on to become a baseball Hall of Famer, it was left to one of Hunter's Hertford pals, the Rev. Keith Vaughan, to deliver the eulogy.

"This is the toughest day of my life," Vaughan began. "My problem is that while Jimmy is home with Jesus, my heart is broken. Jimmy was one of the greatest people ever to come into my life. He made everyone feel like they were the most important people in the world."

Looking at all the ballplayers who filled tiny Hertford Baptist Church, he said, "Your presence here is testimony to how you felt about him, as far away as you all came for a great friend."

Vaughan paused, wiping his eyes with a handkerchief. "Sometimes a sick person needs to die, like a tired man needs to rest," he said. "While I was not really ready for Jimmy to go, I know death is not a dreaded enemy but a welcome friend. I wish [Hunter's time] had been longer, but in God's mind, he had completed the job he had to do.

"I'd like to believe they've got a baseball team in heaven, and that God merely needed a starting pitcher."

From the church, the procession began the final leg of the sad day's journey to the Cedar

Catfish Hunter mows down the Orioles in 1978 at Yankee Stadium. (Keith Torrie/Daily News)

*Catfish Hunter reads mail in the Shea Stadium locker
room. (Dan Farrell/Daily News)*

West Cemetery. Standing in the parking lot, Thurman Munson's widow, Diana, was consoling Helen Hunter.

At the gravesite, you could see the Perquimans County High School baseball field, where scouts first came to see Hunter pitch. On a pole rising from the center field fence, an American flag hung at half-staff. Standing over Hunter's coffin, it was left unsaid among his former teammates that they would no longer think of themselves as forever young.

CHAPTER 6

LABOR
PAINS

As far as I'm concerned the 1994 baseball strike was the darkest time in the game's history. There was no honor to be found on either side.

KAMIKAZE OWNERS CREATE A BLOODY MESS

And so, after granting baseball more death row reprieves than Gary Gilmore, Bud (Dr. Kevorkian) Selig and his fellow Lords pulled the plug on our National *Was*-time yesterday afternoon. Armageddon came by fax from Milwaukee with 26 of the 28 owners signing the names to it.

These are the saddest of possible words, Selig to Ravitch to Fehr.

Undoubtedly, the Lords are feeling quite proud of themselves now. They have stood up to the union that had been undefeated and untied in 20 years of these labor wars. They have shown their might with a willingness to blow off a half-billion dollars in revenues in order to wrest their industry back from their feudal serfs.

"All along, they were looking to say, 'We did it! We hung together!'" said player agent Tony Attanasio, one of the concerned parties who worked feverishly behind the scenes to establish a concept to address the owners' pleas for cost control. "I'm sure this is a sad day for everybody involved with baseball except those 28 owners dancing around the room with their fingers raised in the air, shouting, 'We're No. 1.'

"What disgusts me is Bud said, 'We need common ground to end all this acrimony.' What in the hell does he think this is gonna do? You bomb the town, kill all the people, but what have you won?"

Once again, we heard Selig repeat his tired litany about the short-term pain of blowing off the 1994 season being far exceeded by the long-term pain of not overhauling baseball's economic system. By refusing to budge on their salary cap proposal, the owners are now in position to declare an impasse in what passed for "negotiations" and unilaterally implement their own system this off season.

It is going to be absolute chaos.

You have more than 140 players who are eligible for free agency—or at least *would* have been eligible for free agency had they completed a full season of service this year. No one knows now who's a free agent. Then there are those players with so-called repeater rights whose long-term contracts have expired and must be offered arbitration within five days after the completion of the World Series. But as Attanasio asks: "What World Series? 1995? 1997?"

Taking into consideration the owners' genius history of running their game, one wonders if any of them thought about this. Apparently not. Apparently the game plan is to proceed as if it's business as usual—only business under *their* terms. They have shown the players their united front and now it will be just a matter of time until the players capitulate. Players' wives will see to it.

Joe McIlvaine, speaking on behalf of his fellow GMs who have been kept totally in the dark by their bosses, expressed his frustration with the uncertain and uncharted world the Lords have now created.

"I have no idea what I'm supposed to do," the Mets' general manager said. "I've had absolutely no direction. I don't know what rules we're working under. Reserve lists have to be made up, rosters have to be formulated. You can't even think about free agents or trades. But the owners aren't thinking about things like this."

In all probability it eventually will be left to a judge to give the GMs their marching orders. For as soon as the owners declare an impasse and implement their own system, you can be sure there will be lawsuits everywhere. And all the while baseball's labor war goes on and the 1995 season becomes the next victim of this madness.

"It is going to be a long, long, long time before we see major league baseball again," said another player agent, Tom Reich, in ominous tones. "All you needed to see to know that was how little substantive talking there was last week. The owners are obviously willing to pay an exacting price for bringing the players to their knees. There are going to be many casualties in the meantime. They've found a way to kill something that's fundamentally good, and that's a national tragedy."

There really is no other way to look at it. Baseball is dead for 1994 and an endangered species for 1995. In Milwaukee yesterday, Bud Selig made like Jim Jones and passed around the Kool-Aid to his fellow Lords. Twenty-six out of 28 of them eagerly dipped their ladles in and grinned with satisfaction at having killed a season and shown the players their resolve. They wanted Armageddon. Now they've got it. The blood of a mortally wounded sport is everywhere.

WILPON SPEAKS
HIS PEACE

MARCH 9, 1995

PALM BEACH—Other than Peter Angelos—who doesn't count—Fred Wilpon has been the lonesome dove among the Lords of Baseball in this hideous six-and-a-half-month labor war. And, we might add, a publicly silent one.

In response to all those cries of "where's Fred Wilpon and why isn't he speaking out?" you probably needed to be in the owners' negotiating committee meeting yesterday. It was there that the Mets owner had his say and if everyone was calling him, "Monte" as in Monte "Let's Make a Deal" Hall when it was over...well, so be it.

The thing is, nobody is more distressed, more embarrassed or more disgusted than Wilpon over the carnage from one wrecked season and another possibly wrecked with replacement players. Unlike fellow dove Angelos, the Baltimore Orioles' owner who has defied the Lords over replacement players and vilified acting commissioner Bud Selig, Wilpon has kept his anguish mostly silent. It has been his choice not to make his case publicly. And privately he didn't really have a full audience until the owners convened here this week.

"I said my piece and pulled no punches," Wilpon told *The News* last night after the owners' meetings adjourned for a cocktail reception. "Obviously my views are different from some of the other people. But having said that, I want to make it clear I have complete confidence in our negotiating committee and I'm in the camp."

Basically what Wilpon told his fellow Lords was that the seeds to a settlement are on the table in that owners and players should realize they are at least *both* finally talking about a payroll luxury tax.

Mets owner Fred Wilpon speaks to the media. (Linda Cataffo/Daily News)

Obviously, the gulf between each side's tax remains huge, but in Wilpon's view, there's a deal if only each side will compromise.

"The 'bid and ask' is on the table," he said. "I don't see the ideological differences anymore. That's been worked out."

When it was suggested to him that even the more moderate owners have seemingly begun moving into the hardliners' camp after the union's failure to offer a meaningful tax proposal last week in Scottsdale, Arizona, Wilpon shook his head and waved his finger. Not so, he insisted, because no matter how it may look now, the Lords are not eager to incur more staggering losses and inflict more damage on the game in the absence of a deal.

"I ask myself every day, 'How is the industry—not just the Mets—going to recover from this?'" he said. "And the fact is with every day it goes on it's going to take longer to recover. Even if we settled tomorrow, the gross revenues for 1995 are going to be substantially reduced."

And yet the owners are fully prepared to open the season with replacement players.

"That's a reality," Wilpon said, suddenly sounding almost hawkish. "But given the choice of no continuity of baseball or this, we chose this. It's not something any of us wants. There are two reasons for it: The public has a right to see baseball and the dynamics of it as it regards the two sides making a deal is better."

That is not the way Angelos sees it. Upon arriving at the meetings yesterday in much the same fashion as Daniel entered the lion's den, Angelos was fast discovering what lonesome is. He has isolated himself from the other Lords by refusing to field a replacement team, and there was speculation early that Wilpon had considered taking the same stance.

Had he?

"No," he said. "Like I said, I let them know how I feel about certain things. At the same time, I have great confidence in Buddy's [Bud Selig's] leadership. I was listened to and my opinions are respected.

"I don't believe in being outside the tent. That sends the wrong signals."

In other words, Fred Wilpon remains a dove among an increasingly hawkish group of baseball lords. He is just no longer lonesome.

GEORGE FINDS
HIS CHECKBOOK

Say this about His Bossness, George Steinbrenner—the guy knows what it's going to take to win the fans back to baseball. And it isn't Paul O'Neill shaking hands and signing autographs.

Until yesterday, until Steinbrenner assumed the role of lead vulture and swooped down to pluck relief ace John Wetteland off the ravaged carcass of the Montreal Expos, there weren't a whole lot of fans lining up for tickets at Yankee Stadium.

Strike or no strike, the Lords of Baseball have come to discover there are two surefire means of filling their coffers with ticket receipt revenue—a new state-of-the-art baseball-only stadium with all the amenities of luxury boxes and fine dining, or a championship-caliber team.

Absent the former, Steinbrenner has gone whole hog for the latter. And, presumably, Yankee fans—who have been smarting over being robbed last August of their first postseason experience in 13 years—have reason now to eagerly begin the process of forgiving and forgetting.

For as good as those '94 Yankees were going, they were still missing two key ingredients that conceivably would have separated them from an expanded playoff team and a World Series team. They didn't have a No. 1 starter to take the load off Jimmy Key (whose arm was about shot anyway), and they didn't have a bona fide closer to take the load off Steve Howe (whose relief stints have to be carefully regulated).

Thanks to Steinbrenner and his renewed "open checkbook" policy (and there may well be a direct correlation to this and the "tabling" of revenue sharing and the payroll luxury tax), both those needs have been addressed in a big way. While the strike was in progress, Steinbrenner took advantage of his pal Jerry Reinsdorf's long-simmering feud with Jack McDowell and acquired the White Sox ace in the midst of all the confusion and uncertainty over which economic system the game was going to operate in '95.

When Reinsdorf traded McDowell, it looked like Black Jack was going to be some sort of a free agent and the scant Yankee return—somebody named Keith Heberling—reflected that risk. Ah, but with the owners' bungling lawyers having made certain that 1995 will be played under the 1994 system, McDowell can't go anywhere except to arbitration.

And if you were wondering why Steinbrenner was the first owner out of that "white flag of surrender" meeting in Chicago last Sunday, it was because he was in a hurry to get to south Florida to be first on line when the cash-pinched Expos began conducting the fire sale of all their high-priced, arbitration-eligible stars. The minor league outfielder the Yankees gave up for Wetteland—Fernando Seguignol—well may rise to stardom sometime in the next century. For the present, though, the prime consideration for the Expos was the cash Steinbrenner tossed into the deal.

Suffice to say, it was somewhat more than the $400,000 limit Bowie Kuhn imposed on the Lords years ago. Of course, in the absence of a true commissioner, the owners are pretty much doing whatever they want these days.

"Obviously, everyone is making a statement here—George, the Expos, everyone," said superagent Tom Reich, who represents Wetteland. "But the way I see it, this trade is a win-win situation. George got himself a new Gossage and the Expos are building a new pool of super futures to go along with an already fertile farm system. They won't fall as far as people think and they'll be back a lot sooner than people think."

That may be all well and good for the Expos, but for Steinbrenner, the future clearly is now.

Out of deference to Bud Selig, the man who commuted his "permanently ineligible" sentence, Steinbrenner has kept quiet and played the good soldier these past couple of years—all the while gritting his teeth while the small-market zealots were leading the Lords into another bloody ambush at the hands of the union.

You might say that Judge Sonia Sotomayor's emancipation

injunction for the players last week was Steinbrenner's emancipation, too.

Who knows what the Yankee payroll is going to be this year? Who cares? The Boss is back, eager to once more provide jilted Yankee fans with "the best team money can buy." For them, the scars of the strike ought to start fading a lot quicker now.

Oh, and by the way, don't forget the waitress service in the box seats this year.

Braves Aid Kin of Slain Replacement

There is no telling how long it will take for the scars of baseball's still-festering uncivil war to heal. The scores of empty seats in ballparks across the nation certainly suggest the fans' wounds are far deeper than any of the foolhardy combatants could have imagined.

It is as if the fans are saying: "Hey, while you were gone, we did some thinking and realized there are far more important things in life than baseball." To those fans who worshiped all their lives at baseball's altar, the seven-month players strike was like a death in the family.

Sometimes that's what it takes to put life in perspective.

In the case of David Shotkoski, the replacement pitcher for the Atlanta Braves who was murdered near the team's spring training hotel in West Palm Beach on the night of March 24, it was more than a death in the family. It was a death that transcended baseball. But until that fateful night, David Shotkoski was nothing more than another scab and management pawn in the eyes of the striking major-leaguers.

"Every so often, something has to happen to make you realize that nothing is as important as life itself," Braves pitcher Tom Glavine was saying the other night at Shea. "We're all guilty of losing sight of that. We get so caught up in thinking nothing matters except baseball, and we forget that no matter what, family is still No. 1.

"When something happens to a David Shotkoski, it opens your eyes to that."

Shotkoski, it turned out, was a husband and father just like most of the major-leaguers he supposedly was going to replace. He died trying to make a better

Felicia Shotkoski and her 21-month-old daughter Alexis play in 1996.
(AP/WWP)

life for his wife, Felicia, and their newborn daughter, Alexis.

At least that's the way Glavine and fellow Braves pitcher John Smoltz suddenly came to see it—perhaps because they, too, have baby daughters. So last week, without consulting with Donald Fehr, they decided to take up a collection from the rest of the Braves players to help the Shotkoskis.

"I'm glad they're doing it out of their hearts," Felicia Shotkoski said from her home outside of Chicago yesterday. "I applaud Tom Glavine. I always wanted people to see these players as human beings, which wasn't so evident during the strike. I have to think that if they were in my husband's shoes, they'd have done the same thing. He was in the minor leagues for several years and they come to him and ask him if he wants to try out for their team. What was he supposed to say, 'I'm sorry?'"

"It's so easy to get caught up in the emotion of a strike," said Glavine, the Braves' player rep and a highly visible figure during the strike. "I have a better understanding of the career minor-leaguers...guys with real jobs...doing what they did, than I do for the former major-leaguers.

"The bottom line is, as far as David Shotkoski was concerned, he left a daughter behind. That's what we're all focusing on now. That's what's right."

In an otherwise hideous experience that sullied everyone associated with it, at least something positive finally has come out of the baseball strike. The scars cannot be expected to start healing until there is a labor agreement. But the act of Glavine, Smoltz and their Braves teammates for once looking beyond themselves and the *cause* is a hopeful sign that baseball still has what it takes to right itself.

"I would hate to think," said Felicia Shotkoski, "from the greed of wanting more, this [her husband's death] is what came out of it. Believe me, the replacement players gave up a lot more than the major league players. They walked away from their jobs to help baseball keep going when nobody else would."

TABLE A-ROD OFFER AND PULL UP CHAIRS

AUGUST 26, 2002

After all the divisive and depressing rhetoric that came out of Saturday's labor negotiations, I needed a pick-me-up yesterday, so I decided to go out to Yankee Stadium under the mistaken impression it was "A-Rod Salary Giveback Day."

You probably heard, in the middle of all the much-too-public wrangling over luxury taxes and revenue sharing, that Alex Rodriguez, the Texas Rangers' $252 million shortstop, had stepped up to the plate and said he wanted to do what he could to help baseball solve its labor problems—even to the point where he'd be willing to give back some of his stupefying $22 million per year salary. I suppose I was being a tad naive envisioning A-Rod standing in front of Yankee Stadium handing out $20 bills to all fans 14 and under as a goodwill gesture on behalf of his fellow millionaire feudal serfs.

Anyway, the last-place Rangers, with the second highest payroll in baseball (thanks in large part to A-Rod), beat up on Andy Pettitte and the Yankees and the Baseball Bickersons were back at the bargaining table over in midtown. But cooler heads prevailed and management improved slightly its proposals on the hot-button issues such as the luxury tax, getting the negotiations back on track.

But what's both exasperating and scary about this unseemly squabble is that all the elements for a deal are in place, and yet two decades of mistrust once again reared their ugly head Saturday, threatening to blow up everything and bring baseball to the apocalypse.

Why do I say all the elements of a deal are there? Because, unlike all the previous labor squabbles that have led to work stoppages, this one is about money and money alone, and not a difference in philosophy, which is so much harder to bridge. We've gotten past the "competitive balance" hogwash that originally was supposed to be the basis of the owners' demands for significant revenue-sharing increases, and nobody is bothering to conceal the basic fact that this is really all about welfare.

I never thought I'd see the day again when I'd agree with anything Fay Vincent, the former imperial commissioner, had to say. But when Vincent opined the other day that the owners had already gotten more concessions from the union than he could ever have imagined and that they ought to declare victory and move on, he wasn't far wrong.

Just look at the owners' five principal objectives at the start of these negotiations:

• Significantly increased revenue sharing. Last year, $170 million in revenue sharing was dispersed. Under the latest proposal put forth by the union Saturday, annual revenue-sharing payouts—irrespective of the luxury tax—would increase from $172.3 million in 2003 to $195.6 million, $219 million and finally $242.3 million by 2006.

• Luxury payroll tax. The union had stated from the outset its avowed opposition to such a tax designed to put a drag on salaries—which could also become a form of salary cap. Nevertheless, it has come around on this issue because of management's insistence there can't be a deal without one. And while the ultimate tax won't be nearly the 50percent on payrolls in excess of $102 million the owners had sought, it will be enough to add $15 million to $20 million to the overall revenue-sharing transfer number. From where the parties are now, it's clear that over the life of the agreement the owners will have an additional $100 million in revenue sharing per year.

• Put a major hit on the Yankees. Under the union's proposal alone, the Yankees, who paid $30 million in revenue sharing last year, would be hit for more than $50 million next year and well over $200 million over the life of a four-year deal.

• A worldwide draft. This would have gone a long way toward leveling the playing field in that free-spending clubs like the Yankees and Dodgers could no longer use their resources to procure the prize prospects in Latin America. The union reluctantly agreed to this, too, only to see the owners change their minds. Now owners don't want to reward those teams that, for whatever reasons, chose not to spend in international player development.

• Steroid testing. The union was shamed into agreeing to this given the clouds of suspicion over so many of the game's biggest stars. Granted, the union's initial proposal needs a lot more teeth, but it's a positive start and, considering its past refusal to even consider any sort of testing, a major breakthrough.

So with all this acknowledged progress as their incentive, let the principals go into seclusion, put a muzzle on the naysaying and don't call us until they have a deal.

DEAL IS THIS: WON'T BE BALANCE

SEPTEMBER 1, 2002

When the dark clouds finally parted and the cold mist abated over Park Ave. Friday, it became increasingly apparent that Bud Selig and his welfare recipients had won a significant victory over the players, for which hitting the bricks had little appeal.

In the weeks leading up to the final countdown, Selig had gone a long way toward winning this war with a brilliant public relations campaign in which he managed to convince the public this dispute was really about restoring competitive balance in baseball. And keeping in line with the familiar theme, Selig invoked the term "competitive balance" three times Friday in explaining why the arduous and unseemly process was so necessary.

But now that the onus is off the players—who were admittedly fearful of the public backlash they would have incurred going on strike in the midst of a slumping economy, Wall Street outrage and the anniversary of 9/11—it's squarely on Selig and the owners. For the next four years, they'll have nearly a billion dollars of revenue to transfer from the fat cat Yankees, Dodgers, Mets and Red Sox to the whining welfare seekers, John Moores in San Diego, David Glass in Kansas City, Drayton McLane in Houston, Jeffrey Loria in Miami and Vince Naimoli in Tampa. The Yankees alone will have to fork over nearly $54 million of revenue and payroll luxury tax to the "needies" coffer next year, which, according to the Gospel of Bud, is going to address this huge disparity problem we have in baseball.

Sure it is. And if you believe this revenue windfall is going to be re invested in payroll by these owners, then I've got a beautiful, pastoral stadium in Flushing for you.

Even the players don't care if the owners put their revenue-sharing booty into payroll. For reasons I still don't quite understand, they were disinclined to seek minimum payrolls or any stipulations that revenue sharing be applied to the procurement of playing talent—as Selig managed to convince the general public they would. So if the players don't care, how do you think the owners feel?

Of course, in some cases—like in Miami, where Loria has managed to completely alienate an already diminished and disillusioned fan base—no amount of revenue sharing is going to help. He knows that, and you can be sure the Marlins' payroll will remain comfortably under $50 million while Loria blames the political situation in south Florida for his inability to get a new stadium, then pockets his revenue-sharing largesse.

And you can be sure it'll be the same in Kansas City, Tampa Bay and San Diego. What this revenue sharing does do for these owners, however, is add to the value of their franchises. It's called welfare, and as Selig knows all too well, that's what this whole exercise was really all about. It will be interesting to see how many of these franchises will be sold during the next four years of this labor agreement—for tidy profits—starting with the MLB-owned Montreal Expos, who appear almost certain to be headed to Washington, D.C.

As for the luxury tax—which became the stickiest of all the issues to resolve—I suspect in four years we're going to look at that the same way as we did the long forgotten free agent compensation draft, which was the main bone of contention in the rancorous 1981 labor dispute. Three years later, the owners decided it was a farce and quietly did away with it.

This luxury tax, with all its complicated percentages and formulas, will hit the Yankees for about $8 million and two or three other teams for another combined $10-12 million. It is designed to put an artificial drag on salaries, to encourage restraint. But a funny thing happened last year. With the exception of the embarrassing phoney in Texas, Tom Hicks (who doled out $65 million to Chan Ho Park, $24 million to Juan Gonzalez and another $16.5 million to a couple of retread middle relievers), and Steinbrenner (who lured Jason Giambi away from Oakland for a seven-year, $120 million deal and gave Sterling Hitchcock $12 million for two years), the owners

Bud Selig may have gotten everything he wanted from the players, but you can expect him to have the same look when the same sorry teams are still not competitive. (Thomas Monaster/Daily News)

remarkably showed they could restrain themselves.

Barry Bonds found no bidding war for his services. Neither did Bret Boone (who whined at having to accept $25 million over three years from the Mariners), Moises Alou or Tino Martinez. But as much as their agents tried to trump up collusion charges, it was clear that the floundering economy forced the clubs to show restraint. Even Gene Orza, the union's bullish general counsel, acknowledged Friday that history has shown clubs' spending amounts on players and the state of the economy are directly related. The betting here is nobody, with the possible exception of the Yankees and Mets, will exceed the payroll thresholds established in this agreement after the first year.

Look at the Seattle Mariners. They're the second highest revenue-generating team in baseball and yet ownership told Lou Piniella in July it would not increase the $80 million payroll for a player who could help get them to the World Series. And of course there's Hicks, suddenly proclaiming he's gotten fiscal religion and vowing to get his payroll under the threshold (despite one-fourth of it devoted to one player, Alex Rodriguez).

So there you have it. A deal the owners said had to have significant revenue sharing and luxury taxes in each of its four years. On the surface, for sure, the owners can claim victory. They got everything they said they had to have, including steroid testing and the worldwide draft (which,

for a while they weren't sure if they really wanted after all). And Selig assured us this is a deal that addresses baseball's competitive balance problem. (I suppose he'll be saying that again next month when the Oakland A's and Minnesota Twins are still playing in October.)

I hope he's right and finished now running down the game he governs. But somehow, I suspect we're going to be right back in this same place four years from now where nothing much will have changed. Steinbrenner always has spent much more than any other owner. The only difference between now and the '80s is that he's spent it more wisely. There is no substitute for sound management (see: A's, Braves, Cardinals, Giants) and, assuming the Royals, Devil Rays, Marlins, Brewers and others are in the same plight four years from now, the Commissioner of Doom is going to have a lot explaining to do.

CHAPTER 7

EVENTS

I wasn't even officially working the night Doc Gooden pitched his no-hitter. I was at Yankee Stadium getting material for a future column and stayed to watch the game—at least until somebody got a hit, which, of course, nobody did. Afterward, I had to borrow a colleague's laptop to write this column. ...Watching David Wells pitching his perfect game, while flashing back to when I had been at the Stadium for Don Larsen's perfecto was surreal. ...In retrospect, Mark McGwire's home run feats (and those of Barry Bonds that followed) have certainly lost their luster, haven't they? ...The trip to Havana was enlightening. The sight I'll never forget is the forlorn faces of all those Cubans pressed up against the chain link fence surrounding the airport, watching as we boarded our charter flight out of there.

ORIOLE PARK:
IT FEELS RIGHT

APRIL 7, 1992

BALTIMORE—If he were alive to see it yesterday, The Babe would have heartily approved of what's become of his old man's saloon.

Some 50 years after Ruth's Cafe in Baltimore was torn down, they have built a ballpark in its stead on the grounds of the Camden Yards railroad station. And "ballpark" is the operative word here, for they have spared nothing in combining all the charming elements of baseball's sacred shrines, Ebbets Field, old Comiskey Park, Wrigley Field and Fenway Park, into one spanking new, old-timey baseball park. Without doubt, this is a ballpark The Babe would recognize and love—especially the Ebbets-like right field wall that stands a mere 318 feet down the line from home plate.

"This is as close to Ebbets Field as any place I've ever seen," said the ex-Dodger fireballing right-hander Rex Barney, who has been the Orioles' public address announcer since 1967. "I don't see Wrigley or Fenway [here] like so many other people do. I close my eyes and I see Ebbets— everything from advertisements on the right field fence and the closeness of the field."

Of course, being an old Dodger from Brooklyn it was understandable if that's what Barney chose to see. Longtime White Sox fans, on the other hand, would look at the wrought iron roof that encircles the upper deck and see old Comiskey. And soon Wrigley worshippers can stake their claim on a piece of the Orioles' new playpen once the ivy that has been planted in the center field backdrop takes root and begins to bloom.

"When I look at this ballpark, I can't help but think of all the ones they've torn down," said Brooks Robinson, the

The new Oriole Park is reminiscent of old-time ballparks. (AP/WWP)

Orioles' Hall of Fame third baseman. "This one's their ancestor the way I see it. I always thought it was so sad in the '70s when they built all those all-purpose stadiums that looked the same and had no charm. You'd go into them and look around and scratch your head and say, 'Where am I?'"

Robinson was one of a half dozen ex-Oriole greats on hand for the ballpark's grand opening yesterday. One of them, Boog Powell, has come back to stay, having opened up a barbecued pit beef and pork chop sandwich concession stand on the other side of the rightfield wall. Nattily dressed in a dark blue suit, big

Boog happily signed autographs while his chefs furiously labored over the barbecue pit behind him.

"I'm gonna be here for 90 percent of the home games," Powell said. "I moved all the way up here from Key West, Florida to open and run this concession stand. I figure I'll sign autographs for about an hour every day. We'll let the fans know what time I'll be here.

"The card dealers are upset with me, though. They don't like me signing so many things for free here because they say it's knocking down the value of my cards. Hey, what do I care? This is what this is all about!"

The Babe would agree. Perhaps the most free of all signers in his day, Ruth would smile warmly at the sight of another rotund old left-handed slugger signing autographs and selling sloppy barbecued beef and pork chop sandwiches where the family saloon used to be.

"It's my own special recipe," Powell went on. "This whole thing, pit beef and pork chops, is a unique idea for a ballpark. Nobody's ever done this. I'm more excited about this Opening Day than any I ever had on the field."

Rising just beyond the right-field wall is the restored 94-year-old B&O Railroad warehouse that serves as the most distinguishing focal point of the ballpark. Adjacent to the warehouse is another restored building where it is said president Abraham Lincoln wrote the majority of the Gettysburg Address while waiting for the train to take him to the Civil War battleground.

"I'll tell you one thing," said Powell, gazing at the warehouse. "I guarantee I'd hit that damn warehouse more than a few times during a season. Hell, it's only 460 feet from home plate to the base of the wall."

For left-handed sluggers, the warehouse does make an even more inviting target than Fenway's Green Monster left field wall does for right-handers. There's no telling how many warehouse windows Boog or The Babe might have shattered if they had played here.

Yesterday, however, nobody came close as Baltimore's Rick Sutcliffe christened the new park with a masterful five-hit, 2-0 shutout of the Indians. Sutcliffe's Cleveland counterpart, Charles Nagy, pitched nearly as well, scattering six hits in also going the distance.

Indeed, the only pitcher who wasn't in midseason form for the historic occasion was President Bush, who bounced his ceremonial first pitch into the dirt.

"It was supposed to be a breaking ball," Bush insisted.

Such a disclaimer was about the only thing that would have made The Babe frown yesterday.

DWIGHT DOES IT FOR DAD

MAY 15, 1996

All those bound-for-glory seasons with the Mets, Dwight Gooden never had a New York audience rooting for him like he did last night.

It began when he struck out Ken Griffey in the sixth inning with Darren Bragg on third base. They were on their feet, 31,025 of them, and when Gerald Williams made his second saving catch of the game in center field on Edgar Martinez's sinking liner, suddenly there was the possibility of a no-hitter. On another unseasonably cool May evening, Yankee Stadium was alive with electricity again, the way it hadn't been since October, when the Mariners were here for the playoffs and Dwight Gooden was in Tampa serving out the final days of his year and a half drug suspension.

But as he kept the electricity going, Gooden was not thinking of how he was triumphing over those demons. When his mind was not on the batter, it was on his father, Dan, to whom he had dedicated this game even before he became aware of it becoming the greatest one he has ever pitched. Gooden was unsure whether his father was able to watch the game from his Tampa hospital bed, where he was waiting to undergo open heart surgery today.

"I hope he did," Gooden said, "but I'm not sure he could. I just know I was thinking about him off and on all night. Between innings, [Yankee trainer] Steve Donohue would come up to me and talk to me. Kenny Rogers, too. I needed that."

It was not until the seventh inning that he realized he was pitching a no-hitter. He realized the crowd was larger than usual and sensed its cheering was louder and more imploring, but until then, his mind had only been with his father.

Dwight Gooden is carried off the field by his teammates after pitching a no-hitter. (Linda Cataffo/Daily News)

"It just didn't hit me until then," he said. "I had been thinking about my dad all day and then started focusing on the game. I thought this is what he'd want me to do."

By then, if course, Yankee Stadium was heaving with emotion on his every pitch. A 1-2-3 seventh, followed by a 1-2-3 eighth, and he was three outs from exorcising all those demons that had driven him into a private hell that even his staunchest supporters wondered if he could escape.

What were his emotions as he walked Alex Rodriguez to start the ninth? What was going through his mind with the fans all screaming for him?

"I was just trying to stay within myself," Gooden said. "I knew where I was and I was all pumped up, maybe too pumped up. I had no more legs and I was tired. But once there were guys on base, I was able to think about the game and not so much the no-hitter."

That's what he was thinking, but what was Joe Torre thinking when, after Edgar Martinez walked with one out, Gooden and Joe Girardi got crossed up and Gooden threw a wild pitch, putting runners at second and third?

"I sent [pitching coach] Mel [Stottlemyre] out to talk to him and basically just tell him it's his game," Torre said. "If he said he was tired, Mel was going to bring in John Wetteland. I was smart. I stayed out of it."

So after Gooden fanned Jay Buhner on a 2-2 pitch, that left Paul Sorrento. And when the Mariners' first baseman lofted a high pop into shallow left field that Derek Jeter would grab, Gooden raised his arms in triumph and the crowd exploded.

As he was carried off the field by his teammates, Gooden waved and pointed to the New York fans who have forgiven him his past betrayals. On this, his finest New York night, he took his biggest step yet toward saving his baseball life.

LIKE LARSEN, DAVID QUITE IMPERFECT

MAY 18, 1998

The million-to-one odds of becoming the second imperfect man from Point Loma High School in San Diego to pitch a perfect game at Yankee Stadium was just beginning to sink in on David Wells when Yankees vice president Arthur Richman frantically summoned him into Joe Torre's office to take a phone call.

On the other end of the line was not President Clinton, but Don Larsen, the original imperfect man, as immortalized by *Daily News* baseball writer Joe Trimble in his account of the only perfect game in the World Series, October 8, 1956. Like Wells, Larsen was quite a free spirit and bon vivant, having reportedly partied heavily with Richman on the eve of his perfecto. The two pitchers could only laugh at the incredible coincidence of baseball history.

"I'm honored to share this with you, Don," Wells said. "I mean two guys from the same high school doing this? What were the odds? Who would ever believe it?"

Torre, sitting behind his desk a few feet away, was one who could. The Yankees' manager was 16 years old that October afternoon in 1956 and he was sitting in the upper deck in left field while Larsen was making history.

"I was there as a Dodger fan," Torre said, "but by the time the ninth inning came around, I was rooting for Larsen like everybody else in the park. It is quite a coincidence, isn't it? Both guys free spirits. You don't check their rooms at night."

It is hard to imagine anyone among the 49,820 "Beanie Babies" crowd yesterday rooting for the Twins, but if they were, it

The Yankee Stadium scoreboard shows David Wells's perfect game.
(Linda Cataffo/Daily News)

wasn't for long. Even Twins manager Tom Kelly admitted getting caught up in Wells's bid for immortality.

"As much as we were fighting to win the game, deep down I was hoping to see something special," Kelly admitted. "I like the guy, I really do. He has the charisma for something like this, and I guess his stars were in alignment today."

Actually, they started getting aligned in Wells's last start, when he retired the final 10 batters he faced against Kansas City. If you're counting, that makes 37 consecutive batters Wells has retired, which is four shy of the major league record set by Jim Barr of the Giants in 1972. That's quite a reversal of form from his start before that, when he couldn't get out of the third inning against the Rangers after being staked to a 9-0 lead.

But then that's Wells. Like Forrest Gump's proverbial box of chocolates, you just never know what you're going to get.

Yesterday it was pure domination. About the only time you thought he might be losing his decided edge was in the seventh, when he ran the count full on both Brent Gates and Paul Molitor in succession. The crowd groaned when Wells went to 3-1 on Molitor, and as Torre would say later, "The thing I'll take with me from this game was David coming back from that to strike him out. Getting Molitor, that's when I thought he was going to do it."

And when Wells came out for the ninth, they were all on their feet, imploring home plate umpire Tim McClelland to call everything a strike. By this time, though, Wells seemed almost numb to it all and threw almost nothing but strikes. Barely hittable strikes.

"The way he kept his composure was the most impressive part of the whole performance," marveled Twins pitcher Bob Tewksbury. "I mean just holding onto the ball in Yankee Stadium in front of 50,000 screaming fans and keeping that focus after two long [Yankees] innings [in the seventh and eighth] is incredible. I have to tell you, even from the other side it was pretty thrilling."

"To be honest," said Wells, "I was wishing the crowd would shush. I was starting to get nervous about the seventh inning and the crowd was starting to get to me."

The place really exploded when Paul O'Neill settled under Pat Meares's soft fly ball to right to end it, and suddenly Wells was engulfed by his teammates and couldn't hear anything. The man who made them cringe by trading on-the-air profanities with talk radio shock jocks "Bubba the Love Sponge" in Tampa and Howard Stern was now being carried off the field by Darryl Strawberry and Bernie Williams, the toast of the team.

"I just hope the Yankees treat him better than they treated me," Larsen said. "I barely got a raise from [then-Yankees GM George] Weiss. What David did was quite remarkable. It's tough enough today just to pitch a complete game with all these bullpens."

Was there anything in particular he told Wells, Larsen was asked.

"Oh yeah," he said. "I told David we have to have a few drinks this summer and raise a little hell."

What else would you expect from two imperfect kindred spirits?

PERFECT TIMING

I was 11 years old that October 8 afternoon in 1956 when my father hugged me and just about everyone else around us in the left field upper deck of Yankee Stadium and nearly began crying. On the field, Yogi Berra was jumping into Don Larsen's arms and delirium reigned.

"A perfect game!" my father screamed. "A perfect game! We're all going to be famous!"

Later, as we walked across the McCombs Dam bridge to our car, my father said: "You had quite a thrill for your first World Series game, didn't you? I guarantee you'll never see anything like that again!"

Who was I to doubt him? I mean, really, what are the chances of anyone seeing two perfect games, in the same ballpark, in his or her lifetime? To the best of my knowledge there were only three other people besides myself at Yankee Stadium for David

Wells's perfect game yesterday who were also there for Larsen's 42 years ago: Bob Sheppard, the Yankees' public address announcer, Don Zimmer, and Joe Torre. Zimmer, the Yankees' bench coach, was on the Dodger bench that day in 1956, and Torre, like me, was in the upper deck in left field.

When I told Larsen that yesterday, he laughed. "Yeah," he said, "you and about 10 million other people who claimed they were there."

But I have the scorecard, autographed years later by Larsen, to prove it. It's hard to forget your first World Series game, especially when it turns out to be one for the ages.

Like Torre, the play I most remember about Larsen's perfect game was Mickey Mantle's catch off Gil Hodges in left center. It was about the only hard-hit ball the Dodgers had in the entire game. The only other "scare" for Larsen was Jackie Robinson's hard shot to third that glanced off Andy Carey's glove to Gil McDougald, who made the throw over to first for the out.

Larsen needed only 97 pitches for his perfect game to Wells's 120. But Wells was more dominating. Afterward, Twins manager Tom Kelly was at a loss to single out anything that had even a chance of being a base hit.

After witnessing Wells's feat, I'd like to tell you I've seen everything now. But that's what my father told me, too, and what did he know?

EXCLAMATION MARK:
70 POWERS PAIR TO END '98

SEPTEMBER 28, 1998

ST. LOUIS—Seventy.

Who in their wildest dreams could have ever imagined it? How to digest the sheer magnitude of such a number?

And yet, there it is today, a number to stand for the ages—70 home runs by Mark McGwire, 10 more than The Babe, nine more than Maris, and, you have to believe, more than anyone will ever hit in a season unless they institute batting tees.

Even Mighty Mac, who for weeks downplayed the significance of the eventual record, had to agree after hitting two more homers in his final game yesterday that it is going to take one inhuman effort to ever top his personal Everest.

"It's a huge number," McGwire said, shaking his head. "The magnitude of it will not be understood for a while. It's unheard of. I mean for someone to hit 70 homers in a season...I'm like in awe of myself right now."

He's in awe of himself? What about everyone around him, everyone who was a part of his surreal history-making effort yesterday, from the opposing Montreal Expos who high-fived him as he toured the bases for No. 70 in the seventh inning, to his St. Louis teammates who, like him, were still shaking their heads long after the final out of the Cardinals' 6-3 victory.

"It was amazing to be part of history," said Expos rookie shortstop Orlando Cabrera, who hit his own shot in the fourth inning. "I can tell my kids I hit a home run in the same game he hit his 70th."

"After he hit his 65th, which was the number his son [Matt] had predicted for him, I told him, 'I want you to hit 70,'" Cards reserve catcher Tom Lampkin

Mark McGwire follows the flight of home run No. 70. (AP/WWP)

said. "I was just kidding. I mean, for him to actually do it, I can't even fathom it."

To do it, he had to hit five in his last three games. Yesterday, sitting on 68, he singled in the first inning against Expo right-hander Mike Thurman, then came to the plate with two out and none on in the third. With the count 1-1, Thurman threw a breaking ball, which, McGwire said, "I sat back on" and walloped on a majestic arc that came down in the lower deck in left field— 69.

After he walked in the fifth for the NL-best 162nd time, there were two aboard for McGwire in the seventh and a new pitcher, right-hander Carl Pavano, the rookie obtained from the Red Sox for Pedro Martinez.

Turning on Pavano's first-pitch fastball, McGwire hit a dart that left the park so quickly and landed in a party box below the lower deck in left, the 46,110 fans didn't even have to time to savor it. The time here was 3:19 p.m. The distance: 370 feet—70.

"I wasn't sure if I got enough of a topspin on it," McGwire said, "but I did. My thought going up there was get a good pitch. I had never faced him, but J.D. [Drew, hitting before him] swung at the first pitch for a hit, so I figured I could be aggressive."

"I had not given up a homer in my previous four starts," Pavano said, "but then I hadn't faced the greatest home run hitter in history. I didn't even have to be in the game, but our bullpen is shot, and they've bailed me out all year. I tried to jam him inside with a high fastball, but he's so strong he just turned on it and crushed it."

Now Pavano goes down in the fraternal order of scarlet letter pitchers victimized by historic home runs: Tom Zachary (Ruth's 60th), Al Downing (Aaron's 755th), Tracy Stallard (Maris's 61st), Ralph Branca (Bobby Thomson's 1951).

"Of course my name is going to be forever associated with his," Pavano said. "But I've got all winter to forget it."

Right. Just like McGwire's got all winter to comprehend what he has achieved.

"I can't believe I did it," McGwire said. "Can you? It blows me away. I think it will stand for a while. I know how grueling it was for me to do it."

Perhaps it was Expos manager Felipe Alou who said it best, though. "I'm glad this season is over," Alou said. "The way he was swinging, he was on his way to 80."

ORIOLES' CUBA TRIP OPENS OLD WOUNDS

MARCH 28, 1999

HAVANA—When he heard the news that State Department poobahs had given their blessing to this historic journey by the Orioles to Castro's Cuba, Frank Verdi closed his eyes and felt the bullet grazing his temple all over again.

"It's funny," said Verdi, "it was 40 years ago, but I feel like it was yesterday. It's all still so vivid in my mind."

He is 72 now, living in reluctant retirement in Florida after more than 50 years in baseball as a player, coach, manager and scout. He only made it into one game in the big leagues, with the Yankees in 1953, so the Brooklyn-born Verdi never exactly got to be a household name in baseball.

But he has a place in history. On July 25, 1959, he inadvertently became the cause celebre who touched off the chain of events that eventually led to U.S. organized baseball pulling out of Cuba.

On the weekend of July 24-26, 1959, Verdi's Rochester Red Wings team of the International League was playing a four-game series against the Havana Sugar Kings.

Prior to the Friday night game, Fidel Castro entertained a capacity Gran Stadium crowd by showing off his curveball in a two-inning pitching exhibition. Gran Stadium was a virtual armed fortress that day, as it had been ever since Castro's revolution had overthrown the Batista government a year earlier, with fatigue-garbed infantrymen stationed all around the ballpark.

"I wasn't even on the active roster," Verdi said by phone from his home in Florida. "I had been beaned four weeks earlier and I was still suffering dizzy spells. But I didn't want to miss the trip to Havana, so I served as a bullpen coach, warming up the pitchers.

"Well, in the Saturday night game, we're winning 4-2 in the ninth inning when, with two outs and a man on first, this big first baseman for the Sugar Kings, Borregio Alvarez, hits a home run to tie the score.

"Now we go into extra innings. But at 12 o'clock, all of a sudden all these guns start going off. Bullets were flying out of the sky everywhere, thousands of 'em. We didn't know what the hell was happening. Only later did we learn July 26 was their independence day, the anniversary of the revolution. Players were diving for cover everywhere. There was a Jeep that was used for driving the pitchers in from the bullpen, and that's where I took cover with a bunch of other guys.

"After about five minutes, it all subsided and the game resumed. Needless to say, we were pretty uneasy. Then in the 10th inning, our manager, Cot Deal, got thrown out of the game, and I was asked to coach third base. To this day, I'll always be grateful for the fact that, because of the beaning, I wore a protective inner liner in my cap. With two out, Dick Rand hit a grounder to short for us. Leo Cardenas, the Kings' shortstop, fielded it, threw to first and I started walking off the field. I turned to the outfield and *bang!* down I went. All I could think of is that I got hit by Alvarez's throw back to third base! The third base umpire is standing over me, yelling 'Frank! Frank! Are you all right?' I felt this burning pain on the side of me head and thought I'd been beaned again. Then they

Minor-leaguer Frank Verdi was hit by two bullets during a game in Havana in 1959. (Daily News)

found the .45-caliber bullet lying next to me."

It turned out Cardenas was also struck in the shoulder by an errant bullet, and the next day the reports of two ballplayers being hit by bullets in Cuba was front-page news in the U.S. Meanwhile, the incident prompted International League president Frank Shaughnessy to cancel the Sunday doubleheader between Rochester and Havana. The Red Wings fled the island.

"My mother was home in Bay Shore watching TV when the news came over that a ballplayer had been shot in Cuba," Verdi said, chuckling. "Then she saw that ballplayer was me! Meanwhile, I was on the radio cursing Castro to the UPI."

Despite heavy pressure on Sugar Kings owner Bobby Maduro to move the team out of Cuba, they finished the '59 season and actually won the IL championship.

But the following July, when Castro declared Cuba to be a Communist state and began confiscating all U.S. properties, Maduro had no choice but to move the team to Jersey City, where they were renamed the Reds. On July 13, 1960, the Buffalo Bisons flew out of Havana amid huge, black clouds of smoke billowing from the U.S. oil refineries blown up by Castro.

That was the last sight of Havana by the last U.S. team to play in Cuba until today.

Loss by Birds Would Have Launched Crisis

March 29, 1999

HAVANA—The charter flight that took the Baltimore Orioles out of Castro's Cuba to the U.S. mainland last night was fueled by a huge sigh of relief.

Until Jesse Orosco finished the most important ballgame of his life since Game 7 of the 1986 World Series, Peter Angelos's goodwill ambassadors had done more for Cuban morale than they probably would have liked. The final score, Capitalists 3, Communists 2, was that close a call for Bud Selig and Co.

After all, Selig took such pains to say how sensitive he was to all the outraged Cuban-Americans who failed to see any benefit except to Castro in this first trip to the island in 40 years by a major league team. Imagine if the Orioles had come all this way, broken down all these barriers, only to lose?

For one thing, we probably would have had our second manager firing of the spring, but now, thanks to the unlikely baserunning acumen of Will Clark, Ray Miller will probably get at least a couple of weeks of the regular season to convince Angelos he's got the Birds headed in the right direction. Indeed, the Cubans could learn something about fundamental, alert baseball from the sloth-like Clark, who nevertheless hustled himself into scoring position for the winning run in the 11th inning.

Maybe the Cubans did some unorthodox things because, for them, there truly was no tomorrow. We can only imagine what Fidel Castro, sitting directly behind home plate, clad in his game-day fatigues and flanked by Selig and Angelos, must have thought when his manager, Alfonso Urquiola, intentionally walked Clark with two outs and Brady Anderson on second in the eighth to pitch to Albert Belle!

If El Presidente second-guessed that one, he wasn't alone.

But Bad Albert managed to make Urquiola's move look inspired by rapping into a double play to end the inning.

In the first inning, however, the Cubans paid for showing no respect for Belle, the apprentice right fielder. With nobody out and a runner at first, Luis Ulicia was thrown out attempting to stretch a single into a double. Who knows? If the Cubans hadn't run themselves out of that inning, this might have turned out to be a lot more than just a spectacle. As it is, the impressive, 30-team major league scouting delegation is probably chipping in for a raft for the Cuban reliever Jose Ariel Contreras, who positively stifled the O's batters, striking out 10 over eight shutout innings.

"I usually have a habit of underestimating events," Anderson said. "But in this case, I'm certain our game was the most important game being played today. If nothing else, non-baseball fans who wouldn't be attracted were, because of the circumstances and the attention it's gotten."

Meanwhile, taking it all in from his seat in the dignitaries section behind the plate, 87-year-old Connie Marrero, who had amazed everyone with his ceremonial first-pitch sequence of eight deliveries, beamed with pride at Contreras's performance. For before El Duque, El Tiante and Camilo Pascual, there was Marrero, El Pimero. He was the Satchel Paige of Cuba. He was 38 years old and past his prime by the time he finally arrived in the majors with the old Washington Senators in 1950. But unlike all the others in that last wave of pre-revolution Cubans to come to the majors—Minnie Minoso, Sandy Consuegra—Willie Miranda Marrero returned to his Communist homeland and has remained here to serve as a pitching instructor for all the Cuban teams.

"For me," Marrero said, "this is special. I have not seen a major league team in 40 years. Since I was once part of this, I feel enhanced. I stayed here because my parents were here and they were old. I never made much money playing baseball—$6,500 my first year with the Senators to a top salary of $18,000. This, what I do now, is more rewarding. Baseball is my life. It's in my soul."

It is anyone's guess when another major league team will come to Cuba. Critics of this trip who said it would do more for Castro than for America were probably right. It was a pretty terrific ballgame that came precariously close to raising Cuban morale on this decayed and decrepit island to a level even El Presidente couldn't have imagined.

CHAPTER 8

TRAGEDIES AND TRAVESTIES

I know I'll never forget the night I got a call in my spring training hotel room from my office informing me of the Cleveland Indians' boat tragedy that had just moved on the wires. A tough few days in what is ordinarily the best time of the year for a baseball writer. ...Of all the pieces I've done for *The News*, the one on Tony Horton gave me the most satisfaction, if only because it had been in the back of my mind to pursue for over 10 years. When I was a cub reporter at UPI, Shelby Whitfield, the writer and broadcaster in Washington, D.C., had told me about Horton's breakdown and how baseball had covered it up. I just didn't have the resources then to go after it. ...Poor Darryl Strawberry. If only the tax evasion stories I broke about him were the worst of his life's transgressions. Through it all, though, I've always liked him.

Guidry's $4M Comeback

DECEMBER 16, 1984

LAFAYETTE, La.—Across the Vermillion River, just south of the hub of this peaceful Bayou city, the Bank of Lafayette is situated amid a large complex of Gulf and Exxon office buildings commonly referred to by townfolks as "the energy center." It is here, about as far away as one could imagine from the pitcher's mound of Yankee Stadium, that Ron Guidry has begun the biggest comeback of his life.

It is a comeback that, happily, can now be termed successful, but one that began long before Guidry's frustrating, injury-plagued "season of lost lightning" this past summer. It is a comeback not from too many lost ballgames, but, rather, from too many lost ventures. It is a comeback from debt, the depths of which, Guidry's friends now concede, reached nearly $4 million.

It was almost exactly three years ago—December 15, 1981—that Guidry ended a much-ballyhooed six-week flirtation with free agency and re-signed with the Yankees for a four-year, $3.9 million contract. There was also an option year to the contract, but on the day of the official signing, Guidry's agent and lifelong pal from Lafayette, John Schneider, proclaimed to the assembled media masses: "In all likelihood, this will be Ron's final contract as a major league pitcher. It is our feeling that he probably wouldn't want to pitch beyond the age of 36—which he'll turn in 1986— and this contract assures him that he won't have to. It will make Ron and his wife Bonnie set for life."

And by all rights it should have—just as surely as one presumes all the other multi-million dollar contracts signed since by a multitude of free agents have meant lifelong security. But as Guidry sadly discovered, almost too late, millions earned can quickly become millions lost if not invested wisely.

He discovered it on Nov. 12, 1983, Bonnie Guidry's birthday. Ron Guidry walked into the offices of "Ron Guidry Enterprises Corp." in Lafayette, which had authorization over his assets. Among the enterprises the corporation manages are public relations endeavors and contracts with Puma and Wilson sporting goods companies, plus endorsements and official Yankee appearances. The corporation also serves as a vehicle from which Guidry established his own personal pension.

On this day—according to Reggie Ringuet, a Lafayette accountant who has taken over the management of Guidry's finances—he had come to arrange for the $200,000 payment due on the pension. He was informed that there were no assets remaining in the corporation. "That," says Ringuet, "was the day the bottom fell out for Ron."

Unbeknown to Guidry, the bottom had been gradually falling out for months. Almost immediately after negotiating the $4 million contract with the Yankees, the money was being invested as fast as it was coming in. There was a cleaners equipment business, some real estate, a photo studio on Long Island, and, most notably, the Munro Tool Co.

"The tool company, which essentially leased oil drilling supplies, was owned by a guy named Michael Munro," explains a Guidry friend. "A deal was put together for Ron in which he bought into it."

Later, Guidry ended up as the sole owner.

The fortunes of Ron Guidry and Lafayette are tightly interwoven. Thoughts

Ron Guidry sends a pitch to the plate in 1988. (Keith Torrie/Daily News)

of high finance and its trappings, however, seem distinctly out of place on a recent Sunday in Lafayette. It is 1 p.m. and crowds are beginning to flock into the center of town in anticipation of the annual Christmas parade, rained out a week earlier. Business in Don's Seafood, one of the most popular eateries along East Vermillion St., does not appear to be affected by the festivities a block away. There are only a few empty tables.

"You should have seen it on a Sunday here a few years ago," a waiter relates. "They'd be standing in line to get in. But that was before the oil business went bust."

"The city of Lafayette has been struggling the past few years, no question about it," says Hank Perret, an attorney friend of Ron Guidry's. "When the oil business went to pieces, the economy here was hurt badly. People just aren't drilling any more. In the last 24 months, there have been more bankruptcies in Lafayette than there have been in the last 30 years and it figures to get worse. At the height of things, in 1980-81, the sky was the limit. Oil was up to $40 a barrel. Now it's down to $27-$28."

It was when the oil business was beginning its decline that Guidry bought out the other partners in Munro Tool. The company had borrowed enormous amounts of money to purchase drilling equipment, but now no one was leasing it. And the notes were coming due.

"By then," Ringuet explains, "Ron was coming to the realization that he had no assets. He knew he had this debt, but he didn't know he had *all* of it."

Being informed that the pension monies were gone that November day in 1983 opened Guidry's eyes. His first step was to hire an attorney, Perret, who arranged the formation of the Yankee Tool Co. in order to liquidate the debts accrued by the Munro Tool Co. Not long after that, Ringuet was hired to lend his expertise with the six banks that were calling in all their notes—the total of which had reached nearly $4 million.

By now, the 1984 season was beginning. In early May, word filtered about the Yankee clubhouse that Guidry had severed connections with Schneider. While news of the parting of such good friends was greeted with mild surprise, no one certainly connected it with Guidry's subpar pitching—which would eventually result in his first losing season (11-12) and first-ever ERA of over 4.00 (4.51).

And Guidry did not discuss it. The most private and aloof of all the Yankees—he can be found sitting all by himself reading a book and enjoying a good chew in his corner locker before almost every game—Guidry bore his burden alone.

"It was kind of hard for me to resolve things when I wasn't home," Guidry says now. "I couldn't very well take time out from the season and go home, but there wasn't much sense in talking about it either.

"I don't know if it affected my pitching. It was something I just tried to put out of my mind—especially when I would go out to the mound. Now whether my subconscious took over and wouldn't allow me to put the pitches where I wanted them, I don't know. I know this, when I was out there, I wasn't thinking about being a million dollars in debt."

Guidry was, however, thinking about his burden almost every waking minute he was not pitching. And he was doing something about it, too.

"The thing you have to understand," says Ringuet, "is that Ron could have walked away from this thing very easily and just said 'to hell with it.' He could have declared bankruptcy and all his income would have been exempt from the moment of filing. But he wanted to pay back everything he possibly could."

Guidry thus instructed Ringuet to attempt to arrange an honorable way out of his mess. The accountant began a series of negotiations to work out settlements with the five Louisiana banks whose notes were past due. Then, a meeting with Yankee owner George Steinbrenner was set up and another set of negotiations began with Citibank in New York. "The Citibank people were super, absolutely super," says Ringuet. "They were what made the recovery possible. They understood the problem completely and believed that Ron was the victim here and not the villain."

It is not entirely clear how much of a role Steinbrenner played in the Citibank negotiations, although it is known the Yankee owner was deeply concerned about his star pitcher's desperate situation.

"George has always considered Guidry a 'true Yankee,'" says a high-level Yankee insider. "There were a number of times last year, especially when the club was going bad, that other clubs come to us and asked about the availability of Guidry in a trade. On each occasion, George intervened and insisted that

Guidry was not available under any circumstances. It was George's feeling that, if the debts weren't cleared up, other clubs wouldn't take care of Guidry."

"Essentially what George told me was 'If you can remedy it, remedy it, but don't run away from it,'" Guidry relates.

Which is what has happened. Though he concedes "we had some tense moments." Ringuet was able to work out settlements with the banks. He would not discuss the specifics of those settlements, but a source familiar with the negotiations estimates that "between $2.5 and $3 million" was paid back to the banks.

"Fortunately," says Ringuet, "we were able to accumulate money from Ron's income and we also used his personal pension—which was exempt under law—to help resolve his problems. There was also money in Ron's and Bonnie's personal accounts which was used. I can tell you today that Ron Guidry is no longer in debt and his future is secure again. But for the past year and half, he and Bonnie have been through hell. He was distraught and extremely depressed over everything that had happened."

At least there is a happy ending. The financial impact of Guidry's Yankee contract was such that he could bail himself out of $4 million of debt and probably still not have to pitch beyond 1986. According to Ringuet, even with the huge losses and paybacks to the banks, Guidry, Bonnie and their two children can look forward to retirement and a relatively prosperous life beyond 1986.

"But I think," says Ringuet, "that Ron genuinely *wants* to pitch beyond this contract and it has nothing to do with recouping anything. The fact of the matter is, Ron Guidry is no longer in the oil business. He's a pitcher."

Day of Ugliness and Death

December 10, 1992

LOUISVILLE—The final, emotional day of the grimmest winter baseball meetings in history began with Marge Schott delivering a backhanded apology for all the insensitive racist remarks attributed to her over the last few weeks.

A few hours later, Carl Barger, 62, president of the Florida Marlins and longstanding outspoken critic of the spiraling salary structure that is threatening to bankrupt small-market teams, collapsed outside the owners' meeting after suffering a ruptured aneurysm in his abdomen and died at Humana University Hospital without regaining consciousness.

It took Scott Boras, agent for Greg Maddux, to put everything back into perspective by announcing at 9:15 that his client had finally signed with the Atlanta Braves in a $28 million deal "in which the money was secondary."

You listened to Boras spewing his lies and Schott telling us what a great humanitarian she really is, and then you thought of Barger being carted out of the hotel on a stretcher right in front of you, his face purple with death, and somehow baseball didn't seem like such a wonderful game any more. You wanted to cry for Barger and take a bath for Schott and Boras.

George Steinbrenner, who was banned by his fellow owners from attending these meetings, was home in Tampa when his minions informed him that Maddux had spurned their $34 million offer for the Braves' $28 million. He knew, however, that Boras had told his people that $37 million would get the deal done, and he couldn't help but laugh when told the agent said the money was secondary.

"All I know," Steinbrenner said, "is that I don't want a guy who says he has to take $10 million more to come to New York. He doesn't deserve New York."

By the time Boras finally got around to realizing his scam to use the Yankees to get *someone* up to $30 million for Maddux had failed, most everyone had gone home.

Jimmy Leyland went home Tuesday, and yesterday he was walking out the door to head for the Pittsburgh airport for an emergency return trip with Barger's fiancée, Maureen, when the call came at 3:55 p.m.

It was Barger's secretary, and as he heard her say, "He didn't make it," Leyland trembled.

"I couldn't believe it...I still can't believe it," Leyland said by phone, unable to keep his emotions in check. "I had just talked to him yesterday at the meetings and he looked great and his spirits were up.

"This breaks my heart. He was one of my closest friends. We're going to have our second child next year and Carl had agreed to be the godfather—even if it meant converting to a Catholic. He told me he had even gone to see a priest last week to find out how to go about it."

As Barger's close friends and baseball associates all knew, though, the symptoms of such a sudden end were there: a chain smoker with high blood pressure and a Type A personality. And from almost the day he came into baseball as general counsel for the Pittsburgh Pirates in 1987, Barger seemed to find himself embroiled in high-stress controversy.

His firing of Syd Thrift as Pirates GM touched off a tempest in Pittsburgh that didn't subside for nearly a year. Throughout his three and a half-year tenure as Pirates president, he was easily the most outspoken of all baseball executives about the rising salaries.

Even after his not-so-sweet parting with the Pirates in July '91 to take over as president of the expansion Marlins, Barger was in the forefront of those owners calling for revenue sharing to save small-market franchises like Pittsburgh from extinction.

Ironically, on the day before he died, the baseball owners doled out a record $125 million in contracts. Even Barger's Marlins got into the act, signing Dave Magadan for $1.7 million.

"[That] was the happiest day Carl had had with us," a tearful Marlins GM Dave Dombrowski said. "We were all together celebrating the fact that we had been able to sign a couple of free agents. It meant so much to him—a sign of accomplishment that we could sign players to our team."

Indeed, the Marlins were ready to announce another signing yesterday—All-Star catcher Benito Santiago for $3.4 million—but now that will have to wait. The Marlin contingent, led by Dombrowski, left the media headquarters room in shock after making their emotional announcement.

Across the walkway on the east side of the Galt House, the owners had cut short their meeting and, even though there still was one more chapter of sleaze to be played out, these meetings had effectively ended in gloom.

There are those, however, who might suggest a pall had hung over them from the very outset. Schott, Boras—and Barger—merely ratified that.

RITES OF SPRING LEAD TWO TO DEATH'S DOOR

MARCH 24, 1993

WINTER HAVEN, Fla.— Joe Bick, the agent for Steve Olin, was heading out the door of his Tampa hotel room to meet a few of his other clients for dinner when the phone rang shortly before 9:30 Monday night.

The caller was Patti Olin, who was remarkably composed although she had devastating news for Bick.

"There's been an accident," she began, and Bick instinctively felt numb. "After that," he said, "came the most feared words after you hear *those* words."

Steve Olin was dead.

Some nine hours later, Tim Crews was dead, too.

Death seems far removed from spring training, a time linked more to rebirth, renewal, hope and optimism—not death or finality.

But at that awful moment for Joe Bick, that's what Patti Olin was talking about. Her husband's death. In a boating accident...across the lake...drove under a dock...killed.

"I was amazed at how composed she was," Bick said. "I suppose she was in shock, but she was talking coherently. There was a lot of crying, but she kept going. We talked for about a half hour. What about? Family-related details. I asked her about his parents. I guess there was a lot of silence."

It was the Indians' only off day of the spring. Crews had this house on Little Lake Nellie— actually it was more like a "ranch atmosphere," according to Indians general manager John Hart. There were horses to ride and fishing and boating, and Crews had invited Steve and Patti Olin and Bobby and Ellen Ojeda and their families for an afternoon outing. Fernando Montes, the Indians' strength and condition coach, was there, too.

"Steve came close to not going," Bick said, "because he

had trouble finding the place. Apparently, he overshot the road that turns into the place. But he kept going back and looking for it because he had promised his three-year-old girl [Alexa] she could ride a horse."

They say that's the kind of guy Steve Olin was. Devoted father and family man. One of the most popular players on the Cleveland Indians. Unassuming leader of the bullpen. He was, as Hart said, "an integral part of the club, both on the field and as part of the Cleveland Indians family."

"He and Patti bought a house in Cleveland this winter even though they lived in the Northwest [Vancouver, Washington]," Bick said. "They wanted to be part of the community where he pitched. They never got to live in it."

It all happened so suddenly. One minute Olin and Crews are playing with their kids, grilling steaks and enjoying the good life of a young professional ballplayer in spring training. Ten minutes later, Olin is dead and Crews is dying in a blood-splattered boat that has come to rest under a dock across the lake.

"The wives were up at the house with the kids when one of the other wives came running up shouting there'd been an accident," said Indians vice president of public relations Bob DiBiasio. "Somebody took them

around the lake to the scene, but they wouldn't let Patti near the boat."

Somehow, Patti Olin, who also has six-month-old twins, called Bick to report the tragedy. Her husband was only 27, now forever 27, not even in the prime of his career, much less of his life.

"I was glad Patti didn't ask me to drive out there to Winter Haven," Bick said. "I couldn't have done it. I wasn't in much condition to even hang onto the phone.

"I drove over to the restaurant, the Tex-Mex place, where a bunch of players from the Phillies were waiting for me. They had already ordered. When I told them what happened, they just got up from their tables and left their plates full. We were all sick."

As Indians legend Bob Feller, a veteran of nearly 50 spring trainings, said: "When something like this happens, it makes baseball very insignificant—like with the earthquake."

And even though the season will go on as it always has, spring training will never again be thought of entirely as a time of rebirth. Not now that death has made its unwelcome intrusion into it.

"We'll get over this because we have to," said Indians manager Mike Hargrove. "But I don't know about the Olin and Crews families."

To Hell and Back

Nearly 18 years ago, Bernardo (Bernie) Carbo hit the second most memorable home run in Boston Red Sox World Series history and shouted to Pete Rose as he rounded third base: "Isn't this great? Don't you wish you could hit like this?"

That Bernie Carbo was a fun-loving free spirit who brought a certain irreverence to a game that had always come so easy for him. Or so everyone thought.

When Carbo was winning Rookie of the Year honors or hitting the game-tying three-run homer that set up Carlton Fisk's 12th-inning deciding shot in the classic sixth game of the '75 World Series, no one knew of the demons that raged within him.

To a large extent, Carbo didn't know, either, since he had managed to block many of them out with drugs, booze and pills. Only after baseball discarded him into an empty life on the other side of the cheers did they begin in engulf him.

The day after last Christmas, Carbo sat in his apartment in Winter Haven, Florida, and decided his was a life that was no longer worth living. The parents he hardly knew in his adolescence had died within three months of each other, his mother a suicide. His second wife, Lori, had walked out on him, though not before urging him to get help for his many addictions.

"I had just read where [former Red Sox teammate] Fergie Jenkins's girlfriend had committed suicide and taken his baby girl with her," Carbo told the *Daily News* the other day. "I knew his first wife had died after a car accident, and this hit me real hard. I just kept drinking and sitting on the floor, crying."

In the midst of his crisis, Carbo called Bill Lee, another

former Red Sox teammate, and told him he had reached the end. Lee, in turn, called Jenkins, while another call was put in to the Baseball Assistance Team (BAT).

"Fergie was the first to call me," Carbo related. "I said to him: 'I want to check out, Fergie. I just don't want to live anymore. I'm heading out.' Then Fergie said: 'If I can go on after all that has happened to me, you have to be there too.'"

Shortly afterward, former Indians and Giants pitcher Sam McDowell (a recovering alcoholic) called from BAT, and the next day Carbo checked into a care unit in Tampa.

"I look back and I get chills. I see a grave at the bottom of a hill with a skeleton in it reaching out and that skeleton is me saying 'Come back, come back.' I can say without any doubt BAT saved my life."

But not immediately. First, Carbo had to come to grips with the rage that burned within him and all that had brought him to the brink of self-destruction.

It began with what Carbo now described as "my period of abandonment," when he was six years old and his parents moved away from his aunt and uncle, who had taken care of him since birth. Because his parents both worked, Carbo seldom saw them,

and when he did, they were usually fighting. Eventually, they separated and divorced, and Bernie lived with his mother in Florida.

"I remember up until I was about 12 years old, every year at Halloween my mother always had me dress up as a girl," Carbo recalled. "I never understood that. It wasn't until later that I knew she had been one of eight children and grew up never having her own clothes or her own doll. I guess maybe in her eyes I became a substitution for that."

While relating this to a counselor at the care unit, it was suggested that Carbo needed to make a male bonding. This pursuit unleashed one of those long-suppressed demons.

"I heard her use those words, and all of a sudden I felt cold," Carbo said. "I remembered when I was seven years old, I was in the bathroom taking a bath when one of my cousins came in and invaded my privacy. He wanted me to do everything to him that he had just done to me.

"All my life I had always hated men as a result of that incident, but I never knew why."

If anything, he thought it was because of his father who, he felt, resented his success as a major league ballplayer.

"My father had played in the old St. Louis Browns' minor league system, but when the war came, he gave his career up," Carbo said. "In his eyes, he always hit better than I did, and he wouldn't allow himself to give me any credit for what I did. In 1989, though, I finally got close to him when I went up to Livonia, Michigan, to help him coach a high school team. That's when my mother got upset. She didn't want that to happen. I told her to please not get involved, but she drank a bottle of Roto-Rooter fluid and eventually died after 45 days.

"I blamed my father for her death, and we didn't talk much after that. Three months later, he died and I began doing cocaine, marijuana, pills…anything I could get my hands on."

The drugs, booze and, especially the pills, he says, were a byproduct of his baseball career. At 17, he was signed by the Reds as a No. 1 draft pick and sent to Class A Tampa.

"I was playing with a lot of older guys, and call it peer pressure if you want, I started drinking to be one of them," he said. "It got so I would show up at the ballpark drunk. It wasn't until the next year that Sparky Anderson, my manager at Asheville (North Carolina), called me into his office and told me I was drinking too much and that he was going to stop it. He made me come out to the park from 9 to 11 every morning and then again in the afternoon from the 3 to 5."

A year later, Carbo was in the big leagues and on his way to Rookie of the Year honors in 1970, a season in which he hit .310 with 21 homers for the National League champion Reds. Late in the year, however, a sore arm, a strained leg muscle and overall fatigue from having played baseball the year 'round prompted him to ask for a rest.

"In those days, you just didn't take time off," he said. "Instead, the trainer game me what he called 'vitamins'—dexadrine, benzadrine, Darvon and codeine. Plus they were shooting me with cortisone. The first time I took them I felt like I could run through the fence. Then, because of all the uppers, I couldn't sleep at night, so they gave me sleeping pills.

"We used to have a running joke that we could 'out-milligram' the other teams."

As he reflects, Carbo describes baseball as "mean as the devil" and "the house that Satan built."

"The owners knew the trainers were giving us drugs.

Their attitude was just trade 'em to cover it up. At the end, I was a 32-year-old druggie who had been traded seven times. I was out of the game, still doing drugs, and for a while I was even selling them to other players and sportswriters."

Only after much therapy and a rebirth to Christianity was Carbo able to forgive baseball and see it—and his career—for the positive.

A neighbor in Winter Haven, Karl Schilling, helped. Schilling, a Brooklyn Tech product from Jamaica, Queens, coaches baseball at Warner College, a small Christian school in nearby Lake Wells, Florida Together, with Carbo, he created the Diamond Club Ministry, a vehicle from which they conduct free baseball clinics at schools, churches and even prisons around the country. Or, as Carbo says, "Wherever God calls us."

This is Bernie Carbo today. Free of drugs, free of booze and pills, and, at last, free of the pain of a tormented and broken childhood. All of that, he has "left at the foot of the cross" with the help of God. His sole means of support is a $24,000-per-year pension, but his life has never been richer.

"I had such rage, 45 years of it, there must have been 150 people I wanted to kill."

Now he only wants to help people. He will teach them about baseball, but more than anything he can tell them about life, about how precious it is and how no life should be a wasted one.

"Nobody wants to talk about drugs or alcohol or sex abuse or suicide even though these are the four biggest things affecting kids today," Carbo said. "Well, I can talk about them because I've lived all of them. I've already been to hell and come out."

Luciano: The Ump Always Wore a Mask

He was a true clown prince of baseball, a man of laughter and conviviality, which is why Ron Luciano's suicide last Wednesday seemed so incongruous and utterly senseless to those who only saw that side of him.

It wasn't the same on the other, dark side of the camera, away from the public glare, where, presumably, the phone had stopped ringing.

"It doesn't surprise me that Ronnie was very depressed," said Joe Garagiola, who was instrumental in luring Luciano off the field and into the NBC television booth in 1980. "There was a far more sensitive side of him that few people knew, and I know he was a lonely guy. Everybody thought every day was New Year's Eve for him, but I can attest to the fact that he had a lot of August the twenty-thirds and October the fifths."

When news of Luciano's death spread throughout the baseball community last week, the first thoughts were of the laughter he brought to the game. Those who knew him best—his umpiring crewmates, Bill Haller and Davey Phillips, and Garagiola, with whom he worked for two years in the NBC booth—all wanted to recount the laughs for which he'll be remembered. But as Garagiola observed sadly, this wasn't who he really was or what he was really all about.

"I know he was hurting being out of baseball," Garagiola said. "He needed to be around people and he missed it. I loved him. He was one of the few umpires who didn't act like he was anointed. I *wanted* to see him call a guy out. Baseball wasn't High Mass to him."

Phillips, who went to umpire school with Luciano in 1964 and then worked alongside him in the American League in 1973 and '74, said he never laughed so hard as he did those two years. "But to be honest," he said, "I don't think he really liked umpiring. I think maybe he was really lonely, but he camouflaged a lot of it because he worked *hard* to be funny.

"I'll never forget one game—true story—I'm umpiring at first base and I look down to the plate where Ronnie is and he's not wearing his mask! Campy Campaneris is the batter and he's attempting to drag bunt and the pitcher is winding up when I start running toward the plate to call time out. Campy bunts the ball foul and sees me and thinks I'm calling *him* out. All of sudden, both managers, Kenny Aspromonte and Chuck Tanner, are running out of the dugout and I go over to Ronnie and tell him he has no mask on.

"You know what he said? 'I *knew* I was seeing the pitches good!'"

Umpire Ron Luciano mugs for the camera. (Daily News)

As Luciano's crew chief, Haller can't begin to count the number of times he had to respond to queries from the AL office on Luciano's antics. In one game, Luciano decided to station himself in center field, right next to Tigers center fielder Mickey Stanley. Another time, when he was assigned to a series in Texas, where Billy Martin (with whom he was feuding at the time) was managing the Rangers, he stayed in his hotel room for the entire three days. He could get in trouble with his mouth, too, as when he was asked who he thought would win the pennant one year and replied: "I don't care, as long as it's not Baltimore."

"He hated [Earl] Weaver, and [Jim] Palmer, too," Haller said. "He was a character, but the American League didn't know what to do with him. They allowed him to do some things that were totally unprofessional. Ron was one of the nicest men I ever knew, but the act got in his way."

When Luciano left umpiring to go to NBC, Phillips remembered, he joked that "they were popping champagne in the American League offices after all the turmoil I caused for [AL president Lee] MacPhail."

He may not have been wrong. In all probability, the baseball establishment was relieved to see Luciano leave the field on his own. He would have been awfully hard to fire. Baseball fans loved him, and for the first few years after his retirement they continued to love him through his three very funny books about his umpiring days.

Ultimately, though, Ron Luciano ran out of funny stories. He went home to Endicott, New York, far from the klieg lights and arc lights, and seldom heard from any of his baseball friends. Garagiola suspected he was hurting.

Luciano's final call pretty much confirmed that.

RICHARD REVISITED

There's a big guy in Houston who used to throw a baseball harder than any man alive, until one day, like David Cone, a problem developed in his circulatory system. The difference is that nobody believed J.R. Richard when he said his arm was tired, and because they didn't it almost killed him.

"I guess you could say I was the stepping stone to where they are now with these kind of things," Richard said by phone yesterday. "With me, they didn't give a [expletive]. They thought I was superhuman. 'Your arm is tired; it's not supposed to be bothering you.'"

Sixteen years later, Richard remains one of baseball's biggest shames. At six foot eight with a fastball that routinely topped 100 mph, he was the most imposing and intimidating pitcher in the game. They did think he was superhuman, too perfect a physical specimen to feel tired or weak.

On the afternoon of June 17, 1980 at Wrigley Field, he began to experience deadness in his arm. Fans, the media and even some teammates accused him of everything from dogging it to being jealous of teammate Nolan Ryan's lucrative contract. There were implications he was into drugs.

When he made his next start 11 days later and gave up five runs in three and a third innings, one Houston columnist wrote: "James Rodney Richard's right arm got better Saturday night. It improved from 'dead' to 'tired.' If this convalescence continues at the current pace, his arm may be 'puny' by the next time he pitches."

But that, of course, was only a small part of the shame baseball must forever bear when it comes to the sad story of J.R. Richard.

On July 16, he went on the disabled list and the Astros' physician gave him a clean bill of health, pronouncing the circulation in his pitching arm "excellent." The physician, Harold Brelsford, explained he didn't X-ray Richard's arteries "because you only do that if you have good reason."

A week later, Richard checked himself into a hospital and underwent tests that revealed an occlusion in an artery leading into his arm. Incredibly, doctors told him the clot presented no danger and gave him the OK to resume pitching.

On July 30, after an 11-minute workout at the Astrodome, Richard became dizzy and collapsed on the turf, the victim of a major stroke. He was only 30, two years removed from becoming the first National League right-hander in history to strike out 300 batters in a season.

Which makes it easy to understand why Bob Watson, Richard's teammate on the Astros, inadvertently described Cone's condition the other night as "life-threatening." It took the near-death of one of its biggest and brightest stars for baseball to conclude that numbness and weakness and anything remotely resembling a circulation problem are not things to take lightly.

"I would love to talk to David Cone," Richard said. "I would tell him: 'It was the same situation with me, but don't worry, you're going to be OK.' They caught him early when he could have been dying.

"What they could not explain to me was how this thing started in my arm and why a piece of it broke off and lodged in my neck, cutting off the flow of blood to the brain. Cone needs to know that he'll be fine and that he'll pitch again. Just don't be in no hurry."

If Cone does pitch again, he can look at Richard and feel especially lucky, considering he pitched a complete game with his aneurysm. After having the clot removed from the juncture of two arteries in his neck, Richard made what can only be considered a miraculous comeback. Seven months later, he was working out again and made it back into professional baseball, pitching for the Astros' Class-A team in 1982. But a year later, the Astros released him after he suffered shoulder problems. The flame that struck out 616 batters in the 1978 and '79 seasons had burned out.

Richard later sued three of his doctors and received a $2 million out-of-court settlement. As far as baseball was concerned, though, he was someone everyone wanted to forget. According to him, even Watson, his old teammate, turned his back on him.

"I tried numerous times to get back in the game," he said. "I thought I had a lot to offer as a pitching instructor or in public relations. When I called Bob a couple of years ago when he was the Astros' GM, he told me his hands were tied but that he'd have [team president] Tal Smith call me when he got to the office. I guess Tal Smith never made it to the office.

"I've learned to take it with a grain of salt, that people will keep lying to you until you start believing it."

Bitter as he is over baseball's treatment, Richard apparently has found peace since being discovered living under a freeway in southwest Houston last year. A couple of weeks after that, a bunch of his Astros teammates threw a benefit for him, and he has begun writing a book and working on a movie of his life.

Asked if he can forgive baseball for what it did to him, Richard sighed, "I guess. What happened to me was a blessing in disguise for other players. But if I hadn't gotten sick, I know Nolan Ryan would have never had that strikeout record. I was getting better every year."

BREAKDOWN

When Pete Harnisch left the Mets under a shroud of mystery two months ago, there was a certain chill to the cryptic team announcement that he was being sent home as he was "unable to perform." Those words suggested there was something far more wrong than just physically.

In Harnisch's case, the doctors since diagnosed him as suffering from depression. If nothing else, his frequent appearances in the Mets' clubhouse have given rise to the belief his condition is not so deep-rooted and he may pitch again one day.

No one really knows what demons lurk within the recesses of a person's mind, and there have been countless professional athletes before Harnisch who have had to combat them in differing degrees. Jimmy Piersall had to be institutionalized, but managed to fight his way back and go on to a successful career. Others, like Willard Hershberger, the Cincinnati Reds catcher who committed suicide in his hotel room in 1940, didn't get help in time. Hershberger was said to be despondent over his inability to cope with the pressure of playing in the major leagues.

And then there is the strange case of Tony Horton, the former Cleveland Indians first baseman whose departure from the game in 1970, just as he was approaching his prime, remains one of baseball's most tragic unsolved mysteries.

Horton was 25 years old, a budding star who had hit 27 homers the previous season, when he left the Indians in late August of that year and never returned. At the time of his departure, it was announced by the Indians that he was suffering from exhaustion and was, as the press release stated even then, "unable to perform."

He was a California golden boy, a strapping six-foot-three, 210-pound three-sport Los Angeles high school star who spurned basketball scholarships from UCLA and USC to sign for a $125,000 bonus with the Boston Red Sox. His size, strength and powerful potential were immediately apparent. In 1963, his first training camp with the Red Sox, Ted Williams observed him hitting in the cage and exclaimed, "This kid is a natural. You don't fool with a swing like that."

And nobody did. For one thing, Horton was something of a loner, his self-absorption prompting others to leave him to his own inner thoughts. "I don't think I ever knew a more intense player than Tony Horton," said then-Indians GM Gabe Paul, whose baseball career spanned more than 50 years.

"I was his first roommate with the Indians, and I had to get away from him," recalled former Indians catcher Duke Sims, now a marketing executive in Las Vegas. "He was just so intense, he couldn't ever relax. The fans in Cleveland, all 5,000 of them in those days, really got to him, too. Most of all, though, his father had an extreme influence on him. He had to talk to him every day."

After a rapid ascension through the Red Sox system, Horton played parts of three seasons in Boston (1964-66), only to be traded to the Indians midway through the 1967 season for pitcher Gary Bell. According to those close to Horton then, the trade came as a shock to him and was the first suggestion of failure.

Yet as an Indian, he began to thrive, actualizing his great potential. After hitting .278 with 27 homers and 93 RBIs in 1969, he held out for a salary of $65,000, or about $19,000 more than what was being offered by Cleveland manager Alvin Dark, who had usurped Paul's GM duties.

"Tony was a stud," remembered ex-Yankee Graig Nettles, a teammate of Horton's with the Indians in 1970. "He was as good a hitter as I ever saw. You figured he was going to have a long and very productive career. But then one day he just went crazy."

That winter, when the Indians refused to even talk about his salary demands, Horton began to brood. Recalled Russell Schneider, a reporter for *The Cleveland Plain Dealer* at the time, it was Dark who fueled Horton's inner frustrations by strongly suggesting that Ken (Hawk) Harrelson was a more than viable first base alternative.

"Dark kept telling Tony that if he didn't sign for what the Indians were offering, they'd just move Harrelson to first," Schneider said. "Finally, Tony gave in and signed for the $46,000 the Indians had offered him. Then, the day after he signed, Harrelson slid into third base in a spring training game and broke his ankle. I don't think Tony ever got over what he perceived to be the gods being against him. In his mind, if he had held out one more day, the Indians wouldn't have had any more leverage."

"I never heard that theory," Dark said when contacted at his home in South Carolina. "I just know we didn't have the money. Then, after Tony did sign, the fans really got on him. From day one that season, he was booed more than the average guy.

"I had no idea they would be so constant in their upset with Tony. He gave everything he had and just couldn't understand why they were booing him. As many times as I was fired, I'd have to say there was nothing more painful for me in baseball as my experience with Tony Horton where a life was almost ruined."

The pressure of wanting to prove he was worth the money he requested took its toll on Horton, who got off to a terrible start in 1970 after arriving three weeks late for spring training. It wasn't until late July that he started to get his swing back, but by then there were more ominous signs he was far more troubled than people had realized.

On June 24 in the ninth inning of a game at Yankee Stadium, Horton was facing Yankee left Steve Hamilton, who was known for his "Folly Floater" blooper pitch. Hamilton threw the pitch only occasionally, but had promised Horton before the game he would throw him one if they faced each other. As it was, he threw him two, the first of which was fouled off. On the second one, Horton swung mightily only to pop up to the catcher. In mock embarrassment, he crawled back to the dugout amid howls of laughter from players on both sides.

"That was just joking on Tony's part, but you could see it building with him that year," said Nettles. "I think he felt he was letting his folks down and that pressured him a lot. Then one day he walked into the clubhouse and looked like a zombie with his eyes set back in his head. [Indians infielder] Larry Brown got with him and Tony was just rambling on. He was gone."

As Dark remembers it, there was a game in Cleveland in mid-August which the Indians won, but as the players started making their way back to the clubhouse, he was tapped on the shoulder by Brown, who pointed to the field where Horton was standing at first base.

"He didn't know the game was over," Dark said. "We had to call him in."

Finally, on August 28, Dark, on the advice of Brown and a couple of other Indians players, removed Horton from the second game of a doubleheader. Sam McDowell, the Indians' ace of that era and currently a drug and alcohol counselor for baseball, recalled how he spent most of that day with Horton. "He was deeply troubled," McDowell said, "asking me what was wrong with him. He was wandering around the clubhouse in his T-shirt, shorts and shower slippers, kind of dazed."

Later that day, Horton went back to the Blue Grass Motel, on the outskirts of Cleveland, where he was living, and attempted to take his own life. Larry Mako, the proprietor of that motel (which has since been torn down), says he will never forget that night.

"One of our security people found Tony sitting in his car in the parking lot around 5 a.m.," Mako said. "He had slit his wrists and he was bleeding profusely. I guess it all just got to him. Back then, the motel was a hangout for a lot of the players, although Tony lived there. Hawk Harrelson would come in the bar at night and get a hero's welcome, and Tony could never understand that. Still, we were all stunned at what happened that last night. We rushed him to the hospital, and that was the last I ever saw of him. A couple of days later, the Indians sent a car over to pick up all of his belongings."

Horton's attempted suicide was never reported. Over the rest of that season and the following off season the Indians issued occasional statements saying he was making progress but wasn't ready to return to baseball. Then there were no more statements. Tony Horton was never heard from again.

"I kept in contact with him for a couple of years after he left," said Texas Rangers scout Mike Paul, who was Horton's last roommate with the Indians. "We exchanged Christmas cards, but gradually it stopped. I've come to accept the fact that Tony doesn't want anything to do with his former baseball life."

"He can't," said McDowell. "From what I understand, the doctors told him he had to completely divorce himself from baseball. Baseball was what drove him to his state. He was so high-strung with such a drive to succeed, and when he wasn't succeeding it set him off. It affected him every time he saw a former teammate or had a connection with baseball."

Probably the last person connected to baseball to talk to Horton was Schneider, who called him in February 1973 for an update on his condition. "He sounded fine," Schneider said, "Until I got around to asking him about baseball. That's when I sensed his voice starting to quiver and he cut me off, saying, 'Baseball is no longer a part of my life, and that's the way I want it.'"

Today, Horton remains intensely private in his second life as a telecommunications businessman in California. When a reporter recently paid a visit to his home in Pacific Palisades, an exclusive suburb of Los Angeles, he was first greeted by Horton's father, who told him bluntly, "He won't want to talk to you."

A couple of minutes later, Horton himself emerged from the carport where a gold Lexus was parked. His hair was silver now, but he looked fit in a gray T-shirt, plaid shorts and a Nike cap.

Upon being informed by his father that a reporter wanted to talk to him, Horton said politely: "I'm not interested. You mean a sports story? I'm definitely not interested."

And with that, Tony Horton disappeared into the seclusion of his house, once again shutting the door on anyone or anything that might remind him of a time when baseball so consumed him it almost killed him.

Los Angeles correspondent Dan Whitcomb contributed to this story.

THIS WAS LAST STRAW FOR BUD

FEBRUARY 29, 2000

TAMPA—In the end, after all the consultations with drug counselors, Tampa law enforcement officials and baseball's legal eagles, Bud Selig concluded there was really only one decision he could render, and that was to issue the death knell to Darryl Strawberry's baseball career.

This is why Selig gets the big bucks from his fellow baseball lords—to make decisions such as this for them, decisions that may very well lead to an even worse fate for Strawberry. But you'll notice that even the union isn't vowing to fight this one.

Everyone involved, from the commissioner, to the union, to the Yankees has nothing but the utmost concern and compassion for Strawberry, an essentially good person who has been unable to escape the lure of one of the worst of all addictions. But in situations such as this, the only way to truly help Strawberry is to offer him no hope.

Call it tough love, if you will. Selig agonized over doling out a one-year suspension without a window of early reinstatement to a 37-year-old designated hitter. But to give him such a chance would have made him an enabler. In drug addiction parlance, there is nothing more harmful to an addict than an enabler.

In a lot of ways, George Steinbrenner has been an enabler for Strawberry too. Steinbrenner thought he was doing the right thing when he rescued Strawberry from baseball's skid row, made a place for him on the Yankees, even over Joe Torre's objections, and then helped him deal with his IRS and child support debts. And when Strawberry breached Steinbrenner's faith last spring by getting busted for solicitation and drug possession at the notorious Tampa crime intersection of

Kennedy and Arrawanda, the Yankee boss took him back again.

There were, of course, the extenuating circumstances of Strawberry's battle with colon cancer. It was a sad case, everyone agreed, and understandable why he might have fallen off the wagon. The union appealed his 120-day suspension, and Selig agreed to reduce it so Straw could return to play in time to join the Yankees for the final month of the season and pocket another hefty World Series check.

No one viewed it that way at the time. They all thought they were doing the humane and compassionate thing for a recovering cancer victim and drug abuser. In retrospect, they realize they were not helping, they were enabling.

That's why there are no lifelines for Strawberry this time. Not from Selig, not from the union, not from Steinbrenner.

Painful as it might be for everyone involved, the time has come for Darryl Strawberry to

Darryl Strawberry discusses his drug problems with the media as Joe Torre looks on. (Linda Cataffo/Daily News)

stop thinking of himself as a baseball player and come to grips with the fact he is a recovering addict. He has to get his life together—the reality being a life without baseball.

No one is deluding themselves; this could go either way.

Today, all of Strawberry's friends and supporters are fearing the worst and hoping for the best. If the depression of cancer, debt and being left alone in Florida to continue his rehab last spring could cause him to go looking for drugs, what will the prospect of never playing again cause him to do?

Believe it, this weighed heaviest of all for Selig. And yet, the commissioner had to do what was best for Strawberry and for baseball. What kind of message would he have sent to either the fans or Strawberry if he had levied anything less than an unconditional one-year suspension?

No one was a more dramatic presence at the plate or more of a natural than Strawberry, and that is one tragedy here. But as Torre noted yesterday, the focus—both ours and Strawberry's—should really be on the human side of this.

In all probability, Strawberry weaning himself off baseball and the glamorous lifestyle it has afforded him will be almost as hard as staying off drugs. But the two go hand-in-hand in this crucial battle for him. Selig, the union and Steinbrenner can only hope Strawberry can rise from the ashes of his baseball career and make a clean life for himself.

The debt, the five kids and one on the way, and the uncertain job prospects may all seem like insurmountable odds against Strawberry now, especially when combined with the drug addiction and constant fear of returning cancer. But baseball did the only thing it could in trying to give him direction yesterday when Selig, the union and Steinbrenner got out of the enabling business.

LUMBER'S IN HALL, HE MAY NOT FOLLOW

So much for that enchanting summer of '98 when Mark McGwire and Sammy Sosa held us in rapture with their spirited chase of Roger Maris's home run record.

It quickly became tainted enough with the revelation that McGwire was using muscle-enhancing (but legal) drugs, and now it turns out Sosa may very well have been using a corked bat.

Beautiful. What a game, baseball.

Bud Selig's worst nightmare moved across the AP wires at 8:40 p.m. with the news out of Wrigley Field. Sosa, the Cubs' affable and world-famous slugger, had been ejected when the bat he cracked in the first inning was found to be loaded with cork.

Sosa did not offer his customary two-fingered kiss upon his departure, nor was he immediately available for comment, but what could he possibly say? I didn't know? Somebody else must have done it? It wasn't my bat? It was all a joke? As it turned out, it was a variation of the third.

These were all the sort of excuses offered by baseball's more celebrated doctored-bat miscreants of the past—Albert Belle, Graig Nettles, Norm Cash, to name three—and after all was said and done, their transgressions against the game's integrity were largely dismissed as isolated incidents, more humorous than deceitful. But then none of them could be considered a baseball icon, worthy of a plaque and a hallowed place in Cooperstown.

Make no mistake about this, however: There is no humor in Sosa being caught using a corked bat, only shame and disgrace. Worse, a huge shadow of distrust has been cast over baseball as Sosa, who on April 4 became the 18th player to join the elite 500

Sammy Sosa breaks his bat in the first inning on June 3, 2003.
Umpires noticed cork in the bat and ejected Sosa. (AP/WWP)

club, is now the only one of them known to have used a corked bat.

In other words, unless he can somehow prove otherwise, Sammy Sosa is a fraud and all of his home runs are now tainted. He is the only man in history to amass three 60-homer seasons, and to that, we now say: Yeah, right, and how many of them were hit with a legitimate bat?

Maybe if Sosa was a certifiable jerk as Belle was, we wouldn't care and would merely chalk this up as a legitimate reason not to vote for him for the Hall of Fame. But through all his slugging prowess these past six seasons, Sosa has emerged as baseball's "happy warrior" as well as a goodwill ambassador for the game both here and abroad in Latin America and Japan. Such was Sosa's winning personality that we looked the other way at his own considerably enhanced body.

If Sammy insisted he wasn't then, wasn't now, wasn't ever on the juice, we readily believed him. Now there is nothing we can believe about him.

And here is Selig's dilemma: The very integrity of the game is at stake here and, at the very least, Selig must mete out a lengthy suspension to Sosa. (George Steinbrenner will suggest it should begin immediately.) But what to do about all the home runs, now irrevocably tainted, that have gone into the record books?

It has never been done before, but if Sosa is to have his credibility restored, Selig must order X-rays for the four bats (home runs 58, 62 and 66 in '98 and the 500th this year) that he donated to the Hall of Fame. And, if it turns out any of those were corked, Sosa should be banned from baseball for life and all his home runs be expunged from the record books.

In retrospect, it's probably a blessing Roger Maris wasn't around to watch his record obliterated the way it was by McGwire and Sosa. All those years, Maris had to live with the taint of an asterisk next to his record 61 homers because the commissioner of baseball at the time, Ford Frick, deemed it wasn't the true record since it wasn't accomplished within 154 games.

In light of the events of last night at Wrigley, the present commissioner may have no choice but to resurrect that asterisk and apply it to all of Sammy Sosa's home runs with the denotation "validity in question."

CHAPTER 9

THE RIVALRY

Whether you're a writer or just plain New York baseball fan, it doesn't ever get any better than Yankees-Red Sox.

REMOVING COUCH IZN'T THE ANSWER

SEPTEMBER 1, 2001

BOSTON—For seven tantalizing innings, Frank Castillo, the journeyman junkballer, had given them reason to still dream. To still dream of beating Roger Clemens, at his best, at his own game, in his exalted state among the game's immortals; to still dream of defying their own cursed history.

Of course, you could never ignore the hard reality that this was Yankees-Red Sox late summer pennant race baseball, where the end result is always the same. And so, when the bullpen door opened at the top of the eighth inning last night, winter arrived for Red Sox Nation in the person of Derek Lowe.

It is, as we all know, a whole different game now from when pitchers routinely finished what they started and 130 pitches was considered an average day's work. Red Sox manager Joe Kerrigan, who is now 6-9 since replacing Jimy Williams and more than twice as many games behind the Yankees as his predecessor had been, had all the right answers for removing Castillo after just 89 pitches, none of which was even remotely hit hard by the Yankees.

Castillo has a tender elbow, Kerrigan said, and any time he goes beyond seven innings, it starts to stiffen up. Maybe it does and maybe it would have, but you know what? The guy was beating Clemens, 1-0, completely befuddling the Yankee hitters, even more so than he had in beating them twice earlier this season, and this was the game Kerrigan and the Red Sox absolutely had to win if they were to keep any playoff dreams alive.

As Joe Torre said: "Castillo was unhittable. We didn't get a good swing off him all night, and I imagine my players were just looking for someone different."

In fairness to Lowe, what was ruled a leadoff infield single by David Justice should have been an out, had Izzy Alcantara not mishandled Shea Hillenbrand's throw to first. Suddenly, it was an opening for the Yankees, and on Lowe's fifth straight fastball to Jorge Posada, it was a 2-1 lead for the Yankees and a sudden reversal of fortune for Clemens as well.

The Rocket hadn't pitched too shabbily either—the best stuff he's had in the last five, six outings, in Torre's opinion. There had been only one shaky inning—the fifth, when Trot Nixon and Chris Stynes hit back-to-back two-out doubles to give the Sox their only run. Then there was the sixth, when Dante Bichette doubled with one out and Alcantara singled him to third.

With 18-1 still very much in the offing, Clemens bore down and struck out Hillenbrand and got Mike Lansing to fly to right. He would follow that up by striking out the side in the seventh to move past Sandy Koufax with the third most 10-strikeout games in history, 98. With 11 more Ks, he'll move ahead of Bert Blyleven into third place on the all-time strikeout list. His 14 straight wins tied Yankee Hall of Famers Whitey Ford and Jack Chesbro for the longest such streak in club history.

"I expect to do well," Clemens said when asked if any of this remarkable achievement at age 39—nearly five years into the "twilight" Red Sox GM Dan Duquette said he had reached when he let him walk as a free agent—has hit him. "I do the work and I expect to get the results. Plus, I've got eight pretty good guys playing behind me here. I've been blessed. And then there's the bullpen here—[Ramiro] Mendoza, [Mike] Stanton and [Mariano] Rivera. It's a nice luxury to be able to empty the tank at my age."

For the record, Clemens had thrown 104 pitches when Torre elected to let Mendoza and Rivera finish the Red Sox' season. The outlook for them had not been brilliant to begin with. They had just come off a bitterly disappointing road trip in which they lost the last five games, beginning with an 18-inning killer in Texas.

In the midst of the losing streak, Nomar Garciaparra's wrist flared up again, but instead of finding some reinforcements waiting for them—as the Yankees got yesterday with the waiver acquisition of old friend Randy Velarde from Texas—the Red Sox discovered the couches in their clubhouse had been removed on orders from Duquette.

It seems Duquette was of the opinion there was too much of a country-club atmosphere in his new manager's clubhouse. The Red Sox, it is presumed, will not take elimination sitting down.

Regular Boston Massacre

April 16, 2002

BOSTON—It wasn't until the sixth inning yesterday in Boston—or about the same time the morning fog had lifted and the first marathoners were approaching Heartbreak Hill—when the Yankees began resembling the best team $124 million could buy.

By then, unfortunately, they had done too much damage to themselves, and while their comeback effort may have looked valiant, the overall bottom line on this lost Patriots Day weekend was pretty gruesome: Three losses in four games, all of them by one run; Andy Pettitte a potential casualty; the Bernie Williams-Shane Spencer slumps now a combined 0 for 36; and, lastly, the American League high for strikeouts (by batters, that is) with 116 after yesterday's 12, four of them by Rondell White.

So much for all that improved on-base percentage.

Of course, nobody around the Yankees would blame the early starting time (11:05 a.m.) for their groggy start yesterday. It just looked like they were the only team playing in the fog.

It began with Derek Jeter's boot of Tony Clark's hard-hit grounder to short that, instead being a double play and bailing the wounded Pettitte out of a first-inning jam with only one run on the board, resulted in the bases being loaded with one out. Pettitte then walked Shea Hillenbrand on four straight pitches to let a second run in, and only a freak play—on which Jason Varitek's lined shot through the right side struck Hillenbrand on the leg on his way to second—prevented a totally disastrous start to the day for the Yankees.

That came an inning later when Pettitte's cranky elbow flared up again and Joe Torre took no further chances with him,

Nomar Garciaparra (left) and Derek Jeter talk during a Yankees-Red Sox game. (Al Bello/Getty Images)

bringing in Adrian Hernandez to start the fourth. This is not the first time Pettitte has experienced elbow problems, and in the past he has always been able to pitch through them, but Torre was obviously concerned.

Presumably, he's a tad concerned, too, about the way his team is playing in the early going, both defensively and offensively. Yesterday was a microcosm of this, as Jeter's error in the first kept the momentum rolling for the Red Sox, while the game ended with Ugueth Urbina striking out White and John Vander Wal to leave Yankees at second and third.

"I wish I had an excuse, but I just missed it," said Jeter, who partially atoned for his gaffe by homering in the eighth to make it a one-run game.

By then, it really did look as if the Yankees were reacting to the lifting fog. Williams at least hit the ball hard his last two groundouts, and with one out in the ninth, Jorge Posada singled and Robin Ventura doubled to bring the Fenway crowd to a sudden hush. It revived quickly, though, when White struck out for the fourth time and Vander Wal was left standing at the plate as home plate umpire Larry McCoy rang him up on a pitch that appeared to be well off the outside corner.

"They took me to school today," said White, shaking his head. "I've just got to go home to New York and regroup. I didn't hit the ball well all weekend."

Vander Wal wasn't nearly so charitable.

"Just take a look at the replay," he growled. "In my opinion, it was a ball."

Asked if he said anything to McCoy, he snapped: "Yeah, I told him to have a nice day."

By then, it actually had become a nice day outside as the Yankees schlepped through the corridors of Fenway to the bus that would take them to the train that was to take them home from this dismal 3-5 road trip.

"The way we got to where we were last year was to win series like this," Williams said. "You cannot assume we will just get there."

By the same token, they lost three of four on Patriots Day weekend here last year and wound up 13 and a half games ahead of the Red Sox in October. This is the perspective Torre prefers to use at this 14-game juncture of the season.

"When you make errors early, everyone thinks it's terminal," he said, in reference to Jeter's error and the Yankees' defensive sloppiness in the other losses here. "We just have to play the season out."

Kind of like all those runners, crossing the finish line as the Yankee bus pulled out of Fenway. It's a marathon and still a long, long way before anyone can suggest they've reached Heartbreak Hill.

COLON'S NEW SOX AREN'T RED

JANUARY 16, 2003

Brian Cashman can dance around the Yankees' prime motive for abruptly de-globalizing and downsizing their starting rotation all he wants, but let's be perfectly clear about this: Saving a few shekels, replacing Ramiro Mendoza and adding a promising young arm for the future do not remotely compare to the satisfaction of envisioning Theo Epstein, the Red Sox' "boy wonder" GM, throwing another chair through a window.

Listening to Cashman's soft-shoe routine on yesterday's conference call announcing the three-way trade that sent Orlando Hernandez and $2 million to Montreal, Bartolo Colon to the White Sox and reliever Antonio Osuna to the Yankees, you half expected him to introduce Ginger Rogers as a player to be named later. No way was this a trade designed to keep Colon from winding up with the Red Sox, Cashman insisted.

"We were in separate discussions with the White Sox," the GM said. "We tried to make this deal with them a while back."

Right. And Cashman had no idea the White Sox were going to immediately turn Hernandez around to the Expos, along with pitcher Rocky Biddle and outfielder/first baseman Jeff Liefer, for Colon. So why then did Cashman toss the $2 million into the deal to help offset the $4.5 million or so El Duque will make in arbitration? White Sox GM Kenny Williams surely wasn't asking for that handout.

But you can understand Cashman's reluctance to gloat or rub it in on poor Theo, whose first three months on the job as baseball's youngest-ever GM have been nothing short of disastrous. No point in conjuring up more "evil empire" references to the Yankees from the beleaguered Bosox brass. Cashman, as is his style, stuck to the baseball basics

White Sox starter Bartolo Colon delivers a pitch against the Yankees, his former team. (James Keivom/Daily News)

of this deal—which, for his part, were the shedding of some salary (Osuna will earn $2.3 million next year as opposed to the $3.1 Mendoza will get from the Red Sox) and partially unclogging the eight-deep rotation.

"We're happy to get Osuna and the other kid [right-handed pitching prospect Delvis Lantigua]," a source close to George Steinbrenner said yesterday, "but the objective absolutely was to make sure Colon didn't go to the Red Sox."

Which brings us back to the boy Theo, who, after Colon, Jose Contreras, Edgardo Alfonzo, Jeff Kent and Erubiel Durazo, is now 0 for five in premium players he sought to pick up this winter either by trade or signing. Purportedly, the Kent and Contreras rejections sent him into chair-throwing snit fits, although he has laughingly denied those stories.

Whatever. The Red Sox could have had Colon had Theo been willing to give up their prize young lefty starter, Casey Fossum. Once Epstein balked, it gave the Yankees another opening to orchestrate the Colon sweepstakes.

Fossum may blossom—even into a No. 1-2 starter for the Red Sox. But when he does, where will Nomar Garciaparra and Pedro Martinez be? Boston's two franchise players are both free agents after the 2004 season, and with nearly $100 million tied up in Manny Ramirez alone through 2008, the financially strapped Red Sox almost certainly won't be able to keep them both.

As one baseball person neutral to the Yankee-Red Sox war observed yesterday: "Other than the Yankees, who are always in a win-now mode, no other team in baseball needs to win in 2003 as badly as the Red Sox. Their future is definitely now.

"And yet, they let Casey Fossum stand in the way of getting Colon, who along with Pedro, would have given them the most formidable 1-2 pitching punch this side of Randy [Johnson] and [Curt] Schilling. Can you imagine Steinbrenner doing that?"

Actually, at one point Steinbrenner was willing to give up still-promising lefty slugger Nick Johnson and El Duque to get Colon for himself. That was, of course, before he outbid the Red Sox for Contreras. Now it would seem he's gotten everything he could have hoped for this winter without having to sacrifice Johnson.

To which a resigned Red Sox Nation would only say: What else is new?

CLEMENS TIPS RED SOX & CAP

SEPTEMBER 1, 2003

BOSTON—In the eternal saga that is Yankees-Red Sox, where white-knuckle ninth innings are as much the norm as the name-calling, and owners have been known to evaporate into tears in early July, you always think you've seen and experienced every possible emotion involving these two ancient rivals.

And then something else truly extraordinary happens like yesterday when, in the belly of the beast, Roger Clemens walks off the Fenway Park mound with the bases loaded and receives a standing ovation from a Red Sox Nation that apparently no longer feels scorned by him.

As Clemens trudged to the Yankee dugout, it started almost timidly, with a polite applause, and gradually began to build into a full-fledged "thanks-for-the-memories" salute. This, from a Nation that had endured a crushing defeat from the Yankees the day before and was now looking at an 8-2 deficit that was largely the product of Clemens's superb effort.

Joe Torre, for one, thought he'd spent all the emotion he had in him in Saturday's excruciating 10-7 see-saw Yankee victory and now, here he was, comparing goose bumps on his arm with Aaron Boone.

"As I was standing out there on the mound, Boonie came up behind me and stuck out his arm," Torre said. "I looked at him, at first not understanding what he was doing, and then he pointed to the goose bumps. I had them, too. It was just an unbelievable thing, although, really, it wasn't so unbelievable because the fans here know the game and they appreciated everything Roger did here. It was real classy of them.

"I think they felt they were witnessing something special. This is where it all started for him, where he set the tone for his career. He belonged to them initially and that's why they booed him so passionately all those times he came back here—because they felt he still belonged to them."

Boone, a career National Leaguer, experienced his first taste of Yankees-Red Sox passion. But this was something so spontaneous and so surprising that even Don Zimmer, a hard-boiled veteran of Yankee-Red Sox wars, couldn't help getting caught up in it.

Once Clemens got into the dugout and began collecting his belongings for the trek up the runway to the clubhouse, all of Fenway was standing and clapping. It had been going for nearly a minute when Zimmer grabbed Clemens by the arm and urged him to oblige them with a curtain call.

"I said, 'Go out there. Look at them! They're all standing for you,'" Zimmer related. "Sometimes you're booed, sometimes you're cheered. Roger got what he deserved. They respected him for what he did here. I thought that was great."

Clemens, who won the first three of his six Cy Young awards as well as the 1986 AL MVP with the Red Sox from 1984-96 before his bitter departure as a free agent, admitted that even he had to gather himself in the dugout once the ovation finally subsided.

"I was still just kind of reviewing how I'd walked [Gabe] Kapler [to load the bases, prompting Torre to come and get him] and then I heard them," Clemens said. "It was very special. It gave me the opportunity to say thank you. So I was able to get that opportunity and I was just collecting my thoughts a little bit in the tunnel there and I was pretty emotional. I got [visiting clubhouse man] Tommy [McLaughlin] up there and he had tears in his eyes. He's seen me work here forever."

Because it was probably the last time he will ever pitch at Fenway (you have to believe the Yankees hope they don't have to come back here in October for yet another round of gut-wrenching games), the 41-year-old Clemens wanted to make certain it would be an honorable finale. Yankee pitching coach Mel Stottlemyre worried that Clemens might have trouble containing his emotions, but quickly felt more at ease when the two walked in from the bullpen.

"He was real calm and he had a good game plan, which we talked about as we walked in," Stottlemyre said. "Then the fans out there in the bleachers started yelling 'Good luck, Roger' to him—and most of them were wearing Red Sox shirts—and I kinda figured it was gonna be like that for him today. It was different."

It was definitely that. But after a weekend that started with such promise and great expectations for the Nation, only to end with two disappointing losses, it was a lot easier to say goodbye to an old warrior who was once their own than it was to a season.

CHAPTER 10

GENERAL

Needless to say, I got more letters on the "Hall of Shame" column than any other. …A-Rod lasted three seasons in Texas and had to change positions in order to get his visa out. Somehow, I don't think Bud Selig thought his trade to the Yankees was as much of a "good thing for baseball" as going to the Red Sox would have been.

The Hall of Shame

In about 10 days, the Hall of Fame balloting will be announced. And you have to wonder if, somewhere up there in Baseball Heaven, The Babe is tapping The Rajah or The Iron Horse on the shoulder and saying: "Hey kiddo, there goes the neighborhood again. The old club ain't what it used to be."

Or what it was supposed to be, anyway.

This year's Hall of Fame ballot ranged from the very good (Willie Stargell, Jim Bunning, Luis Tiant, Thurman Munson, Orlando Cepeda) to the pretty good (Ron Santo, Bill Mazeroski, Ken Boyer) to the awfully ordinary (John Milner, Lynn McGlothen, Jim Spencer).

Nowhere, however, was there anyone who fit in the category of "great," which is why, for the first time in seven years as a Hall of Fame elector, I sent my ballot back blank. A bullet ballot, if you

will, as a protest that Stargell, who will probably be elected in his first try, doesn't belong in the same pantheon as Babe Ruth, Lou Gehrig, Rogers Hornsby, Hank Aaron, Ted Williams and Joe DiMaggio.

Used to be that those elected to the Hall of Fame on their first year of eligibility represented the *crème de la crème* of baseball—Mantle, Mays, Musial. But then Al Kaline, three 100-RBI seasons in 22 years, and Lou Brock, .293 lifetime average as a singles hitter and a .959 fielding percentage, made it in on the strength of being in that other tainted fraternity—the 3,000-hit club.

They allot you 10 spaces on the Hall of Fame ballot, and there are those among the voting brethren of the Baseball Writers Association who feel compelled to use all 10 of them. Inasmuch as there are 199 members in the Hall of Fame—and the fact that even the most fervent fans would be hard-pressed to name even half of them—nobody could blame The Babe for lamenting the decline of the neighborhood.

The fact is, there are far too many "very goods" or "pretty goods" enshrined in Cooperstown. Mostly, they have been sent there by the Veterans Committee, which passes judgment on those players who fail to win the writers' approval in 20 years on the ballot. Thus, the Hall of Fame is no longer a sanctuary for the greats of the game—those players who dominated at their positions (See: Johnny Bench on next year's ballot).

So maybe it's time to start kicking some of these imposters out of Cooperstown and return the neighborhood to greatness. There's no better time than the present to use the 10 spots on the ballot for those players who should be voted out of the Hall of Fame.

1. Rabbit Maranville—One of the few errors of commission by the baseball writers. A shortstop with a .258 lifetime average, he was voted in on the strength of a campaign by the Hearst newspaper chain, by whom he was employed at the time of his death in 1954.

2. Joe Tinker-Johnny Evers—"These are the saddest of possible words, Tinker to Evers to Chance," wrote Franklin P. Adams. And indeed they are because there's no way Tinker or Evers would have made it to Cooperstown had Adams not immortalized them in poem. The fact is, Tinker, Evers and Chance weren't that great defensively—as evidenced by the paltry 54 double plays they turned in their heyday with the Cubs from 1906-09. Tinker hit a lifetime .263, Evers .270 in an era when .300 hitters were common.

3. Tom Yawkey—The only "pure" owner elected to the Hall. His contributions? "One of the game's great sportsmen." In the 43 years he owned them, the Red Sox won only three pennants—and no World Series. If Yawkey's in, what about Jacob Ruppert? Or Charlie Finley?

4. Rick Ferrell—When the Veterans Committee elected him and his .281 career average in '84, there were many who thought it had elected the wrong Ferrell, that it had meant to elect his brother, Wes, who may have been a better choice. Wes, after all, was a better hitter—and he was a pitcher!

5. Ray Schalk—Like Ferrell, he was a catcher who got in the back door of Cooperstown with the veterans. He was an even lighter hitter—.253, to be precise.

6. Tommy McCarthy— Another case of mistaken identity? For years, the press steward at Fenway Park was a true gentleman by the name of Tommy McCarthy. And had his name somehow made it on the Hall of Fame ballot, he would have probably received a large number of votes from appreciative writers. This Tommy McCarthy, however, was a diminutive (5'6") outfielder for the Boston Braves before the turn of the century. He hit a career .294 in an era when his Hall of Fame contemporaries were batting 50 points higher or better.

7. Harry Hooper—Played alongside Tris Speaker in the Red Sox' outfield from 1909-15, and that's as close as he should have come to the Hall of Fame. While Speaker hit a career .345, Hooper hit .281 and only once in 17 seasons had more than 65 RBIs.

8. George Kelly—He had a Hall of Fame nickname ("Highpockets"), but that's about

all. His biggest strength was to have three or four of his former Giant teammates, headed by Bill Terry, on the Veterans Committee. They elected him in 1973 even though his .297 average doesn't measure up to his first-base contemporaries, George Sisler (.340), Lou Gehrig (.340) and Terry (.341).

9. Bobby Wallace—Here's a so-called "glove man" the Veterans Committee saw fit to enshrine. Led AL shortstops in fielding all of three times in 22 seasons. His .267 lifetime average is six points lower than Phil Rizzuto's. Then again, Rizzuto played on nine pennant winners to Wallace's none.

10. Eppa Rixey/Rube Marquard/Pud Galvin—Three Hall of Fame pitchers who fit in the same category. They all won lots of games—and lost almost as many. Marquard was 201-177. Rixey had the lowest winning percentage in Cooperstown— 266-251, .515. And Galvin, though he won 361 games in an era when pitchers worked every other day, lost 309!

What does *that* say about the neighborhood?

A Man for All Seasons

PAWTUCKET, R.I.—The eternal cloud that settled over this blue-collar suburb of Providence was now spitting out a light mid afternoon rain. Not enough to force postponement of the International League game that night between the Pawtucket Red Sox and the Columbus Clippers, but just enough to ruin Johnny Pesky's day.

And if you know this man of perpetual joy, you know it takes a lot to ruin Johnny Pesky's day.

"Tarp's on, I guess," Pesky said as he sat in the small, spartan manager's office just off the main lobby of McCoy Stadium. "Damn, I really wanted to have a workout with these kids today. There's a lot of things they need to be working on and not a whole lot of time."

At least as far as he's concerned. Pesky will be 71 in September, and when this, his 47th baseball summer began a couple of months ago, the last place he expected to find himself was sitting in the manager's chair. Any manager's chair, let alone that of the Boston Red Sox' Triple-A farm club.

He last managed in 1964, and after being relieved of those duties by the Red Sox he embarked on a whole new career at the House of Yawkey as a broadcaster, coach, and finally, "special assistant to the general manager." It has been a comfortable life that Pesky has dedicated to the Red Sox (and they to him).

But it has not been so comfortable that he didn't hesitate at saying "sure" when his boss, Red Sox general manager Lou Gorman, came to him in later June with the proposal to go back to the minor leagues and manage.

Pawtucket manager Johnny Pesky fields a question from the media.
(Daily News)

"We had a problem at Pawtucket," Gorman explained. "Our manager there, Ed Nottle, had been there for a number of years and had done a good job for us. But I think he thought he had a chance to manage the big club for us. When we extended Joe Morgan's contract earlier this year, Nottle seemed to lose his enthusiasm. He stopped having workouts, and the players simply weren't progressing.

"The people at Pawtucket have been very special to us. We haven't given them a good team in a couple of years, and when we take away what good players we have had there, they never complain. So when they did complain this time, we knew we had a problem. Originally, I thought Johnny would just do it for a couple of weeks, but I underestimated his enthusiasm. He's handled this like he's 30 years old."

The Organization Man

"I didn't ask any questions," Pesky said. "A guy gets fired, it always bothers you when you take his job. I certainly didn't want to manage any more, but I'd seen these kids in spring training because of the lockout, and I guess the organization felt they were as prepared as they should be at this stage. I really enjoyed working with them in the spring. I feel like I got to know them and well. I'm a guy who loves the field, even though I carry these little business cards around that say 'Assistant to the General Manager.'"

But if truth be told, it goes deeper than just being on the field. Pesky is your consummate organization man, and in this case, the organization runs deep. It is the legacy of Red Sox owner Tom Yawkey that nearly 15 years after his death, his former players and employers remain dedicated to him.

"Back in 1976, I was offered the Pittsburgh manager's job before it went to Chuck Tanner," Pesky related. "That was a helluva club, too. But I have a lifelong love affair with the Boston Red Sox. Mr. Yawkey took care of me, and I never forgot that."

The '46 Series

In Red Sox lore, of course, Pesky is still more remembered for holding onto the outfield relay too long in the seventh game of the 1946 World Series—enabling Enos Slaughter to scamper all the way home from first base with the winning run for the Cardinals— than his hitting prowess. An outstanding shortstop, he led the American League in hits in each of his first three seasons in the majors. He retired with a .307 average over 10 years, which should have been fulfilling enough for any ballplayer.

"I don't think there's a day goes by I don't think about losing that last game of the season in 1949 to the Yankees," Pesky said, recalling that long ago lost Red Sox summer when the Yankees, trailing by a game, beat them on the final two days of the season to win the pennant. "That will stay with me forever...the feeling I had that we let Mr. Yawkey down again. That's why anything I can do, the smallest of things with just one of these kids, if it results in helping the Red Sox win it all some day, this will all be worth it. That would be my payback to Mr. Yawkey."

The Pawtucket club that Pesky has inherited is not overloaded in talent, though. In fact, the PawSox are in last place, 25 and a half games out of first place and 8-20 under Pesky entering the weekend. Moreover, their best player, shortstop Tim Naehring, was recently called up to Boston, presumably never to return. Still, Pesky remains upbeat and enthusiastic in his mission. For him, this is fun and enables him to continue to feel forever young.

Where He Belongs

He couldn't help but laugh the other day when his old teammate, longtime Red Sox scout Sam Mele, sent a letter to Mike Tamburro, the president of the Pawtucket team. The letter was on the stationery of a nearby nursing home and thanked Tamburro for "getting an old guy out of the home to manager." It went on to say that the home planned to send a van to McCoy Stadium every night to pick Pesky up and promised "to keep the light on in case he stays out late."

"People think I'm nuts," said Pesky as he sat back in his chair and stuffed a chaw of Redman tobacco into his mouth. "But I honestly don't feel 70. I really think this is my bag. I have a good rapport with these young players.

"Would I come back next year if they asked? Yeah, I'd say yes. As long as my health is good, I want to be on the ballfield. That's where I belong."

ONE LAST CHANCE TO ROLL THE DICE

AUGUST 8, 1994

The Duke called the other day with a sound of urgency to his voice.

"I need your help," he said. "Charlie's age is really catching up to him. He's pretty much bedridden now, and he's got a catheter in full-time so he's really not supposed to leave his house. But he keeps asking me about Atlantic City. He's got this crazy thing in his mind that he wants to play the craps tables there just once. You know, before it's too late for him."

The Duke is a prosperous New Jersey businessman whose company is next door to Charlie's house. Charlie is an 81-year-old invalid who lives alone. He has never been married and has no family.

His only true friend in life, other than his loyal 32-year-old registered nurse (whom he calls "My Broadway Rose"), is The Duke.

The Duke had already set the wheels in motion to grant Charlie's wish by hiring a stretch limo to transport him to A.C. And he's succeeded in getting Charlie's "Broadway Rose" to agree to accompany him as a medical precaution. (The last thing any of us needed was for this caper to turn into a *Weekend at Bernie's* tragicomedy with Charlie crapping out on *us* and having to be transported back home *au rigeur*.)

The whole gig had to be organized quietly, 'cause Charlie's on a government health plan and is *not* supposed to be able to leave his house.

What The Duke needed now was a place for Charlie to play and then crash for the night. A call was made to Yankees general manager Gene Michael. As only Charlie's luck would have it, Michael just happened to be watching the Yankees game with Donald Trump.

Would The Donald be able to accommodate Charlie? The Trump PR people called The Duke and told him Charlie was set up in a suite at the Taj Mahal.

We were in business.

"What's this?" Charlie asked.

"It's an antique Panama hat and a pair of sunglasses," The Duke replied as he and Charlie's Rose gently slid Charlie out of the wheelchair and into the limo. "You don't want anyone to recognize you, Charlie. You're not supposed to be doing this."

"But what if I run into Frankie down there? I wouldn't want *him* not to recognize me."

Frankie?

"Sinatra!" Charlie replied indignantly, pulling from his pocket a frayed sepia snapshot. "Look here. It's a picture I took of him when we were in Casablanca together during the war."

Charlie and a very young Chairman in Casablanca?

"Well, it wasn't what you might think," Charlie said. "I was winding up a tour in the air force, and Frankie was over there entertaining with Phil Silvers. We had lunch together in the cafeteria."

Although Charlie had requested we stock the limo with Johnny Walker Red, he took only a small sip of it and then stuck a Macanudo cigar in his mouth.

"These were always good cigars," he said. "I used to buy 'em from Nate Sherman himself when he had his store on 57th Street. Then he went over to Fifth Avenue, and I stopped goin' there. This is where I break my fast. They won't let me smoke in my own house now. Can you imagine that?

"I just want to see Atlantic City as it is now. Years ago, it was just a boardwalk with a few big old hotels. I'd a gone there a lot more if they'd had gambling. I played craps most of the time when I lived in Binghamton. They had a parlor there behind a shoeshine store. It was like an open house. I gotta be careful though. Those guys are still around."

Although he had vowed, "It's not gonna stun me," Charlie's eyes widened as his Rose wheeled him into the Taj casino. One of Trump's security people approached.

"You must be Charlie," he said. "I was told to look for a guy with a Panama hat, a cigar and sunglasses."

The plan was to check in, have a little dinner and then hit the tables, but Charlie couldn't wait. He picked a roulette table and played his lucky number, 16. Naturally, he hit it—you didn't think we could make this up, did you?—and so before he even got going, the $2,000 bankroll he had brought was fattened by $175.

After a supper of chicken soup and matzo balls, Charlie was ready to attack the craps tables. Once again, though, his eyes widened at the sight of his Rose attired in a smashing pink pantsuit. They were quite a sight: Charlie rubbing his lucky coin, blowing on the dice and shouting "Little Joe from Cocomo" and "Look down on your son, Cain, and make him Able" as his Rose tossed for him.

"I haven't lost my touch," Charlie said proudly three hours later, after finally agreeing to retire. "I feel like the Prince of the Taj."

The next morning Charlie breakfasted on oatmeal, melon, four jumbo pancakes and four cups of coffee, then asked his Rose to wheel him out onto the boardwalk so he could see the ocean.

"Okay," he said after just a couple of minutes, "I've seen it. Now let's hit the tables once more before we go."

The trip home was happily uneventful. Charlie chewed on his cigar and counted his money a couple of times, satisfied that he had about broken even. His Rose was more pleased with the way he had eaten and how the trip had energized him.

"You know," Charlie said, "I have hopes of one more trip. What's doing next week?"

FREGOSI'S ACHING FOR GOOD OLD DAYS

MARCH 13, 1996

CLEARWATER, Fla.—Jim Fregosi's eyes see nothing but pain.

On the roster in the Philadelphia Phillies manager's office are little red crosses in front of a half-dozen names. "Disabled," Fregosi confirms, "but really that only tells half the story. There are other guys here who are red crosses waiting to happen."

He does not specify who those players are. He doesn't have to. Anyone who has been around the Phillies these past couple of years knows more than they could ever want about Darren Daulton's hollow knees and Lenny Dykstra's aching back.

Between them, they are $11.7 million worth of red crosses waiting to happen.

"Do I expect them to hold up?" Fregosi asks. "In this game, the best-laid plans usually never work. So you count on 'em until they prove they can't do it."

Until a couple of months ago, Fregosi was at least counting on Daulton to take his accustomed position behind the plate for a minimum of 100 games. But that plan was scuttled when Dutch marched into GM Lee Thomas's office and announced that his knees, surgically repaired eight times, no longer could withstand the rigors of catching.

So Daulton, 34, is playing left field this spring alongside The Dude. It is even money as to which of them blows out first, but while everyone waits, Fregosi sees only pain. He remembers what these two were to the National League championship club of only three years ago. Enough that Phillies owner Bill Giles shelled out a combined $43 million to sign them through 1998.

"I'll admit," Giles said, "I got a little starry-eyed. I thought they'd keep doing it. I thought

Phillies manager Jim Fregosi argues a call. (John Roca/Daily News)

they were indestructible because of the way they played."

Dykstra evidently thought so, too. The Dude did everything to the fullest. He partied, he gambled, he bought expensive cars, he bulked up (some say with more than just barbells) and he built car washes. But on the field, he broke down. After playing 161 games in 1993 and leading the National League in at-bats, Dykstra has averaged 73 games the last two seasons.

He was asked recently if he was beginning to feel mortal.

"I don't know, man," he said. "When you've been playing as long as I've been playing and as hard as I've been playing, you just deal with [injuries]. This is the first time I've ever had to put in extra work in spring training. My first seven years in the big leagues, I never saw the disabled list. I admit it's been frustrating not being out on the field, but even more frustrating is the pain I feel every day.

"They took care of my knee with surgery last year, but the pain in my back is something I'm going to have to live with every day for the rest of my life."

Like Daulton, Dykstra, 33, is nowhere close to the same player he was in 1993—even when he does play—and that's the dilemma for Fregosi. These two were the cornerstones of winning Phillies teams in the past and the owner has so much invested in them. But in Glenn Murray, a hulking 225-pound slugger who hits Ruthian home runs, and Lee Tinsley, a burner with excellent center field defensive skills, Fregosi may well have two better players.

"Why do you think we did the things we did over the winter?" Fregosi said, referring to the trade that brought Murray and Tinsley from the Red Sox for last year's closer, Heathcliff Slocumb. "Because those players [Dykstra and Daulton] aren't what they used to be. The best-case scenario is that I get 130 to 140 games out of them. Until then, they've got a lot to prove."

So far it would seem Fregosi has not seen what he wants to see from his two fading stars. Daulton, who has long acknowledged his knees as the source of his hitting torque, has been strictly an upper-body hitter this spring—with predictably sparse results. His play in the field has been equally unsettling. And it is clear, too, that Dykstra no longer will be challenging fences and punishing his body the way he used to.

Dusk is stealing over the careers of Dutch and The Dude. As Jim Fregosi watches the sun setting from center to left field, Dykstra was asked if he has any signals or communications with his new left field partner.

"Yeah," he said, "play deep."

Fat's in Fire in Yankville

FEBRUARY 20, 1997

TAMPA—About four and a half months after the Yankees thought they had arrived there, "Fat City" is taking on a whole different meaning.

We refer, of course, to the two fat guys who are creating quite a spring training stir—one by his absence and the other by his presence—in Joe Torre's world championship stateship. Yesterday, fat guy No. 1, Cecil Fielder, presumably was still angry at the world over the Yankees' refusal to trade him. We say presumably because he was the most notable of the no-shows on the official full-squad reporting day and was not returning phone calls from either the media or the Yankee manager wondering about his state of mind.

Then again, as David Cone noted: "If I were Cecil, I wouldn't show up today either, seeing this mass of media waiting to ask him to explain himself."

Most importantly, Fielder needs to explain himself to Torre, at whom he directed his most stinging barb last month when he said he would "never forgive" the manager for benching him in the first game of the divisional play-offs against Texas. More than his "trade me" demand, the shot at Torre has seemed to upset other Yankee players.

"I don't understand Cecil," said Darryl Strawberry. "Going from last to first, what's not to like about that? Joe was the guy that got us there. He kept it all together last year. You have to avoid being selfish. Guys have to understand you need to be a team. If you don't come here with a team attitude and effort, you won't be successful."

For his part, Torre said he was reserving judgment on Fielder's statements until he talks to Big Daddy himself. He did try to talk to Fielder a while back, he said, but his phone call wasn't returned. "I still haven't heard [the criticism of him] from him," the manager said deftly. "If he did say it, I would want a clarification."

Yankee GM Bob Watson, who has been in contact with Fielder's agent, Jim Bronner, said he has been assured Fielder will be in camp today for the first full-squad workout, so Torre hopefully won't have to wait much longer for that clarification.

At the same time, Fielder has to know he *will* have to wait for some time to get his freedom from the Yankees since no team is interested in taking on his $7.2 million salary. As such, he's just going to have to resign himself to being around next month to receive his world championship ring.

What a pity.

"I talked to him a couple of weeks ago about the impact the things he's saying is having,"

David Wells walks to the dugout in Cleveland.
(Keith Torrie/Daily News)

Cone said. "He's got to face the music and state his intentions. He should just concentrate on getting his 500 at-bats, putting up his numbers and going from there after the season."

Meanwhile, in the midst of the Great Fielder Watch yesterday, there was fat guy No. 2, David Wells, getting more and more testy about his gout condition—not to mention the migraine headache he is fast becoming for the Yankees. Wells reported that he was still in pain and unable to do any running or throwing after being administered anti-inflammatory medication for his condition.

It was when he mentioned being given a book to read by the Yankee medical staff that inquiring minds further inflamed him.

"What kind of book did they give you?" he was asked.

"Why?" he replied gruffly. "What do you mean by that?"

"I don't know," the reporter answered innocently. "Was it the Book of Gout?"

"You're an instigator!" Wells screamed. "I'm out of here. I'm not saying anything more."

The book mystery only deepened when Torre said he had no knowledge of Wells being given any reading material to take home with him. "He does know now he's going to have to watch his diet," Torre said.

Finally, it seemed only right that on this day of diets, fat guys and Yankee turmoil, George Steinbrenner, no stranger to any of the above, should have *his* say on the effect all this might be having on his once-euphoric team. Moments after Wells stormed angrily out of the clubhouse, Steinbrenner emerged from Torre's office beaming.

Was he worried about Wells and all his ailments? "Nah," said Steinbrenner. "I like him. He'll be okay. Besides, I want everybody in baseball thinking our pitching staff is in disarray."

And for Fielder, who wants out? "I don't really believe that," Steinbrenner said. "He likes it here. He just wants an extension."

What was this? The Boss actually defusing Yankee controversy? Removing the fat, if you will, from the fire?

"I don't like things too calm," Steinbrenner assured. "I picture a ship out in the ocean with no wind and all its sails up. You know what happens? It doesn't go anywhere."

Least of all Fat City. The good one, that is.

PAGLIARULO STILL BIG LEAGUE

MAY 27, 1998

BURLINGTON, Mass.— By any stretch of the imagination, these were the strangest ground rules Mike Pagliarulo ever encountered.

The outfield, from left center to right, was a 45-degree incline with a telephone wire cutting across above it. There was no fence at the top of the outfield hill, just a barn-like structure in left center that served as a concession stand.

"As I understand it," Pagliarulo said, "if a ball hits the telephone wire, it's in play. So, too, is the concession stand. I really can't fault my outfielders for dropping any fly balls. It's pretty hard to catch a ball running uphill backward."

If you're Mike Pagliarulo and you've spent the last 13 years of your life in major league ballparks, it is understandable if returning to the sandlots of high-school ball might represent a bit of a culture shock. From a baseball standpoint, Pagliarulo couldn't be any farther away from Yankee Stadium these days, and you know what? He couldn't be any happier.

When his major league career finally ended a year ago this spring with his release from the Texas Rangers, Pagliarulo was presented with a number of options. He could stay with the Rangers as a minor league infield instructor; he could hook on with the Red Sox as a minor league coach and possibly a manager; he could do some scouting and coach in an independent league. Or he could simply go home to Burlington, Massachusetts.

His father, Charlie, sensed that the inevitable day they told him his playing days were over would be as traumatic as anything Pagliarulo had ever faced. "His whole life has been baseball," the elder Pagliarulo said, "so when he called me and told me he was retiring, I knew how hard it was."

Well, maybe it was at first. But a year later, Pagliarulo is

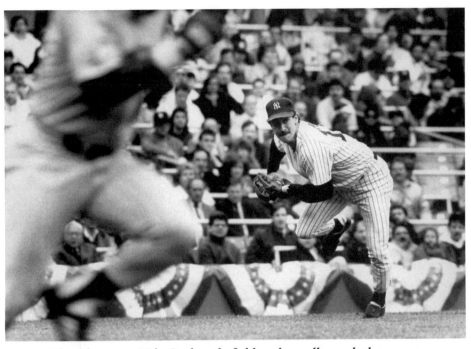

Third baseman Mike Pagliarulo fields a slow roller and throws out the runner. (Gene Kappock/Daily News)

about as happy and at ease with life as a man can possibly be. Baseball still consumes him, but now it is at the far more low-key high school level, where he coaches his local team, the Winchester Sachem. Frequently he finds himself on fields of nightmares such as this one, where merely getting his players through the game without an injury is a victory.

"This is really about the worst field we have to play on," Pagliarulo said. "Most of the others aren't too bad. The kids don't mind. They've never played on the kinds of fields I'm used to."

It is certainly rare—you might say refreshing, too—to see a guy who made a few million dollars playing major league ball returning to his roots. Most players today, when their careers are over, don't even want to go to the minor leagues to coach or manage. Pagliarulo chose to go even further away from the bigs.

"I could have stayed in the game," he said. "I know Texas has something for me if I want it, and maybe down the road I'll take them up on it. But right now I wanted to be home with my kids and be able to teach them how to play this game like my father taught me.

"So when this [high school] job opened, I grabbed it. You wouldn't believe how much bad instruction and crazy hitting theories you see in the high schools and colleges. That's why I'm going to have clinics in the summer after the season is over for all the kids in town. It's not my system I'm teaching. It's what I learned from people like Lou Piniella and Hal McRae."

Watching Pagliarulo at work with his high school pupils, there isn't that same intensity as he brought to professional ball. Work ethic, yes. But these are kids, and though he is 38 now, Pagliarulo still remembers what it was like to be 16.

"It's really kinda cool having him as a coach," said Jeff Daniels, Pagliarulo's No. 1 pitcher, who is headed to Villanova next year. "We know he knows a lot more about baseball than anyone else, but he relates to us, too."

At one point during Daniels's first start of the season, Pagliarulo called him aside and gave him an honest appraisal. "I told him he was really slowing his motion on his breaking ball, and it was tipping it off to the hitters,"

Pagliarulo said. "I also told him: 'I don't know how to correct it. I just wanted you to be aware of it.'"

His means of indoctrinating his kids with the big-league way of doing things are more subtle. On the top of the lineup card he posts before each game is a list of players under the heading "Today's Bomb Squad." And underneath that is inscribed "Work hard, play hard."

"The bomb squad is something I got from Tom Kelly," he said. "The guys who weren't playing in Minnesota were always ready, because you never knew when you were gonna get in there."

Sure enough, on this particular day, Pagliarulo's cleanup hitter was a no-show. No word if he was sick or being kept after class, but he had to be scratched and a bomb squader got into the game. As for the missing player, Pagliarulo laughed when asked about disciplinary measures at the high school level.

"I told them: 'I'm not allowed to put my hands on you and I can't fine you, but I sure as hell can make you take a lot of laps.'"

And with his dad as his guide and only aide, Pagliarulo puts his kids through some rigorous practices.

"I like my practices," he said. "I run them like spring training, dividing them up into three groups. Charlie? I call him my 'Don Zimmer.' He played in the Cubs organization and, really, taught me how to play the game."

And now, you could say, the Pagliarulos have come full cycle. In a couple of years, Pagliarulo's oldest son, Michael, will be attending Winchester High. The program that got its seeds from his grandfather about 30 years ago will be in place for him. By then his dad ought to have gotten used to all the curveballs thrown his way by high school ball.

"My biggest problem," said Pagliarulo, "is getting used to the fact that the seventh inning is not a time to stretch, it's the end of the game. I'm still in the middle of the game!"

SUMMERS OF SMOKE

MARCH 28, 1999

HAVANA—The Great U.S.-Cuban Baseball Detente, subtitled—"Fidel Castro Meet Albert Belle," was, of course, the primary subject of animated debate among the old men who gather every morning at the Esquina Caliente, the Hot Corner of old Havana's Parque Central.

Since there was no complimentary *USA Today* outside my hotel room door yesterday morning, I knew this was going to be the only place on Castro's island where you could get a free morning baseball briefing. The Orioles were coming! The Orioles were coming! By midafternoon the first wave of them, along with Commissioner Bud (Consensus Builder) Selig, had landed at Jose Marti Airport, but by then the old men had already reached their own consensus.

It's going to be a helluva game, they agreed, if only they could see it.

"It's the system," said 69-year-old Marcelo Sanchez. "You can only go by invitation and the invitations are based on what you do and who you are. I'm retired. I have no chance of going. The pure fanatics will not get into the stadium. After 40 years of waiting for this, I'm embarrassed I can't get in. They're concerned about our behavior. I just hope the next encounter will be free."

He was standing in the middle of the crowd of shouting fanatics, this slightly built gray-haired man. His frayed blue-striped shirt had two pockets that were filled with cigars, pens and his billfold. On his head was a shop-worn, stained White Sox cap that only John Wetteland could love.

"Last summer," Sanchez continued, "we argued every day

out here about Mark McGwire and Sammy Sosa and the great home run race. That was the only conversation out here. We didn't care who won the pennants. We only cared about that. Most of them wanted Sosa 'cause we're Cubans. For me, I wanted McGwire."

That was my cue to show him the copy of *Baseball Digest* with McGwire on the cover, which I had brought with me in hopes of settling some of the arguments for the old men.

"For me?" Sanchez said, beaming.

"Well, uh, yes, sure," I replied.

"This is how we get our information," Sanchez said. "It's difficult otherwise. But my house is full of baseball archives. I've been collecting baseball magazines and pictures for 60 years. Come! You must see it!"

Terrific! Out of all these passionate old men, here was a Cuban version of Barry Halper, the New York memorabilia collector.

It would have been impolite to turn down his invitation, so we scurried across the street to a crumbling, light blue, five-story building with clotheslines hanging out of many of the windows. The neo-classical architecture and few remaining

ornate wall tiles adorning the stairway told of the building's former pre-revolution glory, but now it is merely ramshackle.

"The elevator is broken," Sanchez apologized, "so we have to use the stairs."

Four flights up, the old man stopped and grinned. "Halfway there!" he said, happily. "Second base!"

Sanchez's wife, Lucy, and his dirty-white long-haired terrier greeted us as we entered his tiny three-room apartment. In the bedroom, there was a crudely made bookcase stacked with old newspapers and albums. A 1987 set of Topps Baseball Cards was on top of it and, on the bed, Sanchez was eagerly laying out old and new photos.

"Look," he said. "I have them all. My heroes. Minoso! Oliva! Canseco! Palmeiro!"

Then, pointing to a "which-doesn't-belong-and-why" 1988 poster of a pitcher in a Dodger uniform, he added: "And Hershiser!"

Next stop was across the hall to the bathroom where, high above the toilet, was a loft with stacks and stacks of more magazines and newspapers.

"My ladder broke and I have to use the kitchen table to get up there," Sanchez said. "But believe me, my archives are in perfect condition. I'm not afraid of hurricanes or nothing."

I told him it wasn't necessary for him to climb up there. We needed to get back to the debate still raging across the street. As we crossed the street, dodging the '50s Chevys and tail-finned Chryslers belching exhaust fumes, I asked Sanchez how he felt about the Cuban defectors, Livan and El Duque Hernandez, Rene Arocha, Rey Odonez and the others who have found riches in the U.S.

"It doesn't matter to me how many Cuban players go there," he said. "What matters is that they play well and are paid what they're worth. I think Livan is spoiled. He has no discipline. El Duque is better. He's outstanding now that he's in the States. He's older than they they think, though. If he stays in shape, he'll have two, three more years."

Like his "Hot Corner" comrades, Sanchez never read or heard about a ballplayer he didn't have a strong opinion on, and so I couldn't leave this debate without tossing out Albert Belle at him.

"Albert Belle!" he shrieked. "He has troubles with the umpires! He is a very strong character. Here in Cuba we don't accept him."

I was tempted to tell him a lot of people in America don't, either.

CHAMPS KNOW HOW TO STICK WITH IT

OCTOBER 29, 2000

By subway series standards, both teams did New York proud. In terms of baseball for the ages, the Yankees have done New York prouder than it could ever imagine.

We should cherish this Yankee team, savor the memories it has provided us over this incredible five-year run, because we will never see its like again. And, just maybe, no one ever saw its like before.

With four world championships in five years, including a record 114-win season in the middle of it, this can now officially qualify as a dynasty. And you can certainly make a case for this Yankee team being the greatest ever, simply by virtue of having to do more—win more postseason games, go through more layers of playoffs—than any multi-championship team in history.

Casey Stengel's five-straight Yankee teams of the '50s and Joe McCarthy's four-straight Yankee teams of the '30s set the pre-divisional play standard for greatness—and each had its share of Hall of Fame players, from Lou Gehrig, Joe DiMaggio, Bill Dickey, Lefty Gomez and Red Ruffing to Mickey Mantle, Yogi Berra, Whitey Ford and Phil Rizzuto. There's no telling yet if this Joe Torre Yankee dynasty will produce any Hall of Famers, other than the manager, but it is hard to imagine any team ever accomplishing more than it has.

"We may not have the greatest players," Torre acknowledged Friday, "but we have the greatest team. I'm prepared to say that."

Critics will point to the $112 million payroll and maintain that anybody could win with that kind of backing. Hate George Steinbrenner if you will—plenty of people around baseball always will—but if you're a Yankee fan you've got to be thankful for him. Ask the people in Boston how they like John Harrington, or Cubs fans how they like the

The Yankees celebrate their third straight and 26th overall World Championship. (Howard Simmons/Daily News)

Tribune Co. Yet the fact is, money alone does not buy championships, as the Dodgers and Orioles can attest.

It didn't win championships for the Yankees in the '80s, either, because Steinbrenner ran the team badly, didn't listen to his baseball people and thought the only way to go was to throw money at big-name free agents. He had been spoiled by his initial free agent signings of the '70s, the sure things in Catfish Hunter, Reggie Jackson and Goose Gossage, and thought he was bulletproof in signing the Ed Whitsons, Steve Kemps, Dave LaPoints and Pascual Perezes.

Fortunately, it took those failures of the '80s for Steinbrenner to start trusting the judgment of others, most notably Gene Michael. While GM Brian Cashman deserves top credit for coordinating all the scouting and ultimately being the one to pull the trigger on deals, Michael's fingerprints are all over this Yankee team—from his trade for Paul O'Neill to the senior advisory role (aka the last scouting word) he had in the deals for Tino Martinez, David Justice, Chuck Knoblauch, Scott Brosius and Jeff Nelson, as well as the signings of support players like Mike Stanton and Luis Sojo.

What's so often overlooked by skeptics is that there is technically only one "big ticket" pickup on this team—Roger Clemens, who was begat from David Wells. Even El Duque, a free agent of a different kind, makes $2 million per year as compared to the $10 million to $15 million per pitchers of his caliber command on the market.

When the Yankees acquired Justice from the Indians, the same doubters said they were the only team in baseball that would absorb that $7 million salary. But Michael, who liked the way Justice could hit left-handers, helped Cashman sway Steinbrenner away from Sammy Sosa (and the countless millions that would have cost) to make the deal.

And after the way Justice galvanized the stagnant Yankee bats (.305, 20 HR, 60 RBIs in his 75 games for them, three HR and 12 more RBIs in the postseason), is there any team in baseball, especially Cleveland, that could say he isn't worth the $7 million? Off those numbers, Justice would undoubtedly command a sizeable raise if he were a free agent, which he's not until 2002.

What is most noteworthy about this latest Yankee world championship against the Mets is that the core players from '96—Derek Jeter, Paul O'Neill, Bernie Williams, Tino Martinez and Mariano Rivera—again all played key roles in it. So much had been said about the dismantling of this team after the way it staggered down the stretch and into the postseason with a paltry 87 wins, but Torre made it clear he would fight to keep the core intact, noting how both O'Neill and Martinez regained their batting strokes at crunch time and how Tino is arguably the best glove man at first base in the AL.

It is also Michael who has supervised the efficient and thorough Yankee scouting staff which, if nothing else, provided the blueprint for the 16-3 record this team has compiled in its four World Series and overall 46-15 postseason record since '96. Against the Mets in particular, Team Michael's scouting reports enabled the Yankee pitchers to shut down Edgardo Alfonzo and Timo Perez when neither the Giants nor Cardinals could.

The Yankees are the only team to have at least two scouts on every team in the postseason, 17 in all.

"You still need the players to be able to execute," Michael said. "Reports alone don't win ballgames. All I can say is our scouts work really hard."

It has been a collective effort to produce this very special team. For a while there last week, the media, Fox TV especially, was too interested in making the Clemens-Mike Piazza tempest the focus while overlooking maybe the best sports story New York has ever had. So savor this team while you can, New York. It is highly doubtful there will ever be another one like it.

While you're at it, you might want to consider this, too: In the midst of the champagne celebration in the vistors' clubhouse at Shea Thursday night, the normally quiet and reserved Bernie Williams hugged Steinbrenner and said softly in his ear: "Don't worry, Boss, we're not done yet."

A-Rod: Rich Man, Poor Team

FEBRUARY 22, 2001

PORT CHARLOTTE, Fla.—At 10:32 a.m. yesterday, Alex Rodriguez pulled up to the Texas Rangers' spring training complex in his silver SUV, surveyed this God-forsaken baseball outpost and got the first taste of what his $252 million has wrought.

"Port Charlotte is a different place," he said, his eyeballs rolling skyward. "I'm looking forward to finding some nice restaurants here."

It figures to be a long and fruitless search, unless the mini-mart down the road meets his standards. Presumably, the Rangers took pains to assure A-Rod this is only a temporary situation, that they plan to abandon this place after this year and move into a new spring complex being built for them in the middle of Arizona's nowhere.

But once he recovers from the culture shock of Port Charlotte, Rodriguez can then begin to get a feel for the ballclub to which he has committed the prime of his career. Throughout the nearly six-week negotiation process, his agent, Scott Boras, insisted the organization was going to be the primary factor in his decision. A-Rod would not consider non-contending teams, Boras assured.

Nevertheless, when Texas owner Tom Hicks ponied up the staggering $252 million for Rodriguez, Boras somehow ignored the fact the Rangers had just come off a season in which they lost 91 games. And that they have never advanced beyond the first round of postseason play.

Though both A-Rod and Boras professed to have done a top-to-bottom study of the Rangers organization, it is perhaps understandable how 252 million big ones could blind them to the fact the Rangers projected starting rotation of Kenny Rogers, Rick Helling,

Darren Oliver, Doug Davis and Ryan Glynn was a combined 45-48 last year.

Likewise, they must not have bothered to ask who is going to be closing out Ranger games now that John Wetteland has departed. (Psst, it's Tim Crabtree, who was 2-7 with 86 hits in 80.1 innings and a 5.15 ERA as a set-up man last year.)

"I'm glad everyone thinks we have a bad pitching staff, a Little League pitching staff," A-Rod said. "I hope we're gonna surprise a lot of people. That's our challenge."

At least Hicks didn't empty his vault solely on Rodriguez. He saw to it the Rangers would improve themselves in other areas as well. He signed 39-year-old Andres Galarraga to play first base and DH 37-year-old Ken Caminiti to play third and acquired 38-year-old Randy Velarde to play second.

How comforting it should be for A-Rod to be surrounded by all this experience.

Of course, it might have been the Mets, A-Rod's favorite team of his youth, to have signed him. If only they hadn't made such a big deal out of all those marketing perks and stadium office space requests.

Rodriguez once again denied having ever asked the Mets for

that tent in spring training to market his own paraphernalia, or more billboard space than Mike Piazza, or an office at Shea. "Ludicrous," he said, "that I would ever want offices or billboards. I respect the Mets. They were my favorite team growing up."

Maybe the truth lies somewhere in between what the Mets maintained and what A-Rod and Boras adamantly denied. Certainly, the inference of all these perks was there when Boras and Mets GM Steve Phillips initiated talks back in November. But just as Boras would have probably backed off on the tents, billboards and stadium office space, he wasn't about to give the Mets any "favorite team" discount.

By then, the Mets knew the price for A-Rod was going to far exceed the $200 million everyone had projected for him. And they knew Boras was going to demand all the "chutes and ladders" escalator and escape clauses he got from the Rangers. They weren't going to do any of that, so they weren't going to stay in the bidding to help Boras extract his industry-busting deal from somebody else.

"I'm almost embarrassed and ashamed of this contract," A-Rod said. "I've got this 252 tag on my head. But I enjoy the responsibility that comes along with it."

At least the number on his back is the same No. 3 he wore in his six years with the Mariners.

Only a cynic would suggest it might also be the over-under as to the number of years into the contract he demands that the Rangers trade him to a contender.

Soriano Walks Into Hearts of Fans

April 30, 2001

Barry Zito, the delightfully quirky Athletics left-hander, was fully aware he was on the verge of being part of something truly historic when he ran the count to 3-2 on Alfonso Soriano in the third inning on April 29. But even if he wasn't, the buzz in the stands from the near-packed-house crowd of 50,572 had the unmistakable sound of anticipation.

Okay, maybe not the anticipation of a dramatic home run, a rally-ending strikeout or a game-winning hit, but at least the anticipation of a sight many felt might be as rare as Halley's Comet. And so when, sure enough, Soriano did not offer on Zito's next pitch, a changeup high and away, the crowd arose in unison in an even more unlikely event.

For as best as anyone could remember, there had never been a standing ovation at Yankee Stadium for a leadoff walk in the third inning.

"It was fun," said Joe Torre. "I'm sure Oakland wasn't aware as to what was happening."

Maybe not the players on the Oakland bench, but Zito knew that Soriano had been to the plate 103 times this season without drawing a walk.

"If I had thrown it anywhere near the plate," Zito said, "I probably would have gotten him to swing at it. I feel honored."

Nevertheless, the momentous walk came back to haunt Zito when Soriano promptly turned it into a run by stealing second and coming home on Derek Jeter's two-out slow grounder through the left side of the infield. As Torre said, that was the most significant part of the walk.

"I'm glad it [Soriano's walk-less streak] ended because that walk was important for us. Right now, we're winning games with 'little ball' and obviously that run was very big. The last three days I've been telling Jeter, 'This is it. Now the next best thing is for the two of you to walk in the same game.'"

He should not count on that happening any time soon, however.

Delighted as he may have been to get such an unusual standing "O" at Yankee Stadium, Soriano asserted he won't be making a habit of walking.

Rickey Henderson need not concern himself about Soriano going after his newly claimed all-time walks record. This kid is a born hacker and proud of it.

"When I go to the plate I'm only thinking about hitting and putting the ball in play," Soriano said. "I go to the plate thinking aggressive. If [a walk] happens, I'll take it, but I'm not going to change my game."

If he can continue to hit .270 or better and provide the kind of speed the Yankees need from him

Alfonso Soriano scores on a single by Jeter after walking and stealing second. (Corey Sipkin/Daily News)

on the basepaths, nobody will care if he doesn't take a walk. At the same time, though, he should know yesterday's first took him out of all sorts of dubious history.

Going into the game, Soriano had a higher batting average than on-base percentage, a feat no one in the history of the game has ever attained over a full season. Alas, now he's a very ordinary .271 hitter with a .286 on-base percentage. Not only that, he probably didn't even know he was closing in on the immortal Oscar Azocar's last longest streak of walkless plate appearances—129 in 1990.

It is unfortunate the Elias Sports Bureau folks say it's impossible to research baseball's longest walkless streaks, because you have to believe Soriano will continue to make runs at this record, whatever it is. They did, however, offer this bit of esoterica: The record for fewest walks in a season, minimum 500 at-bats, is nine in the AL (by John Leary of the St. Louis Browns in 1916) and six in the NL (by Art Fletcher of the 1915 Giants).

So if nothing else, Soriano is well on pace for either of those marks and thus has a chance to become a real throwback to baseball's dead-ball era. From the reaction of the fans yesterday, they must feel he already is.

"When he got to first base, I said to him: 'What was that, the first walk of your career?'" said Yankee first base coach Lee Mazzilli. "Actually, he got one last year. I was amazed, though, how the fans reacted. It just goes to show how knowledgeable they are here."

It was indeed quite an ovation, one that Joe Oliver, in particular, was sorry to have missed. According to Soriano, of all his Yankee teammates, Oliver had been getting on him the most about the streak.

"That's because I'm pretty much like he is in that I'm hard to walk," Oliver confessed. "But I missed it. I was in the bathroom when I heard the crowd cheering and I came flying out only to see him standing on first. I'm just going to have to get the videotape."

THE PICK:
IT'S D-BACKS IN 6

OCTOBER 27, 2001

PHOENIX—A scout I know, who's been in the business for nearly 50 years, tells me the Arizona Diamondbacks are going to be the Yankees' Waterloo.

"I know all about the Yankee mystique, especially this time of year," said the scout, "and you can't but have an enormous respect for them and all they've done. But I felt from the beginning of this season, if the Diamondbacks could just stay healthy, they'd win the [NL] western division, and if they got by that first best-of-five round, Schilling and Johnson would make them unstoppable from there on out. So far I've been right, and I'm sticking to it.

"The Yankees' run ends here."

What am I to think? More importantly, what am I to do?

Ever since 1996, I have picked the Yankees to lose at least one of the tiers in each postseason, sometimes more than one, only to have them always and relentlessly prove me wrong. It's gotten so ridiculous my colleagues at *The News* have used my Yankee pick as a sort of Groundhog Day barometer. Every time I pick the Yankees to lose, they know they've got at least one more week of extra work. Even my own kids—devout Yankee fans both of them—have gotten to begging me every year at this time to pick the Yankees to lose.

When I picked the A's in five in the division series two weeks ago, my oldest son, Steven, said: "Oh, great. Until now I didn't think the Yanks had a chance. You've made my day, Dad. We're going to the World Series after all."

He wouldn't speak to me last week after I picked the Yankees in five over the Mariners.

But getting back to this World Series at hand with the Diamondbacks. I've got to tell

The Arizona Diamondbacks celebrate their world championship—won in seven games. (Corey Sipkin/Daily News)

you, this scout—who also assured me the Dodgers would beat the Mets in the 1988 NLCS despite having lost 10 of 11 times to them during the regular season—has got me worried. If he's right, that means Jerry Colangelo is about to become the king of baseball.

Colangelo, the Diamondbacks' managing general partner, already is the debt king of baseball. With attendance having decreased each succeeding season since the D-Backs' inception in 1998—therefore falling far short of Colangelo's projections for this so-called baseball Mecca in the desert—the Arizona debt is said to be $148 million. That's on top of the $120 million in deferred money Colangelo owes 10 of his players who heeded his cries of poverty last spring and agreed to take a portion of their salaries down the road, long after they're retired.

Already Colangelo is into baseball for about $75 million worth of cash calls to the central fund, along with another $73 million in bank loans. So if Arizona does unseat the Yankees, this will be a first in that baseball's never had a champion it had to nearly totally subsidize.

Say what you will about George Steinbrenner, at least he bought his championships with cash he had. And, by the way, I had to really laugh last winter when Colangelo, of all people, stepped to the forefront of owners decrying Texas' $252 million signing of Alex Rodriguez and proclaimed: "There's no question there's a tremendous need to do something about this disparity, but when any team does what Texas did, it makes it hard to sell your story."

This from a man who, the minute he was allowed into baseball, sent shockwaves through the game by giving Jay Bell $34 million. He would follow that up with another $45 million for Matt Williams.

So maybe now you can understand my dilemma. I truly believe in this Yankee team. After all they've accomplished, all they've overcome throughout this remarkable streak of championships, their resolve to win should never again be doubted.

At the same time, however, Jerry Colangelo's gotten enough help from baseball to get his team to the World Series. He doesn't need any more help from me.

Take this to the bank, Jerry: Diamondbacks in six.

MAMA MIA!
WHAT A BALLCLUB

The cold, heavy mist, which threatened ominously to become the heavy rain at the end of the supposed four-hour "window," was rolling in from left field, and you could almost hear the echo of Casey Stengel up there somewhere asking plaintively: "Can't anybody win this game?"

The answer was finally provided by Larry Walker, who had been nowhere to be found the day before when the Rockies came up one swing short of extending the Mets' losing streak to seven. And with Walker's mighty 13th-inning wallop off the back wall of the Mets' bullpen, mother's longest day gave way to an even longer flight to the West Coast for Bobby Valentine and Steve Phillips to ponder what sort of Mets team this really is.

Is it a team destined to lead the league in errors, as two more

in the seventh inning yesterday betrayed Steve Trachsel's best pitching effort of the season and ultimately cost the Mets this game? Is it a team that is never going to click at the plate, as Mo Vaughn (0 for 6 yesterday, .247, two HR, 11 RBIs overall) and Jeromy Burnitz (.225, 32 strikeouts) continue to be $20 million worth of clogs in the middle of the lineup, while Edgardo Alfonzo never hits a home run?

Before the Mets snapped their six-game losing streak on Saturday, Phillips had made the very pointed assertion that it was a team with a few players in need of an attitude adjustment. But after the rain-delayed, four-hour, 15-minute debacle, the GM could not be blamed for wondering if there's a more widespread problem here.

A weary Valentine, while doing his level best to defend

The Mets' Rey Ordonez overthrows the ball to first. (AP/WWP)

Robbie Alomar's defensive woes in the critical seventh inning, conceded the overhauled Mets may still be going through a getting-to-know-you process.

"We're still learning about each other," Valentine said when asked if it was safe to say the Mets have not yet defined themselves. (Or if they have, this certainly wasn't what Phillips had in mind when he put this team together in his winter shopping spree.) "Why does it have to be defined? Can't we just be a good baseball team that plays good baseball?"

Well, sure. If only they would start.

For the first six innings, the Mets were a good baseball team because Trachsel was almost unhittable. Actually, he was unhittable until a pair of two-out Rockie singles in the fifth, which went for naught. In the seventh, however, the Mets were a bad baseball team in allowing the Rockies to tie the game thanks to two more errors that gave them 40 for the season.

Todd Hollandsworth led off the seventh with a single up the middle and wound up at second when Rey Ordonez fielded the ball and threw it wide of Vaughn (which isn't easy to do) at first. After another single by Jose Ortiz put runners on the corners, weak-hitting Rockie catcher Gary Bennett hit an appropriately weak pop fly into shallow right. Burnitz, racing in, apparently got a slow break on the ball. It should have been his ball, since he was the only person who would have had a shot at cutting off the run at the plate.

Instead, however, Alomar raced out from second and attempted to make an over-the-head catch of the ball, only to drop it as Hollandsworth scored easily and Ortiz advanced to second.

"I couldn't get to it," Burnitz said, "and that's why I never called for it."

"That's the way I saw it," Valentine said. "It looked to me as if Jeromy slowed down as Robbie ran underneath it."

Call it a fluke play, then, if you will, but there have been just too many plays like that so far this season. If nothing else, the Mets looked to be a solid defensive club, but they are leading the majors in errors by a wide margin. Their 40th came on the next play when Rockie pitcher John Thomson hit what looked like a double play bouncer to short—

except Alomar's relay to first was wild, allowing Ortiz to score the tying run.

After that, the rain-slogged moms were treated to five more innings of futility by both teams. Finally, with Armando Benitez still unavailable to pitch because of a swollen and lacerated index finger, Valentine was down to the depths of his bullpen corps by the 13th and righty Kane Davis paid the price for walking leadoff man Juan Uribe by being too fine with the lefty-swinging Walker, whose monster homer broke the 2-2 deadlock. The day before, Rockies manager Clint Hurdle had refused to call on Walker to pinch hit against Mets' righty reliever, Scott Strickland, with two runners on in the ninth inning, and watched Mark Little strike out to end the game.

"I wanted to give [Little] confidence in that situation," Hurdle explained.

It was the Mets to whom he gave the confidence, but as has been a very disturbing pattern so far, it evaporated quickly in the Mother's Day mist.

YANK CALL GETS MOOSE ANSWER

AUGUST 12, 2002

Throughout these ring-ladened last six years, Joe Torre has uttered a familiar refrain whenever he's been asked to explain his uncommon success as Yankee manager.

It's the pitching, stupid.

And Torre has not in the least retreated from that credo this season, even in the face of the home run might not seen in the Bronx since the summer of '61. Once again, the Yankees' muscle-flexing was the prime topic of conversation yesterday— particularly after Alfonso Soriano moved to within one homer of becoming the first second baseman in history to accumulate 30 bombs and 30 steals in the same season by taking A's lefty Mark Mulder deep in the sixth inning of the 8-5 salvaging win over the surging Oaklands.

But the most important development as far as Torre was concerned was Mike Mussina recovering from a near disastrous three-run second inning yesterday to hang tough against the A's and pick up his 14th win in spite of a yield of 11 hits over six innings. There's a reason Torre hasn't been saluting all these Yankee home runs with quite the same fervor as the media.

It's the pitching, stupid, and the reason the Yankees were in the 0-2 hole in this series to the A's to begin with was the ominous state of his starting rotation. In the first game Friday night, Orlando Hernandez had to leave after the first inning after experiencing mysterious numbness in various parts of his body. (After extensive hospital tests, El Duque was pronounced fit for duty again, but who knows what phantom injury will strike him next?) Then on Saturday, David Wells, whose cranky back remains

Derek Jeter singles and ends up on third on an error.
(Linda Cataffo/Daily News)

a day-to-day concern, was roughed up for 10 hits and seven runs.

So now it was left to Mussina, in the throes of the worst slump of his career, to outpitch Mulder (10-2 in his previous 13 starts) if the Yankees were to avoid being swept in front of three straight sold-out Yankee Stadium houses and one very ornery and increasingly antsy owner. The first inning was promising—Mussina setting the A's down in order while the Yankees were jumping on Mulder for three quick runs.

But as vintage as Mussina had looked in the first, it was right back to his recent horrors in the second as the A's batted around to tie the score, two of their runs coming on Terrence Long's home run that went a third of the way up in the upper deck in right. But when it looked like the A's might be about to duplicate that rally in the third, with runners at first and second and one out, Mussina got Long to hit a comebacker to the mound, which he converted into an inning-ending DP.

"That," said Torre, "was the most important out of the game. I thought [Mussina] battled after having bad location with pitches early. You've got to forget the second inning. I thought it was a quality outing. I think we're making progress."

He hopes so, anyway. For the record, even with yesterday's "quality outing," Mussina has given up 45 hits and 20 earned runs in 22 innings over his last four starts—and there's nothing wrong physically with him, which has not been the case with any of the other four Yankee starters, Wells, El Duque, Roger Clemens and Andy Pettitte. It is an aging and fragile rotation in which the one sound horse— Mussina—has been pitching horribly.

Torre knows he's got to start getting some consistency—both health-wise and stuff-wise—from his starting five or all the home runs on the planet won't be worth a hill of beans come October.

"The pitching hasn't been as consistent as I expected," Torre admitted. "We haven't had everybody healthy at once and pitching the way we know they can at once. But that team (pointing toward the Oakland clubhouse) had injuries to their pitching early—Mulder in particular started the season hurt—and now they're right back in it again. Their pitching is the only reason for that."

He paused as if to reflect on the questions about the Yankee home runs—which, with Soriano's and Shane Spencer's blasts yesterday, ran their major league-leading total to 174, 97 of them in the last 66 games.

"There's no guarantee you can score enough runs to win," Torre added. "You need somebody to get the outs."

Got that, stupid?

Boss's Shadow Grows Longer

All you need is to take a good look at Joe Torre's uncharacteristically haggard face these days to know the Yankee manager isn't just being facetious when he says this hasn't been a fun year for him.

It is not the face of a manager who has had his team in first place since June 11. Rather, it is the face of the only manager in baseball whose team plays 162 separate seasons. Torre has made no secret of the fact that this has been the hardest season of his managing career, harder even than 1995 with the Cardinals when he knew the Budweiser ownership suits cared little about their baseball operation and even less about spending money on players for him, but would fire him anyway.

He has said it on numerous occasions in numerous different ways, but if you're wondering how and why a man being paid $6 million per year to manage the best baseball team money could buy could not be having fun, you haven't been reading the pointed barbs coming from the owner this season. George Steinbrenner says accountability is the key word around the Yankees this year— which is well and good, if that means everybody.

The problem is, as Torre sees it, he and his coaches are being held more accountable than anybody else, and, in the meantime, there is still this "us-vs.-them" Tampa-Bronx schism, which Steinbrenner continues to nurture.

Through all of the Yankees' successes, Steinbrenner has made it a point to say it's been an organizational effort, with everyone in agreement—which, for the most part, it has been. But then you have incidents like a couple of weeks ago, when Jose Contreras, the $32 million Cuban pitching prodigy, hurled seven innings of shutout ball following a lengthy rehab in Tampa, and Steinbrenner goes out of his way to heap praise on his Tampa confidant, minor league pitching coach Billy Connors.

"Billy Connors is truly a guru," Steinbrenner said, and just about everyone in the Yankee inner circle agreed this was a direct shot at Torre and his pitching coach Mel Stottlemyre.

Behind the scenes, there have been a lot more indirect slaps at Torre and his coaches. Don Zimmer, a longtime friend of Steinbrenner's and once his frequent companion at the racetracks in Tampa, still doesn't know what he did to fall out of favor with The Boss. The situation has reached the extent where Steinbrenner, through his underlings, would order the YES-TV directors to keep the cameras off Zimmer sitting next to Torre during games.

And according to two team sources, a couple of weeks ago Steinbrenner sent a team executive down to the clubhouse at Yankee Stadium on an errand, with an additional explicit order "not to go into that coaches room. I don't want you talking to those a————!"

Needless to say, it didn't take long for that to get back to the coaches, and ever since, they've come to kiddingly address each other as "a————."

Even in Steinbrenner's statements of "support" for Torre, he makes it quite clear who he thinks must be most accountable if the Yankees fall short of the World Series this year. "[Torre] picked the team and I gave him everything he wanted," Steinbrenner keeps saying.

The fact is, everybody in the Yankee high command had a hand in putting this team together—for better or worse.

There isn't a team in baseball without major flaws, which is why, regardless of their payroll, the Yankees are no better than even money with the Giants, Braves, Red Sox, White Sox, A's or Mariners to make the World Series. And if David Wells—the Boss's guy—is spent (as it's beginning to look), and Contreras is more the pitcher he was against the Red Sox than the one who mastered the fourth-place Orioles and Bernie Williams doesn't get it together and Derek Jeter is out for a sustained period, the Yankees, despite their lead, might not be even money to even make the postseason.

Torre is fully aware of this grim possibility—if for no other reason than the fact that every

Yankee pitching failure, every Yankee injury, every Yankee loss gets magnified by 10 because of what's expected of them with their payroll and their owner. You're allowed the joy of victory for only a moment, but the losses and problems linger. This is what has taken the fun out of it for Joe Torre, although not so much as to cause him to walk away after the season.

If it does somehow all fall apart for the Yankees because of the pitching breakdown, injuries, internal unrest or whatever, Steinbrenner should remember his "organization" theme. Win or lose, everyone is accountable, even him.

THIS MESS IS NOT
GOOD FOR THE GAME

DECEMBER 21, 2003

Throughout the entire process, so many of baseball's poobahs—from Commissioner Bud Selig on down—said it was important for the monumental Alex Rodriguez-for-Manny Ramirez mega-trade to get completed because it was "good for the game."

I agree with Selig on three points. The deal definitely would be good for the Boston Red Sox, getting the acknowledged best player in the game along with shedding Ramirez and replacing him with a .300-hitting, 100-RBI prince of a guy in Magglio Ordonez.

It would probably be good for the Texas Rangers if only because blowhard owner Tom Hicks was drowning in a self-made sea of red ink, brought about by his own stupidity as Scott (Avenging Agent) Boras's favorite patsy with the signings of A-Rod for $100 million over market value and Chan Ho Park for $65 million. And you have to say it would be good for A-Rod since he was so desperate to get out of Texas that he even was willing to give up some money. If only the union had let him.

But other than that, I fail to see how it was "good for baseball" to allow a certifiable phony (A-Rod) to openly campaign for another man's job when that player, Nomar Garciaparra, was under contract to the team.

How else can you characterize this other than blatant player tampering openly encouraged by all parties—from the commissioner's office to the players association?

In the final analysis, this goes down as one of the more outrageous chapters in baseball history—one in which players were turned against clubs and an owner like Hicks sought MLB's help to get out of his mistake.

Instead of encouraging the parties to work out a deal, Selig should have held Hicks aloft to all the other owners as a poster boy for reckless ownership. "You do these kinds of stupid deals that impact on the entire game," Selig should have said to Hicks, "you live and die by the consequences."

As for A-Rod, it wasn't enough to have a direct pipeline to the owner and a subtle hand in so many aspects of the organization—once he realized his contract was choking Hicks and preventing the Rangers from surrounding him with good players, he decided to bolt.

At the time they did the $252 million deal, A-Rod and Boras never concerned themselves with the impact it would have on the Rangers. Three years and three last-place finishes into the contract, however, and they wanted out of Texas. Incredibly, after all the lasting damage this contract did to the game, baseball was only too eager to oblige them.